OPERA IN ITALY

NAOMI JACOB

has also written:

POWER
JACOB USSHER
ROCK AND SAND
YOUNG EMMANUEL
THE BELOVED PHYSICIAN
THE MAN WHO FOUND HIMSELF
"SEEN UNKNOWN . . ."
THAT WILD LIE
THE PLOUGH
ROOTS
PROPS
POOR STRAWS
GROPING
THE LOADED STICK
FOUR GENERATIONS
"HONOUR COME BACK"
THE FOUNDER OF THE HOUSE
BARREN METAL
TIMEPIECE
FADE OUT
THE LENIENT GOD
NO EASY WAY
STRAWS IN AMBER
THIS PORCELAIN CLAY
THEY LEFT THE LAND
SALLY SCARTH
UNDER NEW MANAGEMENT
THE CAP OF YOUTH
LEOPARDS AND SPOTS
PRIVATE GOLLANTZ
WHITE WOOL
HONOUR'S A MISTRESS
PASSAGE PERILOUS

One-Act Plays:
THE DAWN
MARY OF DELIGHT

Autobiography and Biography:
ME: A CHRONICLE ABOUT OTHER PEOPLE
"OUR MARIE" (MARIE LLOYD)
ME AGAIN
MORE ABOUT ME
ME IN WARTIME
ME IN THE MEDITERRANEAN
ME OVER THERE

General:
ME IN THE KITCHEN

Photograph by Ismay Taylor, Harrogate

Head of Naomi Jacob: sculptured by Eve Atcheson

OPERA IN ITALY

by

NAOMI JACOB

AND

JAMES C. ROBERTSON

With 19 Illustrations

1948

HUTCHINSON & CO. (Publishers) LTD
London   New York   Melbourne   Sydney   Cape Town

Printed in Great Britain
by The Anchor Press, Ltd.,
Tiptree, Essex

ERRATA

Page 11, *line* 7, *for* Pattistini *read* Battistini.

Page 11, *line* 8, *for* Cotagni *read* Cotogni.

Page 11, *line* 17, *for* Maria *read* Ebe.

Page 11, *line* 18, *for* Paccaloni *read* Baccaloni.

Page 21, *line* 11, *for* "*la morta*" *read* "*la morte*".

Page 22, *line* 30, *for* Maschereni *read* Mascheroni.

Page 23, *line* 36, *for* Corbelli *read* Cobelli.

Page 25, *line* 1, *for* Bramonte *read* Bramante.

Page 26, *lines* 2, 6, 10, 17 *and* 29, *for* Constanzi *read* Costanzi.

Page 27, *line* 34, *for* Constanzi *read* Costanzi.

Page 28, *line* 14, *for* Constanzi *read* Costanzi.

Page 30, *line* 7, *for* "*ossia gli Inutile*" *read* "*ossia l'Inutil*".

Page 30, *line* 36, *for* "*d'segui cosi*" *read* "*deh, segui cosi*".

Page 33, *line* 31, *for* Argentini *read* Argentina.

Page 34, *line* 1, *for* "*Sacchini!*" *read* "*Puccini!*".

Page 34, *line* 6, *for* Argentini *read* Argentina.

Page 40, *line* 4, *delete the word* "*La*" *at the end of the line*.

Page 42, *line* 37, *for* "*é Fernando*" *read* "*e Fernando*".

Page 43, *lines* 23 *and* 24, *for* "*é Fernando*" *read* "*e Fernando*".

Page 47, *line* 3, *for* Albanesi *read* Albanese.

Page 49, *line* 26, *for* Alfonzo *read* Alfonso.

Page 49, *line* 34, *for* "*é Cristina*" *read* "*e Cristina*".

Page 50, *line* 13, *for* "*é Pasquale*" *read* "*e Pasquale*".

Page 50, *line* 35, *for* "*La Virtu*" *read* "*La Virtù*".

Page 51, *line* 34, *for* "*é Romeo*" *read* "*e Romeo*".

Page 54, *line* 32, *for* di Carbone *read* del Carbone.

Page 55, *line* 11, *for* "*Arigento*" *read* "*Agrigento*".

Page 55, *lines* 37 *and* 38, *for* "*Un Ballo in Maschera*" *read* "*Le Maschere*".

Page 56, *line* 21, *for* ("*Vietato di Fumore*") *read* ("*Vietato Fumare*").

Page 66, *line* 30, *for* Marquis Bevil Acqua *read* Marquis Bevilacqua.

Page 66, *line* 35, *for* "*banditti*" *read* "*banditi*".

Page 68, *line* 15, *for* Rizza Gilda *read* Gilda Dalla Rizza.

Page 69, *line* 14, *for* "*me creda*" *read* "*mi creda*".

Page 71, *line* 3, *for* MUSECALE *read* MUSICALE.

I

Page 71, *line* 36, *for* "*Florentino*" *read* "*Fiorentino*".

Page 73, *line* 31, *for* "*La Fianna*" *read* "*La Fiamma*".

Page 74, *line* 3, *for* Ducessa Margherita *read* Duchessa Margherita.

Page 75, *line* 13, *for* "*Semirande*" *read* "*Semiramide*".

Page 76, *line* 23, *for* Giomanni *read* Giovanni.

Page 77, *line* 1, *for* "*Museo Teatro*" *read* "*Museo del Teatro*".

Page 77, *line* 19, *for* Claudio *read* Claudia.

Page 77, *line* 28, *for* Gabriella *read* Gianna.

Page 77, *line* 35, *for* "*Ramamum*" *read* "*Romanum*".

Page 77, *line* 40, *for* Eleanora *read* Eleonora.

Page 78, *line* 1, *for* "*di Burottini*" *read* "*dei Burattini*".

Page 81, *line* 31, *for* Lui *read* Liù.

Page 81, *line* 40, *for* Lui *read* Liù.

Page 89, *line* 26, *for* "*La Liara*" *read* "*La Giara*".

Page 91, *line* 34, *for* "*Fantasque*" *read* "*Fantastique*".

Page 91, *line* 39, *for* Pick-Mangia-galli *read* Pick Mangiagalli.

Page 94, *line* 35, *for* Borgiolo *read* Borgioli.

Page 102, *line* 20, *for* Monteverde *read* Monteverdi.

Page 105, *line* 19, *for* "*mezzo-voce*" *read* "*mezza-voce*".

Page 105, *line* 30, *for* Dom Licinio *read* Don Licinio.

Page 109, *line* 35, *for* "*Orseilo*" *read* "*Orseolo*".

Page 111, *line* 26, *for* Oizzetti *read* Pizzetti.

Page 125, *line* 3, *for* Arangi-Lombaird *read* Arangi-Lombardi.

Page 126, *line* 16, *for* "*Ne Andro Lontano*" *read* "*ne andrò lontana*".

Page 127, *line* 13, *for* Paccetti *read* Pacetti.

Page 127, *line* 23, *for* "*L'Amo Ben Io*" *read* "*T'amo ben io!*".

Page 128, *line* 17, *for* priest *read* Padre.

Page 128, *line* 18, *for* priest Melitore *read* Fra' Melitone.

Page 128, *line* 30, *for* "*Rico d'Onore*" *read* "*ricco d'onore*".

Page 129, *line* 3, *for* "*Madre Pitosa*" *read* "*Madre, Pietosa*".

Page 129, *line* 4, *for* "*Sui Finnamenti*" *read* "*sui Firmamenti*".

Page 129, *line* 5, *for* Melitore *read* Melitone.

Page 129, *line* 8, *for* Guardiano *read* the Padre Guardiano.

Page 129, *line* 13, *for* "*Vergina Degli*" *read* "*Vergine degli*".

Page 129, *line* 18, *for* "*in Che in Seno Agli*" *read* "*Tu che in seno agli*".

Page 129, *line* 24, *for* "*Solenore in Quest'Ore*" *read* "*Solenne in quest'ora*".

Page 129, *lines* 25 *and* 26, *for* "*Vergina Degli*" *read* "*Vergine degli*".

Page 129, *line* 30, *for* Melitore *read* Melitone.

Page 130, *line* 14, *for* "*Vergina Degli*" *read* "*Vergine degli*".

Page 130, *line* 32, *for* Lione *read* Leone.

Page 130, *line* 34, *for* Granna Redezini *read* Gianna Pederzini.

Page 130, *line* 37, *for* Baconti *read* Baronti.

Page 132, *line* 1, *for* "*Una*" *read* "*Cena*".

Page 133, *line* 33, *for* Quilio *read* Duilio.

Page 134, *line* 24, *for* "*La Rivedra Nell'Estesi*" *read* "*La rivedrò nell'estasi*".

Page 135, *line* 7, *for* Canena *read* Carena.

Page 139, *line* 20, *for* Giulio Borronti *read* Duilio Baronti.

Page 140, *lines* 16 *and* 17, *for* "*Ma Voi Belle, Breve e Bionde*" *read* "*Tra voi belle, brune e bionde*".

Page 141, *line* 41, *for* Tiliani *read* Ziliani.

Page 142, *line* 8, *for* "*Ma Voi*" *read* "*Tra Voi*".

Page 143, *line* 15, *for* "*Commedri*" *read* "*Commedie*".

Page 143, *line* 16, *for* "*Io Son L'Umileancella*" *read* "*Io son l'umile Ancella*".

Page 143, *line* 17, *for* Manrizio *read* Maurizio.

Page 143, *line* 23, *for* Manrizio *read* Maurizio.

Page 144, *line* 23, *for* "*Cantoni*" *read* "*Cantori*".

Page 144, *line* 24, *for* Manrizio *read* Maurizio.

Page 144, *line* 27, *for* "*L'Anima Ho Stanco*" *read* "*L'anima ho stanca*".

Page 145, *line* 6, *for* Miny *read* Niny.

Page 145, *line* 11, *for* Manrizio *read* Maurizio.

Page 147, *line* 9, *for* "*Quest'o Quella*" *read* "*Questa o quella*".

Page 149, *line* 29, *for* Tiliani *read* Ziliani.

Page 150, *line* 34, *for* "*Ebbezza Delicio*" *read* "*Ebbrezza, Delirio*".

Page 150, *line* 41, *for* cenes *read* scenes.

Page 151, *as a footnote, read* The tenor who appeared in *La Gioconda* in 1946 at Trieste was Nino Scattolini whilst La Cieca's rôle was sung by Wanda Madonna.

Page 153, *line* 19, *for* "*sena*" *read* "*scena*".

Page 153, *line* 28, *for* Zara *read* Iva.

Page 153, *line* 29, *for* Zara *read* Iva.

Page 157, *line* 1, *for* "*Reconsita Armonia*" *read* "*Recondite Armonie*".

Page 162, *lines* 28 *and* 29, *for* "*Ch'Ella Me Creda Libero e Lontano*" *read* "*Ch'Ella mi creda libero e lontano*".

Page 163, *line* 2, *for* Corbelli *read* Cobelli.

Page 169, *line* 9, *for* "*e Morta*" *read* "*è Morta*".

Page 178, *line* 2, *for* Novarro *read* Novara.

Page 179, *line* 26, *for* Novarro *read* Novara.

Page 180, *line* 21, *for* "*Morro, Ma Prima*" *read* "*Morrò, ma prima*".

Page 182, *line* 26, *for* Ferranto *read* Ferrauto.

Page 183, *line* 6, *for* Olivieno De Fabritus *read* Oliviero De Fabbritiis.

Page 186, *line* 20, *for* Rossetti *read* Rossini.

Page 191, *line* 8, *for* 1946 *read* 1948.

Page 203, *line* 16, *for* Parga *read* Praga.

Page 215, *line* 8, *for* Burgamo *read* Bergamo.

Page 217, *line* 24, *for* "*La Rinegata*" *read* "*La Rinnegata*".

Page 219, *line* 4, *for* Burgamo *read* Bergamo.

Page 221, *line* 11, *for* "*è Salvina* " *read* "*e Salvini*".

Page 221, *line* 30, *for* "*Capuletti*" *read* "*Capuleti*".

Page 223, *line* 26, *for* Vaci (also spelt Vacci) *read* Vaccaj (also spelt Vaccai).

Page 223, *line* 29, *for* "*Capuletti*" *read* "*Capuleti*".

Page 224, *line* 11, *for* "*O Promessi*" *read* "*I Promessi*".

Page 225, *line* 1, *for* Burgamo *read* Bergamo.

Page 227, *line* 8, *for* "*Zaza*" *read* "*Zazà*".

Page 229, *lines* 5 *and* 6, *for* "*assoluta mente*" *read* "*assolutamente*".

Page 234, *line* 6, *for* "*Questro e Quello Per Me Pari Sono*" *read* "*Questa o quella, per me pari sono*".

DEDICATION

To the great masters of Italian opera,
To the singers who have interpreted it,
To the conductors who have directed it,
and to
The great Italy of the Future.

NAOMI JACOB.
JIMMY ROBERTSON.

August, 1948.

ACKNOWLEDGMENT

I wish to acknowledge to the following, with my very grateful thanks, the help given to me in making this book:

The Editors of *Musical Opinion*, the *Listener*, the *Gramophone*; Mr. and Mrs. J. Robertson; Lewis Robertson; Geoffrey Handley-Taylor; Signor Ruffini, late of the Italian Consulate, London; Alfredo Alfieri; Signora Giuntini; Signor Beondi; Signor Giovannoni of Mantova; Contessa Cibrario; Signora Rosa Finzi; Pierre Sens; Signora Nadalini Patterson; Audrie Young; Elsa Manley; Signor Vita, Teatro dell'Opera, Rome; Dottore Fausto Maria Bordin; Colonel Andrew Dunn; Signora Guida; La Direzione, Teatro Comunale "Giuseppe Verdi", Trieste; Peter L. Holt; Signora Gina Cigna, the Italian Ministry of the Interior, and Eve Atcheson.

NAOMI JACOB.

CONTENTS

CONTENTS

Part Two : COMMENT AND CRITICISM ON ITALIAN OPERA

by JAMES C. ROBERTSON

Part Three : INDIVIDUAL OPERAS, *by* JAMES C. ROBERTSON

CONTENTS

LIST OF ILLUSTRATIONS

FOREWORD

It is indeed an honour to have been invited to write a foreword to a book on opera, and more particularly to one on the opera of Italy. Apart from being one of those first to interest the author in serious music, I have some small qualifications to express my affection for this form of music. I started my musical education as a student of singing in Milan nearly forty years ago, when Toscanini was conducting at the Teatro del Popolo, when Pattistini was the foremost baritone, Caruso and Martinelli the principal tenors, when Cotagni was the leading teacher and Pusoni presided over the Accademia di Santa Cecilia.

As a soldier six years later, I heard opera five nights a week in Genoa with that excellent baritone Galeffi. I recall the *début* of Gigli at the Teatro al Pergola in *Tosca* and the great bass de Angelis at La Scala. Between the wars, an annual visit to Italy brought me the acquaintance of the lovely Irish soprano Margherita Sheridan, eight years at the Scala with Toscanini, and of Pertile, the most artistic of tenors. Their Butterfly and Pinkerton remain an imperishable memory. As the years drew on came Toti dal Monte, Gina Cigna and Maria Stignani, the finest mezzo-soprano of all time. Pinza, Paccaloni and Pasero among the basses, and Stabile, that great actor supreme, in Mozart and Donizetti. Whether the post war will achieve standards and singers equal to these remains to be seen. I will set down some reasons why the seasons to come should be even more fruitful than those in my past experience.

The very beginning of opera was under Monteverdi in Venice nearly 350 years ago, but it existed largely in the countries surrounding the wealthy patrons, whose munificence made it possible for composers to write and produce their works. This continued during the 17th and 18th centuries, until in Italy, France and Germany in the 19th century, opera houses began to be built and maintained by generous subsidies from public funds. In England, however, this brand of music remained the prerogative of the very rich, who were prepared to support an annual venture lasting only for a few weeks, imported entirely from abroad and sung in Italian, French or German.

Not even the touring companies of Carl Rosa or Moody-Manners or the modest enterprise of the Old Vic succeeded in creating an opera-loving public—it remained a foreign and exotic taste rather like the food one used to eat in Soho.

Today this is changed, and is changing still further. Most of the credit is no doubt due to the Sadler's Wells Theatre. Not only have they built up an extensive repertoire of operas, but they have trained a large number of native people to sing the works under the guidance of imaginative producers with new and admirable *décor*. This company regularly toured the whole country during the War, bringing opera to the multitude at extremely reasonable prices.

Still another stimulus came with the return of the troops from countries where opera could be heard, as in Italy. They had grown accustomed in Naples, Rome, Venice, Trieste and Milan to regular opera-going, where singers were to be heard far superior to those in their own country. This new demand for the best has once more created the supply by the re-opening, under the auspices of the Arts Council of Great Britain, of the beautiful opera house at Covent Garden. A notable company of singers and a fine orchestra have been established with the purpose and intention of keeping opera-going in London all the year round, an advantage enjoyed by no other capital.

So a book like this, *Opera in Italy*, written by an amateur who assures me she is in no sense an expert, may provide our growing audiences of young people with just that sort of information necessary to the real enjoyment of opera. It is written in a style and *format* far removed from the textbook or a book of reference, and is calculated to make the opera-going of its readers as stimulating an experience as it clearly is to Naomi Jacob herself; and to encourage them by her magnificent illustrations to hear and see opera in its original home. Thus only can our own standards be kept up.

Just such a reader would have been James Robertson, many of whose enthusiastic letters during his visits to Italy are included in this book. We shall always need a public as informed and as enterprising as this young man, and I cannot do any young opera-lovers a better service than to hand them over to the tutelage of two such sincere and enterprising guides as they will hereafter find in this book.

W. J. SMITH, M.A.
Director of Music,
Alleyn's School,
Dulwich.

Maderno.

INTRODUCTION

IT is perhaps necessary to explain why I should venture—partially, at least—to write a book about Italian opera. I am not a specialist, my knowledge of music is that of the average intelligent music lover, I am not even quite sure that "I know what I like". I am, on the other hand, quite certain what I do not like! And for that reason there is no reference to certain operas in this book. That may be both unfair and unreasonable, but it remains a fact, and I accept the blame if there is any due to me.

This book is the outcome of two things. First, because Jimmy Robertson—who really had a specialized knowledge regarding opera, and in particular Italian opera—and I liked nothing better than to sit for hours talking and indulging in argument, illustrating our various points by the use of gramophone records, discussing the merits and de-merits of various operas.

We repeatedly promised ourselves that "one day" we would work together on a book dealing with Italian opera. Why that day never came is recorded in another part of this book. As some people are "stage-struck", so Jimmy and I were "opera-struck" and one person I know who speaks with authority regarding theatrical matters holds the opinion that unless a person is "stage-struck" he has no right to attempt to earn his living on the stage. Now, being "opera-struck" is rather different, for neither of us had any futile dreams of ever singing in opera, it was merely that opera—particularly Italian opera—fascinated us, that we not only loved the music, that we not only found pleasure in watching opera, but we wanted to *know* about Italian opera in every possible way. The opera houses, the men who wrote the operas, the history of the operas themselves—had they been immediate successes? had recognition come gradually and often painfully? why had some of them sunk into oblivion?—and so forth.

The result was that I began to collect data concerning opera houses, and here in Italy they abound, and their histories are filled with rich detail and deep interest. In the "old days" before the war, I used to say that as some people "follow the sun" so I followed opera round Italy. When no opera was being presented I studied my Italian *Radio Times* and listened to it whenever possible. Jimmy continued to make his periodic visits to Italy and to immerse himself in the music which he loved to the exclusion of everything else except his long discussions on music with his much-loved friend the great conductor Vittorio Gui. Let me say here that his knowledge was far in advance of mine, his actual musical taste better and finer, his critical faculty more highly developed. I have always allowed my judgment to be swayed by my emotions, which, when you attempt to appreciate music, is a bad thing.

I began to listen to opera when I was still quite young. In those days there were two operatic companies touring England, one the Moody-Manners, the other the Carl Rosa. They had certain artists who, if not actually up to the standard of Covent Garden, La Scala or the Metropolitan, were very good indeed. They toured a good orchestra, carried at least two conductors, and if some of their scenery and effects might have been better, at least they might have been much worse. Their repertoire was extensive but limited, although I know that statement sounds like a paradox. They were limited insomuch as there were certain "surefire" operas which were always included; true, from time to time Charles Manners tried to introduce a "novelty", but in the main both companies stuck to the beaten track of opera.

Wagner was very popular at that time. I remember how the late E. F. Benson and his brilliant brother Mgr. Robert Hugh Benson loved to give long accounts in their novels of visits paid by their characters to Covent Garden to listen to *Tristan and Isolde* or *Lohengrin*. So we provincials were given liberal doses of Wagner with stout sopranos and contraltos wearing unbecomingly girdled garments, and all the basses and baritones looking as if they had made up merely to peer out from immense bushy beards; only the tenors appeared without this "love-in-a-mist" effect. Even in those days, when it was considered little short of heresy to voice such an opinion, I preferred Puccini and Verdi. I recall two operas which seem to have disappeared—and how rightly—*The Bohemian Girl* and *Maritana*. Can it be that our taste in opera has improved?

I used to hear a good deal of opera in Dresden, in the days when Hitler had not made himself acutely unpleasant to people who were actually Jews or who bore Jewish names, and wonderfully good it was. One of the memories which will always remain vividly in my mind was that great open space before the Dresden Opera House, with the State Church facing it, and which at night after a performance looked exactly like a painting by Caneletto. Even then those operas which were "imported" made a greater appeal to me than the Germanic works.

Then came Italy, and I was able to listen to Italian opera of all kinds: I listened in splendid opera houses, where the greatest artists in the world sang; I listened to small unknown companies with poor, thin orchestras and slowly I began to understand something of the shape and form and musical intention of opera. I went to New York, and heard opera in the great and rather gloomy Metropolitan Opera House; I listened to *La Bohème*, when a Scottish Musetta "stole" the honours from poor Grace Moore; I heard the Italians sing the operas of Verdi and Puccini. I came home more in love with opera than ever.

Back in London I went to Covent Garden and heard Gigli and Cigna with Vittorio Gui conducting in more Italian opera, I went to Glyndebourne to listen to the *Macbeth* of Verdi. I returned to Italy in time for the Verona season. I knew that I was slowly and even painfully beginning to understand something about Italian opera. Jimmy came over to stay for the Verona season, and there were long talks and arguments which lasted until the "fisherman's bell" rang at six in the morning, and the light came filtering slowly to touch the waters of the Garda Lake. Again we talked of the book which we were going to write—one day.

The war came, and our beloved opera had to fall back. When Italy was free again, Jimmy wasn't there to work on a book with me, I had to use his notes through the generosity of his father and mother. I wanted to write the book more than ever. Firstly, because I had seen the immediate reaction on the part of the troops—both British and American —towards opera. I had watched how they flocked to the opera houses in Italy, with what attention they listened, and with what just and right appreciation they applauded. In Bari, Naples, Rome, Padua and Trieste I had seen houses packed with eager-faced men who were longing to listen and to understand this—to them, at least—new form of entertainment. In Genoa, Bologna, Udine and Verona I had watched them, and I realized that while they, like myself, were no specialists, it was almost inevitable that they should want to know more about this particular and difficult form of musical art.

So I began this book, in the hope that men who heard opera out in Italy, men who flocked to the Arena at Verona, to the Castello at Trieste, to the Baths of Caracalla in Rome and to the Castello in Milan would be glad to read about the opera houses which they had visited, to read of the artists who had given them such delight, and even to know something about the "men who wrote the operas".

These impressions of Jimmy Robertson's are the impressions of a musically-minded young man who cultivated his appreciation of opera; what I have written is merely the recording of certain knowledge which I have gathered because the subject interested me. And I say with no wish to be sentimental—that I hope Jimmy likes what between us we have prepared to offer to you.

I know that there are going to be a great many people who will ask with a faintly patronizing inflection, "What does Naomi Jacob know about opera?" That matters nothing! I have tried to write what I felt and knew to be true. And my reason has been that I wish to bring those good times back to the boys who were out there and who learned to love and appreciate opera.

It would have been impossible for me to write with profound knowledge—because I lack that profound knowledge; I am ignorant of many of the technicalities which hedge opera round, but if Jimmy and I between us have contrived to bring back more or less vividly the San Carlo at Naples, the Teatro dell' Opera in Rome, the Fenice in Venice and all those other places where you first met Madame Butterfly, Floria Tosca, Violetta in *La Traviata*, Gioconda and the wicked Barnaba, poor Canio of *I Pagliacci*, Mimi and Rudolph of *La Bohème*, Aïda and Rhadames and all those other splendid figures, then we are satisfied.

Nothing could give me greater pleasure than to hear this book referred to as "a popular book on opera". That is exactly what I should like it to be! A book which will awaken memories, a book which will stimulate interest, a book which will make all the men and women who heard opera in Italy long to hear it again in England.

For years many people insisted that opera was a kind of entertainment for "highbrows" and exclusive intellectuals. The war proved that it was the kind of entertainment which was appreciated universally by all types and all classes. There had always been a kind of implication that opera was "difficult to understand", that to listen to it necessitated a special kind of musical training. What rubbish!

Naturally, to understand fully any great form of art needs not only concentration but training; but the stories of many operas are so simple, so direct, so intensely dramatic that not to understand the plot must be to argue yourself a fool. Full appreciation of the music is another matter. I have never felt that I could even *begin* to appreciate an opera until I had heard it at least four times. I hesitate to say how often I have heard Puccini's last opera—and to me his greatest—*Turandot*; yet at each hearing I find something new, something which I have missed at previous hearings. The same may be said of *La Gioconda*, of *Rigoletto*, of *Un Ballo in Maschera*, *La Forza del Destino*, and of *Norma*. To listen again and again to great operas is like going back again and again to stare intently at some splendid picture. With each visit new details emerge, new colours are apparent, greater understanding of the form and pattern is obtained.

If I were asked by anyone how to begin to study opera from the ordinary listener's point of appreciation I should reply without hesitation, "Listen to Puccini." Not because he ranks *lower* than many other great Italian masters, but because he chose simple, direct and dramatic stories, and because his music is so full of lovely melodies. From Puccini move on to Rossini and Donizetti, to Bellini—and now your musical fare becomes slightly more complicated; having learnt to appreciate these, turn to that great master Mozart with all his lightness, his sudden moods of gentle sadness and his heavenly music. Last of all, reach the great

To Mrs. Naomi Jacob
with my best wishes for
her book Benniamino
1947

Gigli

Exterior of La Scala, Milan. The flags are to indicate the visit of the delegates from all parts of the world who attended the opening of the restored La Scala

master Verdi. Don't imagine that I am ranking him as greater than Mozart, for there is in Mozart a charm, a friendliness and a sentiment —and I am not stating that he is "sentimental"—which is not to be found except with rare exceptions in Verdi. But with Verdi what a feast of music awaits you! The grandeur, the great melodies which sweep along, carrying the listener with them, the nobility and the heart-breaking *arias* which occur again and again in Verdi's splendid works!

Later you may add other Italians—Ponchielli, Giordano, Boito and the rest. Masters—but more restricted, both as regards output and sustained beauty.

I have transcribed at the beginning of the chapters in this book a few bars of some melody which is characteristic of the opera or the composer. May I hope that some of you will sit down at your pianos as you read and play them over, calling up memories and giving you sudden pictures of the scenes which you have watched?

Let me say again that this is not a book for the critic, for the highly trained musician. It is a book which I hope—and I know that I can speak for Jimmy Robertson too—will make an appeal to the *average* opera lover. I have included a short chapter on Italian ballet, because ballet— which let me say I do not, never have and never shall understand—does figure in so many Italian operas. I have also a chapter called, "Should Opera Singers Learn to Act?", because I have always held the opinion that one of the reasons why opera presents such difficulties is that to be given perfectly it must be a combination of singing and acting—not of singing with a few stilted and stylized movements flung in as a kind of rather unhappy makeweight.

If in England your chances of listening to opera are remote and slight, then turn to your gramophones! They are not ideal, but they can teach you a great deal, those admirable records—if you will treat them well, and not expect them to give their best under careless and heartless treatment. I have records of Caruso, not those excellent reproductions, but originals. They are over twenty years old, and though the tone is not so rich as the modern recordings, yet they can still bring back to me the most wonderful tenor in history. But they have been kindly and carefully treated. If you would appreciate opera—train your ear, train your powers of appreciation, learn not to accept second rate as anything but—second rate!

If an opera is new to you, study the story of the opera before you go to the theatre. There are certain plots—*Il Trovatore*, for example— which are difficult to comprehend immediately. If you have at least read the story you will be spared the sense of irritation which comes to one who watches something which appears to be incomprehensible.

Demand the best, learn to sift the wheat from the chaff, and then and only then, opera may flourish in England. The air is full of reconstruction, of new means of communication, of plans for better understanding between nations. What could be more conducive to better understanding than to have a regular exchange of operatic companies between England and Italy?

So—here is our book! I don't ask you to praise it, but I do hope that you may enjoy it.

N. J.

Part One

ITALIAN OPERA HOUSES

By Naomi Jacob

LA SCALA, MILAN

IS it because La Scala was almost the first great Italian opera house which I visited, or because I have always found such kindness, gaiety and friendliness in that city, or because the music really was the best in Italy that La Scala seems to me to take pride of place among the famous opera houses of Italy? I cannot say, I only know that the first time I visited La Scala I experienced a thrill of excitement which I have never felt to the same degree elsewhere. Since that time I have been to La Scala again and again and have never failed to feel that sense of expectancy and excitement.

When I heard of the disaster which had overtaken the building, making this home of music, ballet and art one of the victims of the war, I felt what was literally a personal and actual grief. Again and again when I passed that dignified façade, where the traffic of Milan passes with noise and bustle, and knew that within the walls of La Scala workmen were busy, electricians were at work, carpenters occupied in the work of restoration, I felt something like a mental "song of hope" in my heart.

To enter the vast auditorium, to find it rebuilt, ready for those magnificent spectacles which are traditional of La Scala; to see again the beautiful theatre risen and made more beautiful than ever, was a wonderful moment. For the people responsible for the rebuilding have not only been clever, they have also been wise. They have resisted the temptation to rebuild in a "new manner", they have been content with the old form on to which has been "grafted", as it were, every modern improvement, every new technicality, each new scientific improvement, while still preserving the form and style of the building, which has grown through the years to become something woven into the tradition of the great city of Milan.

The theatre stands upon the site of the church of Santa Maria alla Scala, which was built in 1381. The actual building of the theatre began in January 1776, but a disastrous fire occurred which delayed the completing of the building until 1778. The architect was Giuseppe Piermarini, a man of great brilliance and inventive powers who has never received the recognition which was his due.

The opening performance—of a presentation which changed its name many times before everyone was satisfied with the title—was attended by a brilliant audience which included Ferdinando of Austria and Maria Ricciarda Beatrice d'Este.

The success of La Scala was immediate, and the Press was loud in its praise of the whole theatre, in fact the phrases used were filled with super-latives, and every part of the theatre—in addition to the actual presenta-tion which was applauded to the skies—received its due meed of unstinted praise. So on August 3, 1778, the great opera house began its historic career, and was destined to become a veritable temple of art. It was acclaimed also because it would be a means of distracting the people of Milan from thinking and talking exclusively of matters political, and would give them thoughts of a higher and more beautiful kind.

From 1778 to 1788 no less than twenty-two different operas were given, including works of Alessandri, Cimarosa and Zingarelli.

The Scala at this time did not concern itself merely with opera, the management were anxious to provide a musical and theatrical "menu" which should appeal to all classes and all tastes. The Scala, beautiful, with wonderful acoustics, splendid decorations, had not, as yet, a set and determined policy of opera. There were acrobats, ballet, concerts, opera, and in fact every kind of entertainment offered for the amusement of the people of Milan.

In 1871 the conductor's baton was given into the hand of Franco Faccio; he and Arturo Toscanini have done more than any other men to control the destinies of La Scala. These two men, both masters of their art, both filled with a passionate love of their country and her music and with admiration and understanding of the music of other nationalities have made the opera house in Milan among the most famous in the world.

Franco Faccio was to conduct at La Scala from 1871 until 1890 when his lamented death occurred. To enumerate the various operas which were presented during this time at La Scala would be tedious, but among them were a magnificent production of *William Tell*, the first performances of *Mefistofele* of Böito, *Maria Tudor*, *La Gioconda*, *Forza de Destino*, the first European presentation of *Aïda* and the great *Requiem Mass*.

Under the conductorship of Faccio, Adelina Patti came to Milan to give a number of recitals, being paid a figure which was regarded in those days as fantastic. The dresses worn by Patti for these recitals are still preserved in the beautiful museum attached to the Scala. Or more correctly, which was, before the disaster of 1943, attached to the opera house, for it, too, suffered from the incendiary bombs. Happily, thanks to the devotion and courage of the director of the museum, Stefano Vittadini, the treasures were saved, and will be rehoused when the Museum is rebuilt.

In December 1889 the first performance of *The Meistersingers* was given in Italy at La Scala, while two years previously the first presentation of *Otello* had been offered to the public.

At the end of April 1898 the orchestra of La Scala visited Paris for the official opening of the Trocadero, with various conductors, one of whom was Arturo Toscanini.

In spite of its successes, the Scala arrived at a crisis when on the feast of Saint Stéfano, 1897, owing to some difference of opinion between the management and the civil authorities, the opera house was closed. A card of mourning, with a deep black border, was placed in the main doors; the inscription read, *"Chiuso per la morta del sentimento dell' arte, del decoro cittadino, del buon senso."* Virtually, the statement ran, "This theatre is closed because the sentiments of art are dead."

Faccio was dead, but a saviour was at hand, and Guido, Duke Visconti de Modroni, came forward, backed by an influential group of citizens, and assumed the direction of the opera house with the declared intention of protecting it against the entrance of speculators into the management and general direction. The Duke continued to control the destinies of La Scala until his death in 1902, then the duties which he had undertaken passed into the hands of his son, Umberto, who continued to exercise them until 1917.

The Duke appointed Arturo Toscanini not only as conductor but as artistic director (*Direzione artistica*) with Giulio Gatti Casazza to control the administration. The opera house now entered into a period of great success and splendour, for in addition to Toscanini there were other famous conductors to take the baton at intervals. Among them are such names as Serafin, Gui, Mascagni, Martucci and others of equal lustre.

The operas given were many and splendid. Here in 1904 was the first performance of *Butterfly*, which was one of the rare complete fiascos of La Scala. Why this should have been so has never been made clear, it has been said that the clothes did not appeal to the audience, that a jealous enemy of Puccini engineered the adverse reception, and even that the soprano was too stout. The real reason is still unknown. *Butterfly* was originally given as a one-act opera, but after its unfavourable reception Puccini worked upon it, and by the time it arrived in America in 1906, and was offered at the Metropolitan on February 11, 1907, it had assumed its present form and was received with great acclamation. At the present time this opera, in common with others by Puccini, is among the most popular not only in Italy but throughout the world.

The last opera from the pen of this master was given at La Scala, when on April 25, 1926, under Toscanini, the unfinished opera *Turandot* was given and attained an immediate success. There is a tragedy connected with this opera, in which possibly Puccini reached heights which he had never done before. He was concentrating on the duet between the Princess and Calaf; again and again he worked at this music, although he had made copious notes and had roughed out the score for the remainder of the work. He wished this duet to be the "highlight" of the whole tremendously dramatic story, with its music often so barbaric, and at other moments so beautifully tender.

In 1924 Puccini was gravely ill with a disease which had attacked his throat. He visited a specialist in Belgium, and underwent an operation in Brussels. In spite of the fact that his music appears to flow so easily, you have only to read those revealing letters of his to realize that composition was not easy to Puccini. Again and again you find references to the trouble this or that passage was giving him. He writes, "Oh, this terrible *Tosca*" and "Help me with this dreadful *Turandot*." Shortly before his death—for although the operation was successful his heart gave way under the strain and he died on November 29, 1924—he said to a friend referring to *Turandot*, "This opera will be given incomplete! Someone will announce to the public, 'At this point Puccini died.'"

His premonition was fulfilled. As the last passage actually written and completed by Puccini was reached on the evening of its first presentation at La Scala, the music ceased abruptly, and Toscanini, turning to the deeply moved audience, said quietly, "At this point the Master laid down his pen for ever."

Turandot was finished, in the form in which we now know it, from Puccini's rough score, notes and sketches by Franco Alfano.

In the period of the First World War (1914–1918, still called by Italians *nostra guerra*) La Scala was closed, and its auditorium was given over to concerts, exhibitions, great committees for wartime relief and the like, but in 1918 great productions—among them notably *Mosè*—were given to raise funds for the wounded and the orphans and widows, under the conductors Serafin, Maschereni and Toscanini.

In 1920 Toscanini assumed complete artistic directorship, and after certain repairs and renovations had been done the magnificent production of *Falstaff* was given to a crowded house on December 26, 1921.

Later when Toscanini—for reasons which now we may thankfully forget, except that our admiration must always go out to the man who placed the beauty and form of music above political rulings—left La Scala, its reputation continued to stand high. Splendid productions were given, great artists sang there, not only Italians but artists of every nationality and with worldwide reputations.

It is impossible not to record the name of Gino Marinuzzi as a great conductor, also that of Vittorio Gui.

For the theatre itself—the façade is solid and dignified, and differs very little from the original design, except that the present effect is slightly

22

lighter and the arches more open. In the original design the arches were solidly built in with brick, in the later design they are open, so forming a portico.

Inside everything is splendid and dignified—and although this refers to the Scala as it was before August 16, 1943, it will also apply to the new Scala—the boxes rise tier upon tier to the roof, there are six rows of them, all beautifully lit, and commanding a clear view of the stage. The drop curtain is fine, or was, for I have not actually seen the new one. At one time this drop was painted by the great artist Monticelli.

There is the usual chandelier of great beauty and immense size; the attendants move softly and carefully; they, too, are dignified in their black knee-breeches and tail coats, with silver chains round their necks. When last I entered, armies of workmen were in occupation, the boxes were all in place, with a great "Royal Box" in the centre of the second tier. This will, one supposes, be used for important visitors and Ministers. If anything, the Scala appeared to me to be lighter than before. The safety curtain was raised, and I caught a glimpse of the wonderful width and depth of the stage and the mass of mechanical contrivances which have gone to contribute so much to the spectacles given at La Scala. I was assured that there were innovations in the shape of new rooms where the audience would be able to walk and talk between the acts, and a new and admirably fitted buffet. In fact, that every advantage had been taken to make the great opera house worthy of its tradition and its fine history.

Then Toscanini returned to Italy, and took the conductor's chair once more. La Scala had been born again!

Many performances come back to me as I write: Malipiero in *Jongleur de Notre Dame*, an opera given far too seldom; Francesco Merli; Maria Caniglia; Mafalda Favero, who renders Puccini so excellently and with such art; the ever-young and much-loved Toti dal Monte, who has brought such distinction to the rôles of Rosina, Gilda and Lucia; Iva Pacetti; Giacomo Lauri Volpi, with the Duke of Mantua and Principe Ignoto of *Rigoletto* and *Turandot*, so outstanding in his various roles; Gigli, the great and wonderful tenor who is acclaimed everywhere—I heard him at La Scala in *Forza del Destino* before the war, I heard him in Rome and Naples after the war had ended, and only found his voice to be—if possible—richer and more colourful; Giuseppina Corbelli, who made such outstanding successes in the Wagnerian roles; Gina Cigna whose Aïda remains one of the glories of La Scala, as does her incredible and wonderful presentation of the Princess in *Turandot*, and Tancredi Pasero the great bass, with his characterization of Mefistofele and also of Boris—these artists have always seemed to me to sing most beautifully in La Scala, and now again they have an opera house worthy of them and their great art.

THE CASTELLO, MILAN

(Open-air)

ROME has its open-air theatre in the Baths of Caracalla, Milan has one in the Castello of the Dukes of the family of Sforza. Even to mention this family in passing is to open the floodgates of memories of the wild and savage times of the Middle Ages, when, indeed, might was accepted as right.

To read of the rise of Francesco Sforza is to study chapters of history which to us now seem fantastic in their extravagance. He was one of those characters found frequently during the 14th and 15th centuries who made an overwhelming success of the profession of arms. For years he, with his band of fighting men, wandered about the country—both his own and those of other nations—literally tracking war or disturbance as a dog might pick up the scent of game. The war, the dispute to be settled by force of arms, once found, Francesco Sforza sold his services and that of his mercenaries to the highest bidder.

He was energetic, he was vulgar and he was completely unscrupulous. What more could be needed in those turbulent days to mark a man for success? For some years he wandered about North Italy trying, as it were, to find a foothold where he might establish himself. He was employed as a fighting force by the Pope, by Venice and by the Medici. Then it became obvious to his exceedingly quick and active mind that the fall of the Visconti was imminent. He hurried to Milan and virtually entered the service of this decaying dynasty. Slowly he gathered power, until when he felt that the time was ripe he flung off his "badges of service" and during an interview with Filippo Visconti asked for the hand of the Duke's illegitimate daughter. Visconti laughed in his face, astonished at his temerity.

But Sforza was content to wait and while waiting—to work. Slowly he fought his way forward step by step, and finally the marriage was celebrated. On this marriage, Sforza based his claim to the Dukedom of Milan.

Filippo Visconti died, and Sforza, again content to play his "waiting game" entered the service of the Republic; his power grew, until he was able to seize the city itself and to starve it into surrender. He then put into operation his project to rebuild the great Castello of Galeazzo Visconti, assuring the inhabitants of Milan that his one aim was to beautify and enrich the city. Curiously enough, the Milan people believed him, and the castle was rebuilt, fortified, and through the years enlarged and strengthened. It was in part, at least, the work of Bramonte; here Leonardo da Vinci walked, experimented with decorations, worked out his wonderful plans for irrigation, agriculture and the art of war.

Many things may be said to the discredit of Francesco Sforza and his descendants, but it must be admitted that with all their faults they were generous and highly intelligent patrons of the arts. It was that Duke nicknamed "*Il Moro*"—"The Moor"—who first heard Leonardo when he came from Florence and realized that this man with his curious lute "constructed almost wholly of silver and in the shape of a horse's head" was to be one of the outstanding figures of the years.

Slowly the Castello lost its military significance and became one of the greatest museums of Italy, perhaps of Europe. Here the finest treasures of Milan were gathered and displayed, so that it was possible to reconstruct the whole development of life in Italy by walking through its various great rooms and studying the exhibits.

Here, as is fit and right, because music will always play an integral part in the life of Italy, open-air opera is given every summer. A great stage is built, tiers and tiers of seats rise in one of the great courts, and the people of Milan flock to listen to the music which they love. The acoustics are not so good as those at Verona, and I have sometimes wondered if the ghost of Leonardo wanders there and wishes that he might, by some marvel of ingenuity or one of his miracles of intelligence, evolve a scheme to make them perfect. Despite this fault the sight of the Castello, filled with people—*the people*, for this is not restricted to the higher forms of society but is a *popular* spectacle—all intent on their beloved opera is a fine sight. Often the Castello at Milan has served as a kind of "jumping-off place" for young artists in their careers. The stars—or rather the "fixed planets"—shine there, but opportunities are frequently given to lesser-known singers to prove their worth.

As is invariable in the Italian open-air theatres, the productions are excellent and often magnificent; I have seen *Aïda* there given with great splendour, also *La Gioconda*.

Possibly where all these huge open-air stages fail a little is to convey the impression of "small interiors" such as in the first and last acts of *Bohème*. The out-of-door scenes are realistic, great cathedral interiors are credible by reason of the height and dignity, but I have seen the unfortunate Floria Tosca racing about the dining-room of Scarpia like a hare pursued by greyhounds and covering almost as much ground. When I listened to *Tosca* in the Arena at Verona, with its immense stage, where, however, the stage managers did attempt to limit the floor space, the room remained immense and unreal in its immensity; I decided that open-air opera houses should only present "spectacular" productions, if the sense of realism were to be preserved.

TEATRO DELL' OPERA, ROME

YEARS ago the two theatres which Rome possessed were the Constanzi and the Argentina, and in 1926 it was decided to rebuild and reconstruct the former to give Rome an opera house which should be worthy of her.

The Constanzi was built in the middle of the last century, and stood on the Viminale. It was a fine theatre, but there were grave drawbacks to it, such as the fact that it lacked the dignity and space necessary for the entrance of large audiences. It was built in something just over a year by Domenico Constanzi, a man of great energy and commercial courage, who had come to Rome as a young man and had been responsible for the building of several large and well-equipped hotels. The site of one is now occupied in Rome by the great American College. It is said that he hesitated between rebuilding the Argentina, and also considered the possibilities of the Teatro Apollo, but it was deemed that the position of this latter near the Ponte Sant' Angelo rendered it unsuitable.

Therefore in 1877 Domenico Constanzi began to discuss plans with the architect Achille Sfondrini. Sfondrini specialized in the designing of theatres, and was also responsible for the Teatro Verdi in Padova. The building began about the middle of 1879, and the opera house opened— though it was not completely finished—on November 27, 1880 with *La Semiramide* of Rossini.

The new theatre was splendid, well built and large enough to seat 2200 people. It was lit by gas, which was then regarded as a modern form of lighting, but in 1887 the still more modern form of electricity was installed.

The theatre was a success, and record will be made here of a few of the great productions and great artists who appeared there. In 1926 it was decided to rebuild the Constanzi, which, although a fine theatre, presented certain drawbacks, one of the chief being that the entrances were not sufficiently convenient, particularly when huge audiences flocked to hear some especially famous opera. A special entrance was arranged for the Royal Family and important visitors of the State, the whole approach to the building was enlarged, and the fine foyer was also enlarged and beautified. The cupola, decorated in mythological figures relating to art and music, was designed by Annibale Brugnoli; the architectural designs were made by Marcello Piacentini.

A ballet school was added; the lighting system was modernized under the direction of Professor Giannelli. A huge room was built for the painting of scenery, probably one of the finest in the world. Offices for the directors of the various activities of the opera house were added, and some of these are exceedingly fine. The most modern form of heating was installed, and hydraulic lifts for moving scenery, for taking artists to their dressing-rooms and to facilitate the business of the theatre, put in place.

The stage was a difficulty, for while it was thirty metres wide, it was only twenty-one metres deep, but this was atoned for by the installing of the "panorama", a mechanical contrivance which gives—apparent—added depth to the stage.

It has been my privilege to go all over the "back stage" of this opera house, and while my knowledge of theatres is fairly extensive, both as a member of the public and as an actress, I have never seen anything to compare with the Teatro Reale of Rome, now called the Teatro dell' Opera.

The *cuore pulsante del teatro* that is the "beating heart of the theatre" is its great electric system of lighting. Here are to be found all the latest inventions of the art of theatrical lighting; the amount of light can be controlled with an exactitude which is not only wonderful but highly artistic. Ferdinando Bordoni, who is the director of this wonderful system, has every reason to be proud of his achievement.

The "wardrobe" is magnificent. You pass through room after room; here are the costumes for *Aïda* neatly hung, cleaned and pressed, the whole of the clothes necessary for this opera gathered into one great room. Here are the uniforms, the armour and the arms for *Faust*; in another room you may see everything needed in the way of clothes and "stage properties"—or rather what we should call "hand props"—for *Butterfly* or *Rigoletto*.

In February 1928 the work on the new opera house was progressing rapidly, the new frontage was well on the way to being completed. That same year the Teatro Reale was opened in Rome. Since that time the directors have upheld the best and finest traditions of opera; they have given magnificent productions, and have engaged the most famous artists, the best conductors and the most brilliant specialists in theatrical engineering. But since the history of the old Constanzi is really part of the history of the Teatro dell' Opera it is interesting to note some of the famous productions of the old building.

The first performance which might be regarded in the light of a "gala performance" was *Semiramide* by Rossini, given on November 27, 1880, when the house was crowded with all the notable people of Roman society. The audience is described as having been "youthful, beautiful and elegant", and the list of important people present fairly bristles with titles and famous family names—princesses, duchesses and countesses are named in great profusion, and it is recorded that in the

27

first tier of boxes sat the officers of the regiment quartered in Rome at the time.

The King and Queen entered their box while the "Marcia Reale" was played. It is recorded that the opera ended at a quarter to one!

In the part of Rosina it is recorded during the following spring Bianca Donadio made a tremendous personal success. She was acclaimed in a popular song which was heard everywhere, a song which was founded on the music of *"Figaro qua, Figaro là!"*

Roughly translated it runs:

> Figaro here, Figaro there!
> All the world is rushing to the Constanzi,
> Bianca is the star of the town!

1890 was the year of *Cavalleria*, later in the year the great Emma Calvé appeared on the stage of the Constanzi, singing with great success in several operas.

1893 saw the production of *Otello*, produced while its great composer was attacked by nervous fears as to its success and retired to his rooms at the hotel waiting apprehensively for the verdict of the public. Later *Falstaff* was given at a gala performance, attended by the King and Queen, the Queen Mother and other members of the Royal House. The reception was wildly enthusiastic. The house rang with plaudits, and cries of *"Viva Verdi!"*

In the season of 1893 the innovation of giving *Cavalleria* and *Pagliacci* as "twins" or, as the Italians say, *"siamese"*, was first introduced; previously *Cavalleria* had been given followed by a single act taken from some other popular opera.

The opening night of *Tosca* remains as one of the most exciting in the history of the opera house.

As Pietro Mascagni had taken *Cavalleria* from a play offered to the public with the great Eleanora Duse in the leading rôle, so Giacomo Puccini wished to adapt for the opera house the melodrama which had shown Sarah Bernhardt at her finest and most dramatic. Together with his famous librettist Illica, Puccini visited Sardou in Paris. There was a great discussion regarding the last act, and Puccini disliked the first suggestions; he was not even pleased with his own music!

"Questa è l' aria del paletot!" he exclaimed ("This music will make the audience put on their overcoats and leave!"). Sardou was delighted with Puccini's theatrical sense, and said, "Ah, it is plain to me that you are a man of the theatre!" (*"un uomo del teatro"*) The opera was written, and produced at the Constanzi on the night of January 14, 1900.

Something was wrong on the night of the production! Mugnone, the conductor, came to Puccini a quarter of an hour before the curtain was due to go up, and whispered, "They say that a bomb will be thrown in the theatre!" The curtain rose, and the Chief of Police whispered to Mugnone, "At the first sign of a disturbance—play the Royal March!"

For some reason—still unknown—the audience muttered, grumbled and whispered. The artists were upset and nervous, some of them burst into tears, but that "man of the theatre" retained his tranquillity.

"Why are you crying?" he demanded. "Are we all children!"

The noise grew worse; a voice called, "Bring down the curtain quickly." Then gradually—and again the reason will never be known—the noise subsided. True, the audience was not completely silent, there was a nervous tension everywhere, but when the curtain finally came down it descended if not to wholehearted applause, yet to applause which showed that the opera had not proved a failure.

Tosca was given again, and with every performance its popularity grew; now it is one of the established favourites.

To give a list of the artists who have delighted the hearts of the audiences at the Teatro dell' Opera would be impossible—sufficient to say that it would include all the greatest names in the history of opera: Gemma Bellincioni, Rosina Storchio, Enrico Caruso, De Lucia, Claudia Muzio, Toti Dal Monte, Gina Cigna, Caniglia, Lauri Volpi, Gigli. These are but a few of the singers who have delighted the Roman audiences.

Although I have dealt only with the Teatro dell' Opera in Rome, it is interesting to turn for a moment to the Argentina, where was staged one of the most disastrous failures in the history of opera, comparable to the "fiasco" of *Traviata* at La Fenice in Venice, which is still referred to in the annals of that theatre as *"Storico fiasco de La Traviata"*. This was equalled in Rome by the reception of *The Barber of Seville* of Rossini, an opera which is now among the most popular in the repertoire of Italian opera companies.

In December 1815 the manager of the Argentina commissioned two operas from Rossini, and produced the first—*Torvaldo e Dorliska*—which had no marked success. Caesarini, the said manager, suggested that Rossini should write an opera using the libretto of the opera *Il Barbiere di Siviglia* which had been set to the music of Paisiello over fifty years previously. Paisiello was still alive, and the Roman audiences could, many of them, recall the very pleasant music of his work.

It is said that Rossini wrote *Il Barbiere* in a fortnight, but this is probably a slight understatement, although Rossini was a rapid worker. He wrote to the old musician, Paisiello, and virtually asked his permission to use the libretto. The elder man answered that he had no objection to Rossini using it. It is said that although his letter was sufficiently cordial, he was in reality intensely jealous, and that he gave his permission solely because he believed that Rossini would make a ghastly and terrible failure of the attempt. It is also contended that this jealousy on the part of Paisiello had existed since Rossini—who was only twenty-five years old—had scored a great success at Naples in 1815, with *Elizabetta, Regina d'Inghilterra*. Rossini, to use a modern phrase, "boxed clever", and showed the letter from Paisiello to all the musicians and music lovers in Rome; he also changed the title of the opera to *Almaviva, ossia gli Inutile Precauzione* ("Almaviva, or the Useless Precautions").

Nowhere can scandal and whisperings flourish more readily than in the theatre and the opera house, and very soon all Rome was talking of Rossini's "underhand action". There were two camps in every café, the one upholding young Rossini, the other maintaining that he had behaved disgracefully to the elder musician. It is rumoured that Paisiello was not altogether without blame in this matter of spreading dissension, and Rossini was shown a letter in Paisiello's handwriting—sent to Rome from Naples—urging the recipient to do everything possible to ensure that Rossini's opera should be a complete failure.

The story of the first night is recounted by Signora Giorgi-Righetti, who played Rosina and who was held in high regard by the Roman audiences. She tells that Garcia, who was playing Almaviva, persuaded Rossini to allow him to introduce a Spanish song to be sung under Rosina's balcony. Garcia felt that as the scene was set in Spain this would give a greater sense of reality.

By this time the audience were ready in their respective "camps"—the angry supporters of Paisiello and the rather diffident friends of Rossini, who were all too conscious that his last opera produced in the Argentina had met with no particular success.

Garcia made his entrance, with the guitar. It had not been tuned for him to use! The opera was "held up" while he tuned it, and—broke a string! That accident gave the "anti-Rossini" section their cue, and they indulged in whistles and catcalls. They listened quietly enough to the entrance air of Figaro, but on his entrance—the part was played by Zamboni—when he carried another guitar, they burst into roars of laughter, and the solo was rendered inaudible. Giorgi-Righetti—and remember that she was young, attractive and a general favourite—entered to sing *"Segui, o caro, d'segui cosi"* ("Continue, dear, to do always so"). The recollection of the two guitars was too much for the audience and their laughter increased.

The opera seemed doomed, despite the fact that for her solo *"Una voce poco fa"* ("A little voice I heard just now") the *prima donna* received a "triple round of applause"; that ended, the noise grew louder, and Castil-Blaze comments that "all the whistlers of Italy seemed to have given themselves a *rendezvous* for this performance".

30

At the end of the first act Rossini turned to the audience, shrugged his shoulders and clapped his hands. The audience were furious at his obvious contempt and reserved their revenge for the second act—not a single note of which could be heard.

At the fall of the last curtain Rossini left the opera house calmly, as if the attack on his opera did not concern him in the least. The artists, full of sympathy for the composer, hurried into their street clothes and went round to his lodgings to offer him such comfort as might be possible. They arrived there to find Rossini—in bed and sound asleep!

When the opera was produced in Paris its reception was little better; in fact many of the critics declared that it was far inferior to Paisiello's work. Paër, the musical director at the Theatre Italian, stated that owing to a "public demand he would produce the work of Paisiello". This, however, did no harm to Rossini, for the opera was declared by all who heard it to be both dull and old-fashioned.

It is strange how Rossini's work has won its way into public favour until, at the present time, it is offered constantly, and always receives very warm appreciation.

THE BATHS OF CARACALLA, ROME

(*Open-Air*)

NEAR the Passeggiata Archeologica, sometimes called Parco di Porta Capena, may be seen the Baths of Caracalla, one of the most beautiful antiques in Rome, still almost perfect.

Whatever modern science has devised it has never succeeded in providing anything better than the baths which were designed by the Romans, who had apparently a perfect passion for bathing. Whether this came from a longing for cleanliness, or whether they realized—as all civilized people must—the extent of the luxury of hot baths, perfectly appointed, one does not know.

The baths proper are 330 metres along each side, the baths themselves are 220 by 114 metres, and it is estimated that 1600 bathers could be accommodated at one time.

The baths were built by Marcus Aurelius Antonius Bassianus, who was born at Lyons in the year A.D. 188. His father gave him the nickname of "Caracalla", owing to the fact that when he returned from Gaul he wore one of the long cloaks with hoods typical of that country and its people, and known as *caracalla*.

In A.D. 211 his father died, and "Caracalla" and his brother were left to govern Rome. It would appear that Marcus Aurelius Antonius was far from a pleasant person, for he contrived that his brother Publius should be murdered, so that he might have the power vested completely in himself. He went further, and in the next few years caused the execution of no less than 20,000 persons of both sexes who had been his brother's supporters and friends.

His whole reign seems to have been characterized by bloodshed and whole-hearted persecution, tyranny and plots. In the year A.D. 217 he was assassinated, having reigned for six years, leaving behind him very little but memories of hatred and violence; but he left of posterity the magnificent Baths of Caracalla.

These splendid ruins consist of an enclosure within very high walls of Roman brickwork; like all these Roman bricks, they have become mellowed by time, and when at the open-air performances they are flood-lit the effect is very charming.

The stage itself has for a background great blocks of brickwork, which may be joined by suitable pieces of scenery, painted to "fit in" with the brickwork. This setting, simple and almost natural, needs few

The exterior of the Teatro dell' Opera (formerly Teatro Reale), Rome

Exterior of the Teatro San Carlo, Naples

Interior of the Teatro San Carlo, Naples

additions in the way of scenery to prepare the stage for those spectacular operas which are so typical of Italy.

Here, differing from the Castello at Milan, the acoustics are admirable, and in every part of "the house" the music can be heard perfectly. Here again we have the tiers of seats rising, the great stage, the splendid productions and the finest artists in Italy.

This, like Milan and Verona, is an open-air theatre which makes an appeal to every class of music-loving person, and where the prices of the seats make it possible for all classes to attend. The scene is very fine, with the Roman monuments of antiquity on every side, with great arches and pillars rising in the semi-darkness to remind you that you are in "The Eternal City".

Referring to Michael Kelly, who has left such a vivid account of his travels in Italy as a singer, it is interesting to read—though I admit that these remarks have nothing to do with opera—that he drove "with the worthy Mr. Stuart, his amiable wife and sister", they spent their first night on the journey from Naples, where Kelly had been singing, at Terracina; which he records is "a dangerous place to sleep during the summer months, as it is then rendered dreadfully unwholesome by what the Romans call the *mal aria*". The words *mal aria* mean literally "bad air", but many of us who spent time in Sicily and Italy with the C.M.F. during the war have good reason to remember the full significance and the unpleasant results of this *mal aria*.

Kelly is, to me at least, so fascinating that I cannot bear not to quote him further, and this reference will be of interest again, to people who were with the Allies in C.M.F. He notes that they drove to the Piazza di Spagna, where the Spanish Ambassador lived and where his powers were so great that he could, if he wished, give protection even in cases of murder. How many of us remember this beautiful Piazza, where stands the house known as the "Keats and Shelley Memorial". Kelly and his party then visited two opera houses, the Altiberti and the Argentini, and this latter was, during the occupation of Rome, taken over by ENSA, and performances were given for the Allied forces.

It is recorded that the Roman audiences of the 18th century were among the most critical in Europe. Of these the numerous *abbés* were the most severe. There they would sit, each one with a lighted candle and the complete score of the opera on their knees. Should some unfortunate singer be guilty of a mistake, these *clerics* would shout in unison, "*Bravo, bestia!*" ("Well done, you beast!") When it was known that the composer of the opera was present, and these critical gentlemen detected any passage which was similar to some phrase in the opera of another composer, they raised their voices again in shouts of "*Bravo, il ladro!*" ("Well done, the thief!") or called out the name of the composer of

c

the original theme, *"Bravo, Sacchini!"* or *"Bravo, Paisiello!"* It is even recorded that upon one occasion when the *abbés* felt that a very large portion of the opera had been "lifted" from the work of some master, several of them rose and chanted in chorus, "May the curse of God descend upon him who first encouraged you to write music!"

In the Argentini an indifferent tenor named Gabrielli[1] was appearing. His sister was a very successful artist, and it may be that her brother traded to a certain extent on her name.

He appeared, and had scarcely sung a dozen bars when the audience began to show their disapproval, shouting, "Take away the raven!" and "We wish to hear music—not this!" The tenor came down to the footlights, and without anger spoke to the noisy audience in these words: "Ladies and gentlemen, do not imagine for one moment that I differ from your judgment of me, I agree completely. Indeed, I have never appeared on any stage but my audiences have behaved in exactly the same manner as you are doing tonight."

But all this is moving away from the Baths of Caracalla, where tourists from all over the world have gathered to hear Italian opera in its age-old setting. The opera over, you may wander out into the Passeggiata Archeologica, and on every side find memories of that great Imperial Rome which is still—in spite of all her vicissitudes—the pride of every Italian heart.

---

[1] Mentioned as singing in the San Carlo, Naples, and Palermo, Sicily.

THE SAN CARLO OPERA HOUSE, NAPLES

W HEN I saw the San Carlo first, it was long before the war laid its hand upon Naples in common with the rest of the world. The San Carlo is perhaps not so beautifully placed as the Teatro dell' Opera in Rome, but it is in itself such a splendid commanding building that, except on the side of the façade—which admittedly is somewhat hemmed in—it is arresting and dominating.

When next I saw it, the streets were crowded with military, and their cars and *camions*, it was a matter of personal danger to attempt to cross the road from the Galleria to the opera house; in those days you literally took your life in your hands in making your way to that part of the San Carlo which was being used as an officers' club.

The last time, which was in the summer of 1946, Naples seemed comparatively empty; the majority of the troops had gone, the streets were almost empty of military vehicles, and though the Officers' Club still "functioned" it was a shadow of its former self in so far as the number of visitors was concerned.

I have never been able to write about anything without digression, and I shall allow myself to indulge in this failing now for a moment. Whatever may be the shortcomings of the Italians as a nation, they possess to an extent which I have never met in any other country the art of remembering you. True, I was in Naples for several months, true too that I used the Club a good deal; but when I returned after an absence of six months and went there, the attendants recognized me immediately. The same can be said of the attendants actually employed in the theatres, of custodians in museums and art galleries, to say nothing of waiters in restaurants and hotels.

The comment might be, "Well, and what good does that do any-one?" Believe me, a great deal! To enter, for example, the Officers' Club in Naples after an absence of six months or more, having had a long and terribly hot drive from Rome, with your mind filled with business worries and being in the process of recovering from a very unpleasant attack of malaria, and to be greeted immediately upon your entrance, does help to re-establish your sense of well-being and your somewhat battered self-esteem.

Now—the San Carlo!

King Charles of Bourbon decided that Naples should have an opera house worthy of her, and in 1737 he entrusted one of his brigadiers, Giovanni Medrano, with the task of designing the building. The opera house was to be built near the Royal Palace; the machinery was set in motion, the designs made, and in little over eight months the splendid building was complete. The time taken seems fantastic, for the San Carlo is filled with long corridors, great vestibules, many smaller apartments in addition to the actual auditorium and the various rooms dedicated to the general work of a great theatre. The whole place is built of brick and stone of the most lasting and solid type; even after the terrible bombardment which Naples suffered, the damage to the San Carlo was negligible.

On November 4, 1737, the Saint's Day dedicated to Saint Charles Borromeo, Archbishop of Milan, and also the personal "saint's day" of the King, after whom it was named—or would it be more correct to say that it was named both for the Saint and also for the King?—the great opera house was opened.

The first production was *Achille in Sciro*, by Pietro Metastasio, the music was by Sarro and the *prima donna* was Marianna Bulgarelli. The opera was preceded at eight o'clock by a prologue; after which the "Magnificenza", the "Gloria" and the "Celebrità" were recited and the choir hailed the King with the cry, "Long live Carlo!" It is recorded that the whole production of the opera which followed was admirable, the setting magnificent, and the acoustics acclaimed to be perfect.

The opera house was lit with oil-lamps, wax and tallow candles; in every box the social eminence of the occupants was proclaimed by the number of wax candles burning before mirrors at the back of the box. The higher the dignitary the greater the number of candles.

In 1777 the theatre was renovated and redecorated, and it is recorded that the beautiful building was more lovely than ever. Between the years 1810 and 1812 an architect, Antonio Niccolini, added the arcade and façade which extends round the side of the building; at the same time the interior was again restored and decorated. Then came—and how often this has happened in Italian theatres!—a terrible fire which destroyed the work of years and left the San Carlo practically a ruin.

On January 12, 1816, rehearsals were taking place for a ballet, the workmen responsible for the lighting had left everything in readiness for the following day—the day of the actual production. They forget to extinguish one lamp! That was left burning in the "wardrobe". A window was open, a draught caught the flame of the lamp, and the whole place, with its hanging dresses, burnt like tinder. Nothing could save the opera house, despite the frantic efforts of everyone concerned. All that remained were the solid, well-built walls.

On February 22, 1816, a royal decree announced that before the end of the year the San Carlo would "rise again from the ashes".

What workers they were, these Neapolitans; how passionately they loved their opera house and the music which was offered to them within its walls!

The San Carlo entered on a new life, a life of great success and splendour. The architect chosen was Antonio Niccolini, and his new designs contained many features which were innovations of a modern kind and which contributed greatly to the dignity, usefulness and beauty of the San Carlo.

On the opening night, when the Prince visited the theatre and was escorted to the Royal Box, he said, laughing, "It is all splendid; but you have forgotten to give me a private entrance, and so I have to enter with the ordinary public!"

Niccolini, bowing, said, "Sir, this defect shall be remedied."

The opera ended, and the Prince rose to leave. Niccolini was waiting, and indicated a small corridor which led to a separate entrance for the Royal Family.

Immediately the Prince had been seated in the box the architect had rallied a small army of workmen, and had ordered them to make a private corridor by cutting off a piece of the larger one used by the public. It is recorded that the men "worked like demons", and by the time the opera was over the private exit was ready.

There is a sequel to that story. When the Allies were in Naples the opera was always crowded, and tickets were frequently difficult to obtain. Again and again the reply for an application was, "We are sold out!" Yet invariably when the door opened and the audience streamed in it was found that a small number of Sappers were already in their places. At last, after enquiry, the mystery was solved.

These engineers, visiting the theatre and being interested in its construction, had discovered that the wall at the side of the entrance was less solid than the rest. It was evident to them that there was another entrance! So, until the matter was discovered, certain R.E.s had been using the private entrance of the Royal Family of Italy! They bought their tickets early, before the rush for buying, and made their way to the auditorium by way of the "secret passage"!

The manager was the famous Dominico Barbaja, a curious and picturesque character. He had risen from humble birth, he possessed little actual education, he earned a tremendous fortune—completely by his own efforts—and squandered every penny of it. He loved music, and constituted himself the generous patron of two rising musicians— Rossini and Donizetti.

The rebuilding and reconstruction was a triumph. There was the magnificent Royal Box and the tiers of boxes rising one above the other, the splendid painted ceiling by Cammarano depicted "Apollo presenting to the Muses the greatest Greek, Latin and Italian poets". The drop-curtain, which was painted by a band of artists under the direction of Niccolini, was applauded as a work of art, the stage and its arrangements, the fine staircases, which still remain, all went to make up a theatre which is one of the glories of Naples.

The curtain was replaced in 1854 by one which was the work of Giuseppe Mancinelli, which shows the Muses and Homer with eighty-three poets and musicians gathered round them.

Then followed the question of the *foyer*. There was no room sufficiently large for the audience to gather between the acts—and as we know the waits in Italian opera are very long—to talk over the performance, to smoke and meet their friends. If they walked in the long corridors they were not allowed to smoke, if they went out into the porch or the *portici* they were, to all intents and purposes, in the street itself.

At last after endless discussions, arguments and conferences, permission was given in 1936 by Prince Umberto of Piedmont to build on an immense hall, on the condition that exactly the same materials as formed the remainder of the opera house were used. This great hall, which is reached from the original vestibule after crossing a circular hall where a fine marble bust of Verdi is standing, is decorated in the most magnificent fashion. Giovanni Brancaccio, an artist of the Neapolitan school, executed a frieze, there is a great amount of inlaid work, much use of fine wood and many mirrors; to this add a large number of divans upholstered in soft blue, and you have a room which is breath-taking in its splendour.

I find here that I am writing as if the San Carlo were completely given over to opera again; it may be that this fine room is still the restaurant of the Officers' Club, but that it will be back in all its old beauty before long cannot be doubted for a moment.

The size of the stage is tremendous, covering an area of 10,045 feet. That is twenty-four feet wider and also much deeper than the stage at Covent Garden. The lighting is the best that modern knowledge can produce, its wardrobe is extensive and—at least until the war, when its resources were called upon to assist productions in smaller and less fortunate opera houses—excellently kept. The device known as the "Fortuny[1] cupola", invented, as its name implies, by the painter of that name, forms a great addition to obtaining effects of "distance". This invention is used in every Italian theatre, where it has come to be regarded as an essential part of the equipment.

During the war the San Carlo was perhaps the first opera house to make a real appeal to the Allied troops. Many of them had never had any

---

[1] Note: Referring to Fortuny, I find that Mr. C. B. Cochran in his delightful book, *Showman Looks On*, makes the following remarks: "Many of the so-called inventions of the modern stage are in reality the inventions of MacKaye or others before him. . . . He preceded Fortuny with machinery to produce cloud, sun, rain, wave and rainbow effects, and substituted overhead lighting for footlights."

opportunity to watch opera, and to learn, to understand and appreciate its beauties. Once the boys realized that opera was not some strange kind of "highbrow" entertainment, when they understood that many of the operas were fine, full-blooded dramas, that the music was not incomprehensible, but suitable for "whistling in the bath", they began to flock in greater and greater numbers to the San Carlo. I believe that in this opera house were sown the seeds of a real and actual interest in opera, seeds which grew and flourished among the Allied troops.

Certainly no better audience ever existed; they were punctual, they gave rapt attention, and their appreciation was unstinted.

I remembered so well the first time that the greatest tenor of our day appeared there—Gigli. I had not seen or heard him since the last Italian Season at Covent Garden, and I admit that I went to the San Carlo wondering if that wonderful voice would have survived the years of the war.

The production was *La Tosca* of Puccini, which I still regard as a work having all the elements of a magnificent dramatic opera. The story is good, a story dealing with human passions and emotions which can never change and which never grow stale.

The house was packed from floor to ceiling, everywhere you looked were uniforms and men's heads bent over their programmes to study the "story of the opera"; which, as I had written it myself, pleased me considerably. This pleasure was somewhat mitigated when various soldiers told me, "Yes, we can understand the story now, but you've robbed us of a lot of laughs." This because, frankly, the former stories were written in some language which might have been many things, but which was certainly not English.

The curtain rose—for in *La Tosca* there is no overture, merely a few masterly chords—Gigli entered. The effect of his entrance was electric, his ovation tremendous. I could not see that he had changed; if anything I felt that his actual acting had improved. His voice, that wonderful voice, might have lost a little of its "freshness" but there was the same magnificent artistry, the same ability to move the hearts of his listeners. In short—Beniamino Gigli had "come back" to enter the hearts of the Allies.

In order to give some idea of the working of the stage of the San Carlo, I am giving extracts here from an article written for the programme by one of the British Military executants who was in part responsible for the productions. The article is signed "F.P.F."

"Every morning at 7.30 five electricians and twenty stage hands report for duty. When we have ten operas running, as we had at Christmas, it is impossible to raise scenery to its exact position and leave it there. Therefore the previous day large backcloths have to be taken off their battens and moved to the rear, doubled up and raised to the roof. . . . If we have *Faust* and *La Bohème* in one day that means nine different scenes in all: six in *Faust* and three in *La La Bohème.*[1]

"All the scenery in the San Carlo is built on the stage, and unlike Rome we have no workshops or doors through which the scenery can be brought in. The scenery is "put together" on the stage between 9 and 11.30 a.m. if there is no rehearsal, while the orchestra is rehearsing in the orchestra pit with the safety curtain—which is almost sound-proof—lowered. At 11.30 the afternoon opera must be prepared and the stage cleaned. At 12.30 the opera house is peaceful except for the whiff of vacuum cleaners as the final touches are given. At 13.30 activity starts again, when fifteen electricians and twenty stage hands arrive to help to move scenery as quickly as possible. When the performance begins we have about twenty electricians and forty stage hands all working. Unlike Rome, we have no 'lifts' on the stage, and all our platforms and staircases have to be built by hand—no easy task."

Here is his last paragraph, and I ask you to read it, and remember it when you next listen to Italian opera in Naples, Rome, or any other city.

"Perhaps you think that the intervals are rather long at times, but I can assure you that Antonio di Scala, the hardest-worked man in the opera house, and his staff do a very fine job of work, and that it would be almost impossible to cut down the length of the intervals."

That I consider a very fine tribute made by a British officer to the Italian staff with which he worked. It is all over now, the great opera house will be run again by its own management, but I venture to think that both British and Italians will look back with pleasure to the time when the San Carlo Opera House was run—and run under great difficulties—by the British Military Authorities in Naples.

It is of interest to read something of the original San Carlo Opera House, destroyed by fire as I have related. This is an account of the opera house given by Michael Kelly, who visited it in 1779 when he arrived in Naples for the purpose of having his voice trained.

He tells us that even in the middle of the 18th century the seats in the pit (by which he means the floor of the opera house as opposed to the boxes—what we called "the stalls" and the Italians "*poltrone*") were

[1] It is true that there are three different scenes, but there are four acts, thus four changes of scenery: the Studio, the Café Momus, the exterior of the inn, and back to the Studio.

40

all provided with stuffed cushions and arm-rests, but there was an arrangement that each seat was kept *locked*, the subscriber retaining the key after each performance. There were seven tiers of boxes—before the bombardment La Scala had four tiers and two galleries—the front of each box being a mirror illuminated by two large wax tapers (probably he means candles.—N.J.) and these, multiplied by reflection and added to by the blaze of light from the stage, gave a dazzling display.

Each box on the grand tier (*La prima fila*) had a small withdrawing room, where the pages of the theatre were waiting to hand ices and sweets to the patrons.

Kelly further records that the ballets at the San Carlo were staged with great lavishness and splendour; four hundred persons and eighty horses appeared in *Il Disfatta di Dario*, when the famous Madame Rossi was the *prima ballerina*.

THE CARLO FELICE OPERA HOUSE, GENOA

THERE is something tragic in writing of many of these magnificent Italian opera houses which suffered so badly during the war. Never again can they be quite the same; they may be rebuilt, the result may be splendid and satisfactory in every way, but the actual link with the past cannot be repaired.

The Carlo Felice, which was over a hundred years old—for it was opened in 1828—was terribly damaged (as was so much of the city of Genoa) by the air raids of 1944. The stage and much of the auditorium have gone; only the façade, so dignified and beautifully proportioned, is left.

The last time I heard opera in Genoa was in 1945, when it was given in a small, experimental theatre, totally unsuited to opera—or indeed to my mind to anything except some "intimate" plays—and the effect was depressing when I remembered the beauties of the Carlo Felice.

There is a kind of tradition in Italy that the Genoese are avaricious and that they hold their purse-strings with a tightness that may be compared to the belief that all Scotsmen are mean! Whatever may or may not be the characteristics of the people of this great city of Genoa, they most certainly never showed any signs of meanness when it was a matter of spending money for the advancement of any of the arts. Their opera house was one of the most splendid in Italy, second only in musical attainment to La Scala at Milan.

The Carlo Felice was designed by Carlo Barabino, an architect possessing a brilliant and fertile imagination. He was educated in Rome, and was awarded a prize for a design for a theatre, to be built in that city, by the Accademia di Santo Luca. This design made such an impression on the Genoese authorities that they gave him the work of building the Carlo Felice, the first opera house worthy of the name to be erected in Genoa. The authorities and the people of the city were generous, nothing was spared that would contribute to the beauty of the building. The façade was classical, beautiful in its grand simplicity. The acoustics were admitted to be perfect, and the corridors, vestibules, the various rooms and the auditorium contributed to make one of the most beautiful and satisfactory opera houses in Italy.

The opera house was opened on April 7, 1828, when Bellini's opera *Bianca é Fernando* was given. King Felice and Queen Maria Cristina were present at this performance, and the Royal Hymn was sung, set to music for the occasion by Gaetano Donizetti. The opera itself had been produced two years before in Naples, and Bellini came over from Milan to superintend the production of the new version which was to inaugurate the splendid Genoa opera house. With him came also many of his Milanese friends and admirers, and on the opening night the great building was packed with a most brilliant and enthusiastic audience.

Here we come to one of those charming love stories which seem to open the door in order to admit us into the more intimate life of great artists. The Duchess Litta, daughter of the Marquis Lomellini, had arrived from Milan, returning to her native city of Genoa to be present at the opening of the opera house. She knew Bellini very well, and introduced him to the most artistic and wealthy people in Genoa; he was entertained everywhere in a most generous manner, which seems to contradict again the "tradition" regarding the tight-fistedness of the inhabitants of that city.

At the house of the Marquis Lomellini, the great composer met the woman who was to influence his art so much; she was a native of Lombardy, by name Giuditta Turina. The moment that Bellini saw her he fell violently in love with her beauty and charm. She was very gracious to him, and with each meeting Bellini fell more deeply in love. Then Giuditta Turina fell ill and Bellini, half frantic with anxiety, spent his time visiting her, calling to enquire as to her progress, and lavishing flowers upon her. He dedicated the "rondo" of his opera to her, and she was sufficiently well to attend the first performance at the Carlo Felice.

What happened—why did this charming interlude come to an end, as it did with the fall of the curtain on the last performance of *Bianca é Fernando*? Did Giuditta return to Lombardy? Was she already married, or promised to some young man living in her own part of Italy? Whatever may have been the reason for the abrupt termination of this romantic friendship between Giuditta Turina and Bellini, the story ends here.

The Carlo Felice prospered, the Genoese were proud of their opera house and supported it magnificently; it was in those years that the artistic life of the town centred round the opera house.

In 1828 *The Barber of Seville* and *The Siege of Corinth* by Rossini were given, followed by Donizetti's *Queen of Golconda*. In 1839 Rossini's opera *Semiramide* ran for thirty performances, the *Lucrezia Borgia* of Donizetti was presented thirty-six times, and in 1844 Verdi's magnificent opera *Ernani* was given at the Carlo Felice for the first time. Its success with the Carlo Felice audience was great and immediate, and this opera has remained ever since one of the great favourites of the Genoese operagoers.

In the year 1852 the figure of Angelo Mariani takes the stage of the Carlo Felice. The two distinct positions of Director of the Orchestra and *Maestro al Cémbalo* were abolished, and the Municipal Orchestra was instituted under Mariani's direction. He no longer played the violin

43

as "leader of the orchestra" as was then the custom, but constituted himself the conductor. This may seem sufficiently trivial in itself, but it was in reality a revolution as regards the music of opera, and the position in opera of the orchestra. Whereas previously the orchestra had merely "accompanied" the singers, it now became a definite force in opera and was acclaimed as such. In short, the orchestra not only more than justified its position as part of the production, but it assumed an importance barely second to that of the artists. In future, critics not only wrote of the singers, of the general production, but also commented upon the ability of the orchestra and the art of the conductor.

Mariani was called "Garibaldi of the opera", and greatly through his influence and artistic capability the Carlo Felice rose to be acknowledged as one of the most important opera houses in Europe. For twenty years the reputation of this opera house flourished and grew. New works were produced—*Faust, Mignon, Carmen,* and so forth; the newer school of composers, Franchetti, Puccini and Mascagni, made a great appeal to the public; the success of the Carlo Felice was unbroken.

During the war of 1914–1918 the opera house was closed, and when the war ended it was still left apparently abandoned; there was even at one time a suggestion that it should be demolished to make way for street improvements!

Then came the revival of opera in Italy, and whatever sins and mistakes may be laid at the door of the Fascist regime—and Heaven knows there are many—it was under this rule that opera once again began to flourish as it had not done for many years. Opera houses all over Italy flung open their doors, they were redecorated, in many cases remodelled —among these was the Carlo Felice.

Then came the Second World War, and tragedy laid its hand everywhere. The beautiful opera house, with its hundred and more years of tradition, with its long history of successes, was almost destroyed by the air raids of 1944. The stage and auditorium were completely destroyed, only the fine portico and the walls remained.

What was it like before this disaster? It was one of the most elaborate and beautiful opera houses in Italy, perhaps in the world. The people of Genoa have always loved rich decorations, splendid and heavy velvets, shimmering silks, gold and silver wrought and chased, precious stones and the like. All this elaboration and decoration was lavished on their opera house—there were polished woods, inlaid work of great beauty, marble from Carrara, granite polished until it looked like glass. Lights abounded, branching from each box, chandeliers of cut-glass looked like clusters of great diamonds. In short, the whole atmosphere of the Carlo Felice was one of richness and elaborate decoration which yet contrived to be in the best possible taste.

44

The tiers of boxes go right up to the ceiling, and at a packed performance it was literally hair-raising to watch the people in those upper boxes. I have seen them when it seemed impossible that they should not crash down into the auditorium.

Now—for I see that I have been using the present tense, as if the opera house were still existing—we wait to see what will happen to the great Carlo Felice. La Scala at Milan has been rebuilt, it is beginning a new lease of life; the opera house at Rome—once the Reale—is undamaged, so is the San Carlo at Naples. At Verona the beautiful little opera house is damaged beyond repair—or so it appears at the moment—the fine opera house at Brescia is closed. What is the future?

To Italians opera, music and singing are almost as important as food and *vino*; opera is not solely a "fashionable" entertainment, it is "popular". More, it is known and understood; you can enter almost any small *caffè* where the radio is playing, and hear the proprietor telling his customers that at such an hour opera is to be relayed from Milan, Rome, Naples or some other town. The time arrives, by common consent there is silence except for the gentle singing of the patrons who know every note of the opera. I have had carpenters working for me at my house, and as they worked they sang the beautiful aria for the tenor in the last act of Puccini's *Tosca*; I have heard the washerwoman singing Madame Butterfly as she washed the sheets. These people not only know their operas but they love them; they are literally part of their daily life.

So for the sake of those proud, city-loving people of Genoa, let us hope that a wise government will rebuild their Carlo Felice. At this moment, as I write this, there are difficulties—money is lacking, there are other forms of reconstruction which are more important, but one day that opera house, in common with many others, will ring again with the music which in Italy has been called "The very soul of the people".

TEATRO COMUNALE, BOLOGNA

THIS fine theatre was built in 1756, and designed by the celebrated architect Antonio Galli Bibiena. His work was always acclaimed as admirable, and nowhere is his skill shown to greater advantage than in this excellent building.

The style is of correct and reasonably restrained *barocco*, but the restraint is marked and the simplicity is a characteristic of the building. The exterior is particularly dignified, but the interior is full of fine plasterwork, good decorations, and there are the usual great and splendid chandeliers, which are a common form of decoration in practically all Italian opera houses. Not only do the thousands of cut-glass ornaments and "lustres" form a sight which is very pleasing, but when lit the effect is one of great brilliance.

The stage is one of the largest in Italy, and has an area of more than one and a half times the size of the floor of the opera house itself. This stage has always called forth much attention from the management of the opera house, and again and again the newest forms of mechanism have been added for its improvement. The stage can be lowered so that it is on a level with the floor of the house—that is, to what is called the *golfo mistico*.

There is also a fireproof curtain which appears to be a source of pride and considerable satisfaction to the patrons. It certainly saved the opera house when the fire—and how common these disastrous fires seem to have been in most Italian opera houses!—which occurred in 1935 broke out. The fire began in the wings, the curtain was lowered and the auditorium suffered but little damage.

The Bolognese claim that the tradition of the theatre and the admirable taste of the patrons entitle it to be ranked only second to La Scala. Without wishing to express any doubt as to the veracity of this statement, I must in common fairness state that I have heard the same claim put forward by quite a number of opera houses and their patrons in various parts of Italy.

Bologna was one of the first opera houses to accept the Wagnerian operas, which they did with wholehearted enthusiasm; it is curious to note how different was the reaction to this form of opera in places not very distant one from another. For example at Mantova, Wagnerian opera on several occasions met with a very lukewarm reception.

The acoustics are very good in this opera house, and the stage can be seen perfectly from every seat. There are five tiers of boxes, and the house can hold 3000 people.

The theatre has a fine record of productions of considerable note, and also for the excellent symphonic concerts which have been given there. I have visited this opera house only once, when I heard Albanesi sing Butterfly. All Bologna was excited over the appearance of this young artist who had made a surprisingly rapid ascent to "stardom". A few years previously, I was assured, she was singing in the chorus of opera in Bologna.

Her performance impressed me up to a point. I have no doubt that now the defects which were apparent then have been rectified. Her appearance was pleasing, her acting—except in the death scene—quite passable; in her voice there was a certain unevenness, particularly in the middle register. Her high notes were good and powerful, and her diction excellent. The names of the rest of the cast and even the conductor have escaped me, but I remember that the orchestra was very good indeed.[1]

---

[1] Note: I find that the artists taking part in *Madame Butterfly* on the occasion to which I referred to above were: Butterfly, Licia Albanese; Suzuki, Maria Marcucci; Pinkerton, Giuseppe Lugo. The conductor was none other than the justly famous Gino Marinuzzi. No wonder that I remembered how excellent had been the orchestra on this particular evening!

THE TEATRO SOCIALE, MANTOVA

IN the strange, rather sad town of Mantova, which had such a glorious history under the Gonzagas, there are at least two theatres, where music if not actually opera was given. That is, the smaller one offered only symphonic music, while the other has a splendid history of successes derived from the operas.

The town is rich in artistic history, for the Gonzagas were great patrons of the arts. It was due to them that the painter Andrea Mantegna came to the town and painted those wonderful frescos depicting the Court of the Gonzagas. When the pupils of Raphael were dispersed after his death in 1520, the most famous of them all, Romano, settled at the court of Francis the Second in Mantova and decorated the well-known Palazzo del Té there. To Mantova also came the great architect Leon Battista Alberti, brought thither by Lodovico the Third. Among other notable structures he designed the great church of Sant' Andrea, wherein is the tomb of Mantegna.

Tucked away in a quiet and secluded street, attached to a great and ancient Palazzo, stands a beautiful little theatre.[1] In order to find it the seeker must make a careful search and enlist the good services of many passers-by to aid in giving directions. But once found, the reward is more than adequate.

The place is very small, it might be a miniature opera house. It was designed and built in 1768 by Antonio Galli Bibiena. There is a "built set" and three tiers of boxes as in an opera house. The fittings are of wood, and the set on the stage of the same material. The effect is very subdued but charming, though when I last visited the place I was told that the boxes were unsafe.

I was assured that Mozart conducted the first symphonic concert here, which would appear to be something more than the truth, for Mozart was born in 1756 and the theatre was surely not unused for so long after its building. Be that as it may, the little place is charming and well deserves a visit. It is now used only for conferences and lectures.

The Teatro Sociale of Mantova possesses much interest. Originally the theatre of Mantova lay outside the city, and was finally moved into the precincts between 1816 and 1822.

There had been two theatres, one standing near what is now known

---

[1] Note: I have since been told that this tiny theatre is attached to the Accademia Virgitiana. I have been talking to a man from Mantova, I have consulted various books (Baedeker, Quigley, etc.), and the Mantovanian declares that this small theatre is not attached to the Accademia; the books do not mention it.—N. J.

48

as the Piazza della Arche, which was open in autumn and winter; the other situated near the Palazzo di Corte and which was used only in spring and summer.

Neither appears, for some reason or another, to have been completely satisfactory, and there is a contemporary record which complains that the inhabitants, "a music-loving people, are often forced to travel to Verona to hear music and opera". The record adds that this is manifestly an absurdity, as it allows money to be taken out of Mantova which might—if the town possessed a good opera house—be spent within its boundaries!

The project for the new theatre was set on foot in 1816, and on January 12, 1817, a commission was appointed, after a conference which was attended by the leading citizens of the town. It was determined that an architect of note should be appointed, and after a search in such towns as Milan, Verona, Brescia and Cremona the services of the artist Cannonica were chosen. The decorations were in charge of Tranquillo Orsi, the painter pupil of Sanquirico. With him was associated the Mantovanian painter Carlo Bustaffa; the committee were also fortunate in obtaining the services of the celebrated Professor Hayez, who greatly assisted in the building and various designs.

In particular he was associated with the designing of the vast and splendid ceiling.

The theatre was completed and opened on the night of December 26, 1822, when the "elegance of the spectacle and the excellence of the taste displayed called forth the admiration of all patrons".

The first production was a melodrama entitled *Alfonzo and Elisa*, which was followed by a ballet *eroico* of Gundeberga. This work does not appear to have been particularly successful, but in 1823 we read that the company offering comedy of Luigi Velli played at the Sociale, giving no less than fifty performances.

1823–1824 finds that the opera being offered was *Margherita d' Anjou* of Meyerbeer, and the *Barbiere di Siviglia* and *Aurelian in Palmira* of Rossini. The following year Rossini is again the author of one of the works given, *Edoardo é Cristina*. The records tell us that it was received with great acclamation.

1825 has "particular importance for the Teatro Sociale", when the Emperor and Empress of Austria visited Mantova and came to the opera house to witness two "farces with music", one of which was by Rossini.

Although this is a digression, it is of interest to note that when the opera house was first built, the site bought being the Casone Gervasoni, it was decided to build in addition to the actual theatre a special hotel with a small restaurant for the artists; it was claimed that this was a "great convenience" and one wonders a little if the convenience was not for

D

the managers. When we recall the escapades of singers such as the high-spirited young Michael Kelly it was no doubt thought to be good to have the artists "under the eye of the management".

1827-1828. Rossini's name again appears in two productions, one tragic, one a comedy: *Otello* and *L'amor pellegrino.*

Later in the same season there are two more works of Rossini—*Cenerentola* and *L'inganno Felice*—as well as an opera by Donizetti. This is excluding two others less well known, and it is recorded that five operas—four from the pen of Rossini—were produced, owing to a "gift" to the management of *L.*3000 (*lire*, of course).

In 1828-1829 we read that contrary to the many successes of Donizetti with Mantova audiences, he failed to please them when he offered his opera *Olivo é Pasquale* for the first production. Reports said that its reception was "glacial".

1829-1830 is recorded as a year of great and continuous success; the orchestra is now increased from thirty-six to thirty-eight. In this year the celebrated Giuditta Pasta, first singer to King Francis of Austria, appeared with various well-known artists from the Scala of Milan.

Note here the prices of admission—the floor and single seats in the boxes are *L.*2.50 and in the smaller and higher boxes *L.*1.50![1]

During the season of *Carnevale* of 1830-1831 the name of Vincenzo Bellini occurs for the first time. He was born at Catania in Sicily in 1801. His *Norma* was produced in 1832, and given in Mantova with enormous success in 1833. The following year is recorded as the "greatest possible success of the opera, of the artists, of the ballet, the dancers and the mime actors". *Stagione Fortunata* indeed! For always it must be remembered that ballet was run concurrently with the opera.

So the history of the Teatro Sociale continues, seasons of great successes, but occasionally one where they "declare a loss of *L.*3000". In the 1840-1841 season the ballet of Coppini, *La Caduta di Messulungi*, was given. It is reported to have been nothing short of a disaster, the public "disapproving" at the first presentation, while at the third they apparently did nothing to hide their dislike of the work. As a result the theatre was closed for three nights in order to have time to produce a new ballet, *La Virtu Premiata.*

On December 26, 1841, *Il Templario* of Nicolai was given. This also did not please the Mantovanians, being heavy and Germanic in character. Later the same author offered *Le allegre comari di Windsor* which, as a kind of "musical comedy", both vivacious and amusing, made an immediate appeal. In this unfortunate season the ballet by Casatti also proved unpleasing to the public. Even the *Gemma di Vergy* of Donizetti,

---

[1] Naturally the *lira* was worth considerably more than it is today; even so, the prices are moderate.

did not make any appeal, and they appear to have shown their disapproval throughout the whole first act, and for every single line sung.

The next year saw the production of the *Stabat Mater* of Rossini, and of this the audience could not show sufficient approval. It was a great and unqualified success. The orchestra for this production was augmented, and a visiting artist was the Director Nicola De Giovanni, who was leader of the orchestra for the Duchessa di Parma.

In 1845 from May to December the theatre was closed while great improvements were made; heating was installed, two artists from Milan were in charge of complete redecoration, and the accommodation for the orchestra was made more commodious. A magnificent new "drop-curtain" was designed by the two Milanese—Galli and Borghi-Carati.

To record from year to year the activities of the Teatro Sociale would be not only impossible but tedious; it is only possible to give one or two "highlights" in the history of this opera house. December 7, 1852, is a tragic date for the city, for it marks the Austrian invasion, and in spite of all protests the theatre authorities were ordered to keep open the theatre. The takings on that evening amounted to *seven lire*. The takings for forty-five productions amounted to a sum of *L.*4719. As the brilliant recorder of the history of this opera house, Signor Giovannoni, remarks, "This was not sufficient to pay for the lighting!"

The season which followed, owing to the political disturbances and the general unhappiness of the people, left the theatre practically deserted. In 1853 *Il Trovatore* of Verdi was given for the first time in this city with great success, and at the end of the curtain seven or eight "calls" were taken amidst tremendous applause.

During the seven years from 1859 to 1866 the theatre remained closed, while Italy went through "seven years memorable for the story of the Risorgimento; years of fear, of mourning, of blood and heroism to win the great ideal of a united nation" (Giovannoni). The King visited the theatre on November 16, 1866, and on March 9, 1867, the people of Mantova greeted the hero Garibaldi. Tablets in commemoration of these two visits were placed in the Sociale.

The following year *Giulietta é Romeo* (Bellini) met with a very poor reception.

In 1886–1887 the *Mignon* of Ambrose Thomas (Charles Louis Ambrose Thomas) was received very poorly, and none of the artists pleased the public.

1888–1889 saw the first production of *Lohengrin* of Wagner. The orchestra and the chorus were both augmented for this opera. It is evident that the public of Mantova were not "easy", for in this same season they expressed their disapproval of Lucia Cavallini in *Ballo in Maschera*.

They certainly did not like *Lohengrin*, finding the music too heavy and Germanic for their taste. Twelve presentations of this opera were given, and the deficit was considerable! Mantovanians had decided to "stay away".

In 1889–1890 we find mentioned for the first time, as master of the chorus, the name Marco Finzi. I am unable to say if this is a member of the same family as the lawyer Finzi, who later in the history of the Sociale played such a large and valued part in its management, but it seems probable.

In 1892–1893 the conductor Gaetano Cimini was particularly enamoured of Wagner's *Tannhäuser*, which was produced with an augmented orchestra and chorus. The music left the audience indifferent and cold, and after the production on January 10, 1893, the reception was such that it was decided—in compliance with the requests of the patrons—to substitute another work. In consequence *Roberto il Diavolo* was presented, but the public again disliked the soprano and the tenor. 1895–1896 saw the first production in Mantova of *Manon Lescaut* to an enraptured audience; applause was given particularly to the tenor Coppola. Again, in 1898, *Lohengrin* was given; at the rehearsal there was one of those "minor incidents" which so often occur in an opera house, a discussion between director and conductor. The opera was given with scenic effects of great luxury, the interpretation was excellent, the audience remained—cold.

Fedora, by Giordano, that opera which is given so seldom, was produced at the Sociale in 1899. A tremendous audience attended—from Verona, Brescia and Cremona, as well as the Mantovanians themselves. The applause was wonderful, the success immediate.[1]

Tosca appeared for the first time in 1902–1903, and while during the opening scene the audience were not particularly impressed, their enthusiasm grew as the opera developed.

Electricity was installed as a means of lighting in 1905, and this season was a great success, both artistically and financially.

The 1906–1907 season saw Gino Marinuzzi as the director of the orchestra; 1911–1912 brought the name of Concetta Supervia in *Lohengrin*; 1912 the first production in Mantova of *Fanciulla del West*, and the name of Amelita Galli-Curci appeared in *Rigoletto*. The years of the First World War were dedicated to concerts in aid of various charitable organizations, but in 1920, when we find the name of Avv. Ciro Finzi as secretary to the Teatro Sociale, the year was marked by the visit of Arturo Toscanini, when he conducted a splendid orchestra in works of Rossini, Verdi and Beethoven.

---

[1] It should be noted that in this opera—and how good it is!—the much-discussed "entrance of the bicycles" appears to have been dropped in all recent productions.

This will give some idea of the magnificent work done in this opera house, of the critical faculties of the people of the ancient town, and of their real and glowing love for music.

For not only has opera at its best been offered, but the management of the theatre have always been ready to give concerts for the benefit of deserving causes. Truly a magnificent record.

LA FENICE, VENICE

VENICE is one of the few cities which really lives up to its reputation for being both beautiful and romantic; other places lauded and praised may disappoint the visitor, Venice remains "*La grande Signora*".

To be in Venice is in itself sufficiently exciting, but to go to the Opera in Venice is almost too much! Leaving the Piazza of Saint Mark, you walk through narrow, twisting streets until you find yourself in a small square which I cannot believe has changed very much since the rebuilding of the opera house in 1836.

There is the old well-head, the staircase with its jutting window and the very paving-stones worn smooth by the passage of many feet through the years. To the left is the opera house, La Fenice, with a fine portico in the style of Palladio.

The original opera house was called the San Benedetto, and in the British Museum an old print may be found of the interior of this building on the occasion of a fête given on January 22, 1782, in honour of "the Russian Grand Duke and Grand Duchess". In this year the Irish singer, Michael Kelly, came to Venice. He records his arrival in October, when he immediately began rehearsals for Anfossi's oratorio and took up his residence with Signora Teresa de Petris. Kelly tells us that all through the time of the Carnival he lived "in the lap of luxury and in a vortex of pleasure".

To Venice at this time, too, came the astonishing English *prima donna*, Nancy Storace; she was only sixteen, and such was her success that she was the first performer to be given the privilege of a "benefit" in Venice.

Her success in Venice was without parallel. The theatre was packed to overflowing, and Nancy Storace's mother stood at the entrance of the opera house to receive the gifts—rings, chains, jewellery and money—which the generous and warm-hearted Venetians showered upon this talented young *prima donna*.

The Storace had to pay the penalty of fame, for a woman arrived and took lodgings in the disreputable Calla di Carbone—the part of Venice where the law permitted prostitutes to live—and here it was customary for these women to hang out their portraits from their windows to attract custom and visitors. This new arrival duly exhibited a picture outside her lodgings which bore the inscription, "The portrait of Signora Storace's sister".

In vain did the Storace and her mother protest that the woman was no relation of theirs, that the Storace had no sister; the story had spread round Venice, and for days the impostor reaped a rich harvest, her rooms being besieged with visitors anxious to see the sister of the popular *diva*. Finally, Storace sought the protection of the law, the impostor was imprisoned and later banished from the State of Venice.

In 1787 the new opera house La Fenice was built and took the place of the San Benedetto; this is six years after the arrival of Michael Kelly, when, after considerable success, he found himself stranded in Venice for want of funds! The new opera house was built on very much the same lines as the magnificent La Scala, with tiers of boxes, and with decorations which were both costly and magnificent. The official opening was on May 16, 1792, when a new opera by Giovanni Paisiello called *I Giochi di Arigento* was presented, the opera being followed by a ballet.

In 1836 a disastrous fire caused the Fenice to be closed for repairs until February 18, 1837, when it opened with an opera by Donizetti. Curiously enough, the last performance given before the fire had been the opera *Belisario* by this composer.

Since that date the Fenice has continued successfully and has been the scene of magnificent spectacles, as when Vittorio Emmanuelo II witnessed a presentation of *The Masked Ball* (*Un Ballo in Maschera*). The Fenice was also the scene of one of the greatest fiascos in the history of opera in Italy, recorded as "*Storico fiasco de La Traviata*". This production took place on March 6, 1853, and whether the contemporary setting provoked antagonism—for the setting was later changed to the period of Louis XIV—or that the music of Verdi on this occasion made no appeal, the reception was so cold and the audience showed such marked disapproval of the work that the night of March 6, 1853, has become historic in the annals of La Fenice.

In 1854 the opera house was improved and redecorated, and in March 1857 Verdi's *Simone Boccanegra* was given. This was the last work specially written by the great *maestro* for La Fenice; the reception was completely lacking in enthusiasm. It seems evident that the Venetians were a critical and difficult audience! In 1874 the first performance was given in Italy of Wagner's opera *Rienzi*. Wagner died in Venice nine years later.

In 1900, living up to the reputation for being highly critical, the audience at La Fenice received, with no warmth, the opera by Wolf-Ferrari *Cenerentola* (*Cinderella*), and the following year *Un Ballo in Maschera* of Mascagni met with a scarcely better reception. In 1912 Mascagni directed his own opera *Isabeau* at La Fenice with great success, and in 1925 Wolf-Ferrari achieved tremendous approbation for his work *Gli Amanti*.

In 1938 the opera house was again redecorated, and very beautiful those decorations are.

I visited this opera house first before the war; the month was January and Venice was cold—as cold as that beautiful city can be in winter, which is very cold indeed. In summer it is possible to reach the opera house by gondola, and there these graceful vessels remain in the canal waiting for their owners, swaying and dipping, looking like huge black swans.

The entrance of La Fenice is beautiful, and immediately you get an impression of light. The Fenice is what Italians call *carina*—lovable. It lacks the grandeur of the old Scala, it has not the restrained magnificence of the Reale at Rome (now called Teatro dell' Opera, since the word *"reale"* has vanished with the Royal Family), it has not even the height and dignity of the opera house at Brescia; but it remains charming and completely delightful.

In the entrance, which is decorated in white marble and gold, stands the major-domo, magnificent in cocked hat, white velvet breeches and a coat heavily trimmed with gold lace, wearing a white wig. He carries his staff of office with its huge golden knob. He is dignified, aloof, apparently immersed in his own lofty thoughts; but let some unfortunate venture to light a cigarette, and see how that major-domo is galvanized into immediate life, and how promptly, with a wave of his staff, he indicates that "Smoking is Not Allowed" (*"Vietato di Fumore"*).

The auditorium makes you catch your breath; it is beautiful, filled with bright colours which never become garish. From the roof hang magnificent chandeliers made in Murano (one of the Venetian islands). The tiers of boxes are painted white, and every one is decorated with a design of flowers, fruit and knots of ribbon. Between these come plaques depicting famous musicians. The whole effect is delightful. There is no heavy red plush, and the gold is applied with care and discrimination. The seating accommodation is ample and comfortable.

The attendants are all dressed as they were in the old days of the San Benedetto, when young Michael Kelly listened with all his ears to the voice of La Storace, and later possibly forgathered with his friends at the nearby restaurant—La Taverna—to discuss the opera and criticize the singing; when Casanova, plunging headlong from one amorous adventure into another, fluctuating between being the favourite of the Great and the prisoner of the Venetian State, swaggered and philoso-phized—and wondered how on earth he might pay his debts. Between the acts—and in Italian opera houses the intervals are very long, because the Italians still "nail" most of their scenery together and are addicted to heavy "practical" staircases and the like whenever possible—you may mount the marble staircase and find yourself wandering through spacious rooms where the furniture, if not all completely authentic, is so arranged as to give the impression that you are in a private palace, where the host has been sufficiently thoughtful to supply his guests with an admirable buffet.

The lighting system is admirable, there is no sudden switching on of brilliant light or immediate descent into darkness; the lights rise and dim slowly and steadily.

The present drop-scene was painted in 1878 by Ermolao Paoletti, and shows the unloading on the quay of the spoils and trophies of Lepanto. The name "Fenice" means Phoenix, the legendary bird which when burnt rose in new beauty from its own ashes. Thus after the destruction of San Benedetto the new opera house "rose from the ashes" of the old theatre. As we have seen, again fire destroyed the theatre, on December 13, 1836, leaving only the façade, the entrance hall and the rooms above which I have mentioned.

La Fenice has had its historic moments as when, on March 23, 1848, to commemorate the fact that the theatre had been given back to the Free Republic of San Marco, a gala performance was given. That night the President Manin sat with all his ministers to witness a performance of *Hamlet*. Before the curtain rose, amid scenes of incredible enthusiasm, the hymn "The Patrol of the Civil Guard" and the hymn to Pope Pius X were sung. Not long afterwards the cannon thundered, the air was filled with tumult; war had Italy in its grip and the beautiful theatre was closed.

It was reopened by the Austrian General Govzkowski. The arrogant and overbearing Austrian governor, afraid that certain operas might result in patriotic demonstrations, actually changed the names of many of the operas. Verdi's *Battaglia di Legnano* (*The Battle of Legnano*) was renamed *The Siege of Haarlem*, and *The Lombards of the First Crusade* became *Jerusalem*!

In 1859, when so many patriotic dreams seemed to have faded, the Society owning the Fenice decided to close it until happier times should come, and until November 1, 1866, the opera house remained in darkness. Then, for the ceremonial visit of Victor Emmanuel II, with Prince Umberto and all the Italian ministers, the lights blazed out again and once more the Phoenix had risen from the political—if not actual—ashes, in new beauty and dignity.

I saw it again in the August of 1946—there was no performance, for the open-air theatre was being used for a summer season; but the stage doorkeeper remembered me, and with pride and pleasure showed me the auditorium, raised and lowered the lights, and we both—without speaking—looked towards the royal box.

I said, "It is beautiful—this Fenice."

He answered, "Indeed yes—La Phoenix."

TEATRO REGIO, PARMA

FEW cities in Italy have greater musical connections than Parma, where not only has music but the pictorial art flourished for many years. The history of the town is rich in memories, and although the opera house whose history is given here has been terribly damaged by the war from the air, yet that demand for music which has always been one of the characteristics of the people of Parma will without doubt assert itself, and—as in so many other Italian towns, both in the past and present times—another "Phoenix will rise from the ashes of the old".

The last season of opera given at this opera house was 1938–1939, when the success was tremendous. The operas given were *Bohème* of Puccini, *La Sonnambula* of Bellini, *Madame Butterfly*—again Puccini—*La Traviata* of Verdi and *Il Piccolo Marat* of Mascagni.

Verdi is of course beloved and admired everywhere; but at Parma there is the splendid memorial erected to him, which fortunately suffered little actual damage during the war. This great semi-circle of stone has niches in which are placed statues depicting all the great characters of his operas, and very well done they are. What a procession of well-known figures from operas whose fame is world wide!

To stand before the fine bust of the master himself is to realize the essential greatness which was the source of his music. The splendid forehead, the eyes with their overhanging eyebrows, deep-set and thoughtful, and the sense of power which radiates from the whole statue are almost overpowering and certainly call forth both admiration and veneration.

The history of music and the theatre of Parma goes back to very early times, when Paolo III Parnese made his son Pier Luigi the Duke of Parma and Piacenza, September 16, 1545. The standard of music given appears to have been very high, compositions by the greatest masters of the time being offered to the public. In 1600 Parma was able to witness a great fair organized in the city, where, although business was its first aim, fine musical productions were included. The celebrated Teatro Parnese, which was constructed by order of Ranuccio I but was not opened—although plans were made in 1618 and 1619—until 1628 for the marriage of Margherita, the daughter of Cosimo II Medici and Odoardo Farnese. Chronicles of the time record this performance as being so magnificent that it called forth admiration from everyone.

The Farnese family encouraged the building of theatres, and about 1688 Parma possessed several. There was a theatre at Rachetta, the theatre Ducale in Parma itself, a smaller theatre for the court dated 1689, the theatre of S. Caterina which was reconstructed at a much later date (1804) and other theatres of minor importance.

After many years of successful productions in Parma came the building of the new opera house which was called Il Regio. This was built at the wish of the Duchess Maria Louise, ex-Empress of France, the wife of Napoleon I. It was opened on May 16, 1829, and was destined to carry on the noble traditions of the Ducale.

Maria Louise wished Parma to have a theatre "which for size, beauty of design, of painting and ornament would rank among the first in Europe". The old theatre with its high tradition was followed by one which was no less successful.

It is worth noting before we leave the Ducale for the Regio that among other great artists who had appeared there was Nicolo Paganini, named in the records as "the God of the Violin". He played there in 1812 and also conducted. It is said that the success of his concert was "prodigious and insuperable". Napoleon and Josephine Bonaparte had attended a performance at the Ducale in which some of the greatest artists in the world of opera had appeared—such names as Grisi, Pasta and Malibran—with an orchestra under the direction of a fine conductor, playing for an opera, which had the lyrics written by Carlo Goldoni, who was the court poet of the Duke of Parma.

The architect of the new theatre was Nicolo Bettoli, and the painter —or, rather, the designer of the decorations for the interior—the great Battista Borghesi. In 1853, when the theatre was redecorated, a simple and more dignified style was adopted in place of the rather flamboyant *barocco*.

The opera certainly gave its patrons "value for money", for again and again we read in the chronicles of productions which began at half past eight and ended at half past twelve, though even in more modern times it is quite customary for an opera to begin at nine and not to end until long after midnight.

Then follow many productions, including four memorable productions of *Anna Bolena*; *Norma*, 1834, given for twenty-one performances; *Lucia di Lammermoor* in 1837 for twenty performances; and in 1842 came the *Stabat Mater* of Rossini, under the direction of De Giovanni, which was acclaimed as being "not inferior" to the conducting of the orchestra at Bologna under Donizetti.

In the May of 1843 *Nabucco* was produced, with Verdi himself attending all rehearsals. The success was tremendous, and it was during this time that after the noise and tumult of Milan and La Scala he and Giuseppina Strepponi wandered together in the quiet gardens of the Ducale enjoying the peace and tranquillity of Parma. Here they began their lasting and romantic affection for one another. Verdi was a native of

59

Roncole, near Busseto in the Duchy of Parma, where his parents had kept a wine shop and grocery store. To return to Parma, therefore, and to hear his opera hailed with delight must have been an added joy to him. From 1835 to 1872 the Parma opera house boasted a permanent orchestra, and not one which was gathered together to meet the special requirements of various productions. This orchestra was considered to be among the very finest in Italy. The contemporary writers say, "The strings are the first in Italy, the scenic artists and engineers of Parma have no equals."

One success followed another: *Macbeth* (1849) for thirty-four successive performances; *La Traviata* (1855) for nineteen; *Sicilian Vespers*, which had its first Italian production in Parma in the same year; and, five years later, *Un Ballo in Maschera.*

From then on we can read of an unbroken and splendid record with one success following on the heels of another. The orchestra continued under its various conductors to be admirable. The names of the conductors alone are sufficient to guarantee the excellence of the orchestra—Nicolo Paganini (1835),[1] Bernardo Farrara (1836), Nicola De Giovanni and Giulio Cesare Ferrarini.

The opera house possessed—I have not been able to ascertain if this was damaged during the war—one of the most famous drop curtains in Italy. I remember seeing it before the war, and the beauty of design and execution of "The Triumph of Knowledge" by Borghesi impressed me very much indeed.

In addition to the opera house itself and the music offered to patrons there, the standard of ballet at Parma was very high indeed.

At the last season, before the disaster of the Second World War overtook the country, the *prima ballerina* was Bice Del Frate, the sopranos Magda Olivero and Iris Adami Corradetti; singers in the various casts were Renato Gigli (so far as I have been able to ascertain, not a brother of the great Beniamino), Maria Farnoraro, Luigi Borgonovo, Giuseppe Lugo (whose voice I have not heard since the war), Lyana Grani, Renzo Pigni, Maria Carbone, and Giovanni Malipiero (who gave such a magnificent rendering of the hero in *Le Jongleur de Notre Dame* at La Scala).

Poor Parma, which has suffered so much, the city which has always been a real home and testing-house for opera, must surely again have an opera house worthy of it and of its great traditions?

---

[1] Lest it should seem extraordinary that the great Paganini should also have been conducting the orchestra at Parma, it must be remembered that frequently the conductor was also the "leader" of the orchestra. I believe that I am right in thinking that the innovation—for such it was at the time—of the conductor retaining only his baton instead of his violin was inaugurated at the Opera Reale in Rome.—N. J.

THE TEATRO VERDI, PADOVA

THE city of Padova has been famous through the ages for her culture; here is one of the oldest schools of medicine in the world, here science flourishes, here too is the great church—Il Santo, dedicated to Saint Antonio of Padova—and also, close to the church, one of the most entrancing art galleries and museums I have ever seen.

This building is not very large, neither was the collection very extensive; but to walk round the gallery at Padova is, to me at least, to find more beauty than I have found in the larger collections. The building was damaged by an air attack launched—and I record it with a certain thankfulness—by the Germans. The treasures had, however, all been taken to places of safety in Venice,[1] and two years ago (1946) many of them were shown in the fine exhibition which was organized at Venice, and there I saw again many of the pictures which I had come to know so well in the museum at Padova. Particularly delightful to see again were the two Giorgiones, although I was told that some authorities doubt the authenticity of "Il Mito di Erisittone" (though again many aver that there is no doubt as to its being genuine) and the charming "La Nascita di Adone', both from the Padova collection.

There is a rhyme regarding the towns of Northern Italy, age old, which, being translated, runs:

> Venice is the great lady,
> Padova is the great doctor [or, more literally—
> the great intellectual];
> In Verona everyone is mad,
> In Brescia they all eat cats!

Being, therefore, essentially a city of the arts and the dignified professions, it was necessary for Padova to have an opera house, and the matter was decided by the nobility of the city in 1748. The theatre—for want of a better name—was known as the New Theatre and was designed by the architect Antonio Cugini and the construction carried out under the direction of a native of Padova, Giovanni Gloria.

The first production was of *L'Artasserse*, a melodrama by Metastasio. After the fall of Napoleon, musical concerts of songs to salute the return of the Austrians were given, and—proving the lethargy of the feeling of patriotism which existed at that time—we find similar concerts being given for the birthday of the Emperor (February 13, 1815). In the

[1] Capolavori dei Musei Venete (St. Mark's Square).

autumn of 1817 the *Barber of Seville* of Rossini was given for the first time at the Padova opera house.

Then came an unfruitful time for this house; the theatre was closed in 1820 by the order of the Austrians and the public were forbidden to attend the "dress rehearsal". Then occurred one of those "explosions" between the students and the Government which are common to all university towns where the undergraduates believe that they have a just grievance. On this occasion, however, the actual force of police supported the students, and it would appear that the order was either disregarded or annulled.

1821 saw a production by the company of Elizabeth and Charlotte Marchionni, and at the same time the Austrians gave another of those foolish and—to the populace—irritating orders, which seemed so senseless. The audience were forbidden to applaud the artists except when they came to take what we should now describe as "calls before the curtain" at the end of every act. This time the police remained on the side of the authorities, and riots ensued. 1825 saw the production of Meyerbeer's opera *Il Crociato in Egitto*, and in 1829 Gustavo da Modena presented *Francesca da Rimini*, the tragedy by Silvio Pellico.

1831 saw one of those strange exhibitions of which we have read regarding many operas. On this occasion during the scenes of an opera by Bellini, of which I have not been able to trace the name, the whole company were greeted with "whistles and cries"—or, as we should say in England, they were given "the bird". Whether this was due to the fact that their singing was indifferent, or because the opera did not meet with approval, it is not possible to say.

Three years later *Norma* and *La Sonnambula* of Bellini were given with immense success. In 1842 *Nabucco* of Verdi was given and gave great satisfaction. A contemporary chronicle says of the applause which followed this opera: "The applause given in Padova is unlike that given in other cities. Because Padova is always young, always a queen and a lady of culture, the applause is spontaneous as in no other city." Two years later Verdi's *Ernani* was offered, and two years later still the theatre was reconstructed. The work was in the hands of the architect Giuseppe Japelli, who had already achieved fame by his design for the famous Caffe Pedrocchi.

This *caffe* is still open, and is famous because—through some charter granted at the time of its construction—it is never allowed to be closed. One door at least must remain open night and day, so that students working late at the university shall always be able to call there and get some refreshment no matter how late—or how early—the hour.

The reconstruction of the theatre was finished in 1847, when it was decided to find a new name for the building. The style was considered modern, the arches which surrounded the building were designed on the model of those in the courtyard of the Ducal Palace at Venice, the frames and decorations of the windows were elaborate and in the baroque style. The four statues which ornamented the roof were the figures of the four great Italian poets. Inside, the roof gave the illusion of representing the sky, with figures of "Love" and the twelve hours; the models for the hours were the twelve most beautiful women of Padova.

The beautiful *ballerina* Fanny Essler was in Padova during the opening season, and constantly spoke and wrote of the success of the theatre and the enthusiasm of the audiences. Possibly the Essler may not have been a completely unbiased judge, for, with her art and her great personal magnetism, a chronicle of the time says of her, "Even the most serious and well-conducted man after witnessing a performance by the Essler found it impossible to go home and sleep tranquilly."

For two years (1848–1850) the theatre remained closed owing to the war of the *"Risorgimento"*; later in the year 1850 the theatre was opened by order of the Austrian police, and the people of Padova made a "passive protest", entering the theatre in mourning for the state of their country. The result was a manifestation of a violent nature.

1856 found the theatre open again, with a new curtain designed and painted by Vicenzo Gazzotto, showing the "Festival of the Flowers", a carnival which had been given in Padova in the Middle Ages.

In 1858 Ristori presented *Giuditta*, and its success was immediate, for it roused all the patriotic fervour of the audience; then the opera house again remained closed—owing to the second and third war of the *"Risorgimento"*—until the August when the war was over, and on the 27th of that month Victor Emmanuel attended the first presentation in Padova of *Faust*.

In 1882 the opera house was again restored and redecorated, under the direction of the architect Sfondrini. Everything was renewed, and various additions were made—staircases, the entrance hall, and various corridors. Then came another war to prevent the continuity of the operas presented at Padova—the First World War, when from the air the Austrians bombed the city in 1917. Again the theatre was redecorated, and paintings of the chief characters of the numerous operas of Verdi served as decoration, the theatre being formally given the name of Teatro Verdi.

In 1921 and 1924 Toscanini came as a guest conductor for several concerts, and in the time of *Carnevale*—the period immediately preceding Lent—the first presentation was given in Padova of Puccini's last great opera *Turandot*. 1929 saw the first production in the city of Boito's splendid work *Nerone*.

In 1938 the Teatro Garibaldi in Padova ceased to be a theatre for purely theatrical performances—*di prosa*—and the Teatro Verdi became not only devoted to opera but also to legitimate drama.

Again, during the Second World War, the theatre remained closed, and reopened in the June of 1945 with a company presenting legitimate drama.

What will be the future of this opera house no one can predict; an Italian friend wrote to me the other day that "its future direction lies with the stars".

TEATRO GRANDE, BRESCIA

THE town of Brescia lies between Milan and Verona; it is on the main high road to Padova and Venice. A busy manufacturing town, where the people are always friendly, and which also contains far more beauty than the average tourist realizes. I have been visiting Brescia for many years, and am still discovering new beauties, fine pictures and little out-of-the-way churches, each containing some treasure.

Brescia suffered during the war from the air raids, and more than one of her fine churches were damaged badly; but with the fall of the Fascist Government visitors to Brescia were spared at least one horror—the "more-than-life-sized" statue of "Young Italy" which stood in the big square: a monstrosity, crude, hideous and of little or no merit.

It was said—with what truth I do not know—that this statue was offered to Mussolini for the Foro Mussolini at Rome and he refused it. The story continues that having some slight grudge—over a political matter—with the authorities of Brescia, Mussolini disliked the town, and when the question arose as to where "Young Italy" was to find a home, Mussolini's reply was, "Send it to Brescia!"

But—the opera house!

There are certain seasons of the year when you may find this beautiful place given over to cinema programmes, but three times a year opera claims its own, and you may hear opera sung there with an admirable orchestra and fine production.

The three seasons for the opera are *Fiera* (the Brescia Fair which takes place in August and September); *Carnevale*, which is the season which precedes Lent; and *Quaresima*, which is the season of Lent itself. At the present time as I write this (March 1947) the opera house has not yet been reopened after the disasters which befell it during the war, but it is impossible not to believe, and to hope, that it will soon be restored and put in order to give the people of Brescia the joy of hearing opera once more.

The opera house was restored and redecorated in 1863 under the direction of the celebrated architect Magnani, and of it, when ready for use, Andrea Sala said, "The Teatro Grande of Brescia, with its solidly constructed walls with their harmony and artistic proportions, with the exquisite taste of its decorations, merits to be acclaimed as one of the first opera houses in Italy." The cost of the reconstruction, the re-decoration and general restoration was paid for by the generosity of the Comune and also by the openhanded and music-loving citizens of the town.

E

There must have been a former opera house, and one of considerable importance, for Michael Kelly was engaged to sing there in 1782, for the *Fiera*. He records that he received the sum of eighty golden ducats for the engagement, which lasted for two months. The *prima donna* was the beautiful Ortabella, with whom Kelly had sung in Florence.

Bertini, the manager of the opera house at that time, arranged for Kelly to have rooms at the hostel "The Sign of the Lobster", a place which I have sought for in vain, and which must have been pulled down. Rehearsals continued for *Il Pittore Parigino* of Cimarosa; Kelly is full of praise for the theatre, which he states was decorated in the style of the San Carlo at Naples, "with tip-up seats". Ortabella lodged also at the "Lobster",[1] and owing to this fact, the proprietor of the theatre, one Manuel—who had been nicknamed "*Il Cavaliere Prepotente*" ("The Self-satisfied Gentleman")—grew jealous of the hours which Kelly and Ortabella spent together. This man had already "made proposals to the *prima donna* which she had the courage to reject", and her refusal of the favours offered her by "*Il Cavaliere Prepotente*" made him certain that she was in love with young Kelly.

The hatred which Manuel felt for Kelly grew; Kelly, full of high spirits and a certain recklessness, did nothing to appease the wrath of the proprietor. Finally Manuel threatened to have Kelly assassinated, and as he was known to employ a band of paid ruffians to dispose of people whom he disliked, known as *sicari*, Kelly realized that discretion was the better part of valour and went to ask for the protection of Conte Momolo Lana. This gentleman advised Kelly to escape as quickly as possible and to put himself out of the reach of Manuel.

While the stage was being set for the grand ballet of *The Siege of Troy*, Kelly made his escape from the theatre, and found the travelling carriage of his friend. Lana had sent a letter recommending Kelly to his friend the Marquis Bevil Acqua of Verona, and in the night the escape was successfully made.

It is curious to read Kelly's comment on the journey to Verona from Brescia. He says, "I arrived safe in Verona, which I thought rather fortunate as the greatest part of the road from Desenzano is infested by numerous *banditti*. I scarcely travelled a quarter of a mile without seeing a little wooden cross stuck by the roadside, as a mark that someone had been murdered on the spot."

That was in 1782, and now that road is as peaceful and tranquil as any you could wish to find.

The present opera house at Brescia is a handsome building with wide

[1] To my great pleasure my secretary "found" "The Sign of the Lobster" a few days ago in Brescia. It is still named "The Sign of the Lobster" (*gambero*—which is literally a crayfish of a large size). The hotel has been enlarged and modernized, but it holds the same position as it did when young Kelly first visited Brescia.—N. J.

semicircular stone steps leading to the entrance, and an immense portico supported by massive pillars.

The opening was with *Ballo in Maschera* of Verdi, followed by his *Trovatore*. From then until 1900 the Brescia Opera House gave its patrons a succession of splendid operas, magnificently produced. Reading down the list of productions many names appear of operas which have long ago sunk into obscurity and been forgotten; but again and again the names of Verdi, Boito, Donizetti, Puccini, Bellini, Meyerbeer and Bizet occur and recur. Brescia was always ready to accept the innovations, but was always loyal to the established favourites.

Turning to the opera house itself, the auditorium is veritably a miniature La Scala with tiers of boxes rising to the roof; there is the royal box which looks almost too magnificent for actual comfort. The scheme is red and gold, yet here as in so many opera houses the use of these colours has been done delicately, and the effect which might so easily have been garish is soft and restrained. Imagine it, five tiers of boxes, amounting to 150, rising in smooth ascension to the roof of the theatre. Here are, as usual, the great and splendid chandeliers of cut glass, and over the stage the clock without hands. That is to say, the hours and minutes are recorded on two slits, one showing the hour, the other moving every five minutes.

Before you reach the auditorium itself you pass through the vestibule, or *ridotto*. This room is magnificent. True, the frescos are of no great artistic merit, there is much baroque decoration—if you like this style, as I do, then you admire it very much; if not, then you must piously turn your eyes from it. The pillars are of marble, the ceiling is painted, much of the decoration being in that well-known "trick style" which appealed so strongly to the Italian artists. You may find the same style—though naturally in a superior manner—in the castle of the Gonzagas at Mantua, where complete miracles are performed in the use of paint and perspective. I recall one ceiling where an angel with a trumpet is depicted, and this trumpet appears to "follow you round the room"; another where a chariot drawn by three horses appears to be facing you no matter in which part of the room you stand. Italian artists admit that it was *una gherminella* with paint and brushes, but the art—if art it was—is lost.

Here there are decorations of balconies from which lean beautiful ladies and children, apparently bending forward over the balustrades. There are also swags of flowers which appear to hang down quite apart from the canvas on which they are painted.

Green, cream and gold are the prominent colours, and the whole effect is quite delightful. Here between the acts patrons walk up and down discussing the music, the artists and the general *décor* of the opera.

The buffet—which received a good deal of interest when the opera house was restored within the last years—is disappointing. With the exception of the fine marble mantelpiece, which looks rather lonely and slightly out of place, the buffet is ordinary and completely modern.

The stage itself is good, deep and wide; the lighting is excellent, and the dressing-rooms adequate. The acoustics could not well be bettered.

The Teatro Grande has a magnificent list of artists who have sung there. Toscanini conducted there in 1890 when *Le Villi* of Puccini was given, and followed that with two concerts before he left for America. He again conducted here in 1921 after his American visit.

Among the artists who have sung in Brescia are—and lists are always unsatisfactory for one is liable to leave out some of the most successful and satisfactory—the great bass Tancredi Pasero, Tito Schipa, Margherita Carosio, the magnificent soprano Gina Cigna, Malipiero, Borghese and Rizza Gilda.

These are a few of the great artists who have given delight to the people of "Brave Brescia".

The first time I visited the Teatro at Brescia I went to hear *Fanciulla del West* of Puccini. My good friend Leo Ferrari had booked my seat. I thought that the performance was for the evening, whereas it was an afternoon show. I was quietly eating my luncheon when Ferrari telephoned to me.

"Tell me, are you playing a little joke with me?"

"A joke, Leo, what do you mean?" I answered.

"The performance is for three o'clock, it is now half past two."

The distance from my house to Brescia was thirty-five kilometres. We did it in twenty-five minutes, and we had to stop to get petrol on the way!

We entered the auditorium just as Maestro Podesta lifted his baton. The first act of *La Fanciulla del West* had begun. The setting is unusual, though the first chorus of cowboys and miners is—to my mind—one of the best things in the opera. Once Viglione Borghese had made his first appearance as the Sheriff we realized that here was another Scarpia, and knew instinctively that unless the tenor "watched his step", and if "The Girl" did not prove herself to be as "slim" as possible, we were out to watch another tragedy cast in the same lines as that of Cavaradossi and Floria Tosca.

A fine dramatic opera this *Girl of the West*, possibly lacking something of Puccini's lovely melodies, but a fine opportunity for a singer who can act as well as sing. That scene where we watch "The Girl" playing poker, and slipping that extra card for a "straight flush" into the top of her stocking, and generally "getting away with it," is good robust stuff.

68

For me, too material—I prefer the misjudged Amelia of *Un Ballo in Maschera*, Gioconda, poor Butterfly, the splendid Aïda, Violetta or "darling Floria Tosca" to this very practical young woman in a cowboy's shirt and top boots.

In the last act there was a certain amount of difficulty with the horse. Horses from time immemorial have been bad actors and temperamental at that. Either the horse is obstinate and obviously unmusical, or the sheriff cannot ride. Borghese at this performance was evidently distinctly uncomfortable and apprehensive.

Then at the very end of the opera—which Puccini adapted from the play by David Belasco which he saw when he visited New York—came the great "highlight". Mario Bianchi, playing Johnson, a word which no self-respecting Italian could possibly pronounce, sings his lovely aria, *"Ch' ella me creda libero e lontano"*.

Here was the Puccini we all knew and loved, here was sentiment without sentimentality, here were the beautiful melodies which we have come to expect from this master of sweet music. Bianchi sang with the rope around his neck, but it was removed in order that he and his Minnie might live "happy ever after".

It is not my place in this book to write about opera in a critical sense, I am leaving that to my dear and good friend, Jimmie Robertson; but to me this *Girl of the West* is the most neglected of all Puccini's works, with the exception of the charming *Gianni Schicchi*. It has drama, movement and much of the music is well worth hearing and remembering. It may be that one day some impresario with courage will give it again to the world outside Italy.

The next time I went to Brescia was to hear another of Puccini's operas, *La Tosca*. Surely here are all the elements needed for a fine, full-blooded dramatic opera! The Floria was Gina Cigna, that soprano who played such a brave and courageous part in the war and during the time of the German occupation of Milan. But in those days—I am writing of 1938—except that some of us were vaguely worried about the number of Germans who were visiting Italy—"tourists"—we had not begun to think seriously of war. What a performance!

Cigna, who does really know something about "costumes", wears the traditional clothes of the period. Recently I heard of a *prima donna* who dressed Tosca for her first entrance in black and white. I am assured that she looked like a—penguin.

At the end of the performance I went "back stage" and began to talk to the stage manager. He asked if I had been to Rome. I replied that I had. And the castle of Saint Angelo, had I seen that? I said that I had seen it several times.

He said in a confidential whisper, "Of course, *signora*, we don't allow

Cigna to fall as far as she would from the tower of the Castle of Saint Angelo, understand."

Well, I look forward to the time when the opera house where young Michael Kelly sang, and where so much beautiful music has been given, will be open again, and the people of Brave Brescia will be able to find the music which their souls love.

TEATRO COMUNALE, FLORENCE
TEATRO PERGOLA, FLORENCE
IL MAGGIO MUSECALE, FLORENCE

THIS opera house, which is now owned by the Comune of Florence, was built in the year 1862, when the private society responsible for the erection of this theatre decided to provide Florence with an opera house which should be worthy of her historic and artistic traditions.

The construction was in the hands of the famous Bonaiuti, and his work was highly successful. The acoustics were admirable, the ground floor spacious, with tiers of boxes and a ramp fitted with seats so that all members of the audience obtained an uninterrupted view of the stage. The theatre was capable of holding 5000 people, and was one of the largest in Italy.

It was opened on May 17, 1862; then occurred one of those disastrous fires, which seem to descend like an evil fate upon so many of Italy's opera houses, and immediately the work of rebuilding was put in hand, for the theatre reopened in 1863. In 1895 the whole place was modernized, and the most effective mechanical devices were installed, together with the newest system of lighting.

In 1932 the opera house was bought by the Comune, when this body decided to inaugurate performances of the very best and finest kind. No expense was spared, the community was fired with the wish to possess an opera house which for equipment and modernity of stage mechanics could take its place with the foremost opera houses in Europe. The Comunale was completely transformed, redecorated and modernized.

The old theatre, or rather the Teatro Comunale before it was so renamed, had been called the Politeama, and held a fine record from 1862 until it was taken over by the community. All that was best and newest in opera was given there, and the list of successes is noteworthy.

Traviata which was given during those years no less than 200 times, *Aïda* which was given for sixty, *Tosca*, *Iris*, *Gioconda* all had fifty performances each, *Bohème*, *Isabeau* and *Carmen* all had more than thirty performances each. In addition, of course, all the other operas of Verdi, Rossini, Bellini and Donizetti were produced at the Politeama, as well as many German and French works.

In 1932, when the *Maggio Musicale Florentino* was inaugurated, the opera house, acquired by the Comune, became the "headquarters" of the famous Florentine Festival. Between 1933 and 1947 ten of these *Maggio* Festivals had been given.

For the purpose of possible reference the dates were as follows: 1933, 1935, 1937, 1938, 1939, 1940, 1941, 1942, 1944 and 1947.

It is necessary to make fuller reference to this great Festival which is one of the features of musical life in Italy, and is regarded as one of great and real importance by the whole of the world of music lovers.

In 1928 the Permanent Orchestra of the Comunale was formed, and a season of symphonic music was given. The greatest soloists and conductors in the world were invited to come as guest artists. The orchestra was trained with strict discipline, and attained a very high point of excellence. Such men as Strauss, Stravinski and Toscanini praised the work which the orchestra did.

The orchestra was launched, was a success and the opera enthusiasts began to devise some scheme which might raise the standard of opera given in Florence to the same pitch attained by the orchestra. It was not considered that the opera in Florence would be worthy of the traditions of that beautiful city of the arts if it were to be left in the hands of speculative theatre managers and commercially-minded impresarios.

The scheme finally evolved was the Triannual festival to be held in the late spring, which was to be known as the *Maggio Musicale* or "Musical May".

The first of these festivals took place in 1933, and it was such a success that it came as a surprise to everyone. The idea had fired the imagination not only of Italians, but of people all over the world. Rosa Ponselle travelled from America to sing in the opera *La Vestale* by Spontini. The finest conductors in Europe were glad and even proud to participate in this festival.

So great was the popularity of the *Maggio Musicale* that it was decided to make it not triannual but annual, and from 1937 the festival was given every year and continued until 1944 when the world upheaval rendered it impossible, and when the stage of the Teatro Comunale was partially destroyed during an air raid.

The festival was revived in 1947, but the stage was not yet in complete order and the activities were restricted to symphonic concerts.

In 1947 the Florence Symphony Orchestra was engaged by the Combined Services Entertainments and Army Welfare in Italy to give a series of concerts which were primarily for the troops still in Italy, but to which Italians were also admitted. The concerts were given in Padua, Trieste, Udine and Venice. The two conductors were Guido Cantelli and Igor Markevitch, the leader was Antonio Abussi. The concerts covered the period from April 21 to April 30 when the orchestra returned to Florence for the opening of the *Maggio Musicale*.

I believe that this short tour was a great success, and I am assured that Cantelli was a most admirable conductor. I was not able to be present,

A corner of one of the rooms in La Fenice, Venice. The pianoforte and furniture
are authentic

The Arena, Verona.
begin, the conductor

Tancredi Pasero, the great
Italian basso, in the character
of 'Don Carlos'

formance is about to
io Gui) has just entered

Vittorio Gui

Jimmy Robertson

and I must admit that the programmes were something of a surprise to me. Verdi was the only Italian composer included while Wagner was favoured with two items—the Overture to *Rienzi* and *Siegfried's Journey to the Rhine.*

The programme "notes", things which I detest, have a short commentary on *Forza del Destino* which frankly amused me. The statement ran: "Verdi in 1862 journeyed to St. Petersburg to attend the production of *The Force of Destiny.* It was not unreservedly successful, owing to the fact that the Russian audience expected Italian Opera to be light and fluent" (I feel that what was really meant was not "fluent" but "fluid"; I may be wrong.) "Since *The Force of Destiny* is one of the gloomiest operas ever written, their disappointment is scarcely a matter of surprise."

However, to return to the *Maggio Musicale,* whose reputation grew year by year until it ranked with Salzburg and Bayreuth. It was always given careful and thoughtful notices in the European Press, and tourists flocked to Florence for the Festival, for not only were operas given which were known throughout the world, but also those which were either old and had lain neglected, or those which were modern and might be classed as "novelties".

The opera *Nabucco* and also *Luisa Miller* as well as Verdi's *Simon Boccanegra* were all revived in Florence, and after being too long neglected again took their place in the repertoires of various great opera houses. An interesting performance was given in 1940 of the *Dido and Æneas* of Henry Purcell, which was very successful.[1]

The Festival has always had the courage to present "novelties" and among their ventures are: *Volo di Notte* by Dallapiccola, *Cleopatra* by Malipiero, *Re Lear* by Frazzi, *Il Deserto Tentato* by Casella, *Don Juan* by Alfano. All these had their first productions at the *Maggio Musicale.*

The Paris Opera Company visited Florence to give Debussy's *Pelleas and Mélisande* and Rameau's *Castor et Pollux;* the Budapest Opera Company came with Respighi's *La Fianna* and Kodaly's *Filanda Magiara.* Stravinski conducted his own opera *Persephone.*

Florence has yet another theatre, the Pergola. This is the oldest theatre in Florence, and was built in 1652. It was designed by Tacca, and constructed of wood. In 1738, with the designs of the architect, it was rebuilt in concrete. Again, in 1837, it was "modernized" under the direction of the architect Baccani. It could accommodate 2000 people and had sixty-six boxes.

The building was the property of the Academy of the Immovables, which had for its sign or crest a windmill. The boxes, as was the case in the majority of old Italian opera houses, were the property, or held

[1] I believe that the Milan Philharmonic Society plan to present this work—but as a symphonic performance only—shortly, with Cigna in the leading role.—N.J.

in lease by the various noble families of Florence. Until a comparatively few years ago, the doors of these boxes bore the coats of arms of the various nobles.

The first performance was of the opera ballet *Ercole in Tebe*, which was given on the occasion of the marriage of the Ducessa Margherita Luigia, daughter of the Duc di Orlèans, to Prince Cosimo de Medici. Verdi visited Florence in 1847 when his opera *Macbeth* was given for the first time. For this performance Verdi also conducted the orchestra. The performance is said to have been a tremendous success, "and the applause worthy of the greatest Italian musician".

Of late years few operas have been given at this charming theatre, the seating accommodation is small and the size of the stage renders anything in the nature of "spectacular" opera impossible. During the *Maggio Musicale*, operas have been given such as those by Mozart, Handel, Rossini, Ravel and Debussy.

At present the Pergola is used as a home for legitimate plays; its opera days are over, and only the spoken word is heard. It remains a charming and historic opera house, and is well worth a visit.

TEATRO COMUNALE GIUSEPPE VERDI AND ITS MUSEUM, TRIESTE

ON the evening of April 21, 1801, all Trieste waited for the opening of the new and splendid theatre, then called the Teatro di Trieste. The building was admirable, with its fine, restrained front and the large, dignified porch. In appearance not altogether unlike the splendid Scala of Milan.

The work chosen for the opening performance was *Ginevra di Scozia* by one Giovanni Simone Mayr, the teacher and master of Gaetano Donizetti. The production was an unqualified success, and the theatre was launched on a successful career which has continued for more than 140 years.

On May 21, 1801, a production was given of *Annibale in Capua* by Antonio Salieri, who was the master of both Beethoven and Schubert, and on April 19, 1802, *La morte di Semirande* by Sebastano Nasolini with the singer Caterina Guidarini, the mother of Gioachino Rossini.

Rossini was at this time eleven years old, and came with his mother to Trieste. For some reason the public resented the choice of Caterina Guidarini, and pressed the claims of a *prima donna* named Grassini in no uncertain terms. Young Rossini flung himself into the discussion with immense vigour, defending his mother's claims in a most unchildlike and courageous fashion.

He himself used to tell in later years that this action of his convinced his grandparents that he was unfitted for the career of a singer for which they intended him, as it would afford too many opportunities for his high and spirited temper! Instead they decided that the child should be trained as a musician. Trieste claims therefore to have some part in the decision of Rossini's career.

I can find no trace of this story in his life, though it is certain that his mother was a singer of some repute, and that she travelled Italy in a touring company. Also it is true that at the age of ten Rossini was earning sufficient money through his singing to support himself in a very modest fashion.

On November 20, 1829, *Gli Illinesi* was presented with immense success. The opera was the work of Feliciano Strepponi, who was then impresario of the New Theatre. He died in Trieste on January 13, 1832, leaving his family in grave financial difficulties. In 1835 his daughter, Giuseppina Strepponi, who later married Verdi, made her début at the Trieste Opera House in *Matilde di Shabran* by Rossini. This was the beginning of her long and very successful career.

A number of other notable productions followed, but although they are recorded as having been tremendous successes, their names are unknown to present-day opera-goers.

On January 11, 1843, came the production of *Nabucco*, the original name of which was to have been *Nabucodonosor*, the first full-scale opera of Verdi. The composer himself could not attend the performance at Trieste, but the success was immediate.

The records of the Trieste Opera House record that Verdi composed especially for them *Stiffelio*, which was produced on November 16, 1850; this opera was later revised and renamed *Aroldo*. For the production of this opera Verdi was the guest of the city of Trieste. It is stated to have been received with great enthusiasm, but some other records state that it was a complete failure, and that even when it was revised and renamed the Italian public would have none of it.

On March 10, 1870, Trieste saw the first presentation of the *Mignon* of Ambrose Thomas. This is also stated to have been well received, and a letter from the composer is preserved in the theatre museum, written in French, and describing his delight at the reception of his opera.

During the years which followed many well-known works were offered to the public of Trieste, and it is said that "authors both sought and feared the severe but just criticism of the Trieste public, then considered one of the most competent and authoritative in Italy".

A document which is preserved in the museum tells the story of the first impresario (1801–1810), Giomanni Drosso Plastera. He discovered that he was completely ruined in 1811, and sold all his possessions. The articles for sale are recorded as follows: ". . . shields, halberds and spears of tin and pasteboard, chandelier of pasteboard, swords with antique handles of wood gilded and silvered, false precious stones, bellows, a wooden trough to hold rain water . . ."

Whether the money obtained by the sale of these properties was not sufficient to pay the debts of this unfortunate impresario does not appear, the record merely states: "Then he killed himself."

The theatre has always given a warm welcome to musicians and composers, both Paganini and Liszt appeared there.

The name of the theatre has been changed frequently. Originally named in 1801 Teatro Nuovo, it was renamed Teatro di Trieste. In 1820 it became Teatro Grande, in 1861 Teatro Comunale, and on January 29, 1901, it took its final name—Teatro Comunale Giuseppe Verdi.

THE MUSEUM OF THE GIUSEPPE VERDI

Nestled away among the labyrinth of passages that honeycombs the building a veritable paradise for connoisseurs of music lies concealed.

Surprisingly few people know about the "Museo Teatro"—and indeed, it *can* easily be overlooked. Its treasures are housed in a cool, dim suite of rooms, and directly you enter the outside world seems far distant and remote. This museum possesses all the mellow dignity of age—not the customary decay and mustiness that you invariably associate with such a place—but an atmosphere that is vividly redolent of the eternal inspiration, that lives on in the world of music. The past glories of the artists of a bygone era are linked with the triumphs of the celebrities of today.

The first thing that strikes the eye upon entering the doors is a large photograph of the ravishing Gina Cigna, clad in the rich, oriental robes of Turandot, whilst directly opposite is a portrait of the distinguished American contralto, Marian Anderson. Close at hand are ancient prints, in a remarkable state of preservation, of such almost legendary figures as Grisi, Mario, Malibran and Viadot-Garcia.

A closer inspection of the glass cases reveals a signed photograph of every celebrity who has sung at the opera house since the early years of the century—some even before.

There is the ill-fated Claudio Muzio; the Spanish tenor, Michele Fleta, stiffly erect in a high-winged collar, taken shortly after his début at the Teatro Verdi; a very youthful-looking Beniamino Gigli, in the costume of Mario Cavaradossi; the imposing figure of Bianca Scacciati as Norma; the fabulous Mattia Battistini; Adelina Patti; Luisa Tetrazzini; Tita Ruffo; Stabile; Giuseppe Lugo; Carlo Tagliabue; Lucrezia Bori; Toti dal Monte; and Gabriella Bezanzoni. One could go on interminably.

A little further away we see the magnificent Galliano Masini, who *should* have attained a world-wide fame with his glorious voice; the sultry Carmen of Gabriella Pederzini; the incomparable Tito Schipa; the handsome smiling "close-ups" of Mario Fillipeschi and Alessandro Ziliani; Gina Cigna again—this time in a close-fitting hat of the 1937 period; and the immortal Caruso, taken in 1901, even before his historic début at the Metropolitan Opera House, New York.

Then we are able to see the original manuscripts of Verdi, study his actual handwriting. Here are the delicate, almost crumbling parchments of a *Dugenhardt Prinmiciste* (dated 1581), *Missale Ramamum* (dated 1607), and a *Madrigale* (dated 1617).

The Teatro Verdi has also been visited by many theatrical celebrities throughout the years. There are faded daguerreotypes and photographs of the great Salvini, of Mariana Torelli (1871), Virginia Marini (1881), Eleanora Duse and Sarah Bernhardt, and the celebrated Dina Galli of the present day.

Then there are musical instruments: a tapestried harpsichord, with a keyboard brown with age, oboes, violi, hautboys and the intricate mechanisms of an entire puppet theatre, *Teatro di Burottini.* You can see the grinning, painted faces and carmined lips of the puppets, the ingenious details of their costumes and the ropes and pulleys which made them come to life.

Lastly, the playbills dating back to the early 1800s, and preserved with the care and tenderness of those who are fully aware of the importance of their task. There is so much to see in this delightful little retreat in the Teatro Verdi that you can discover something new each time you go there. It is certainly worth a visit, even if time only permits it to be a brief one.

THE ARENA, VERONA

(Open-air)

ITALY is famous for her open-air theatres, where, during the long summer evenings, opera may be heard by great audiences seated with the wide dome of the starlit sky overhead. Milan, Rome, Florence, all have such theatres, but none is more impressive than the great Arena at Verona, that beautiful town which Ruskin called The "peach blossom city".

The date of the building is uncertain, it has been given by some authorities as early as the 1st century A.D. There must originally have been two walls, an inner and an outer; of the outer wall only a fragment remains, but the inner walls have been carefully preserved through the ages and are almost intact. The seating, formed of great blocks of stone, rises in tiers ; there are seventy-four exits with internal staircases, numbers of smaller rooms which were probably used by the gladiators, and even housed some of the prisoners.

It is claimed that the Arena at Verona is one of the oldest in Italy, and some authorities have stated that its origin is Etruscan, but this is generally believed to be incorrect. Nevertheless, Capua, Lucca and Pola all have arenas older than the one at Rome, and Verona may also have the same antiquity as they.

The Arena was intended for horse and chariot races, for games and gladiatorial displays, but it is known that during the persecution of the Christians by Diocletian many people were put to death within its walls, including the two saints—Saint Fermo and Saint Rustico.

The Arena itself is 168 yards long and 134 yards wide; to stand on the topmost row of seats and look down into the Arena is an impressive sight; it is said that Dante stood there, lost in contemplation, and from the scene which met his eyes evolved his idea of the "Inferno".

The Arena was also used as a place for public executions. In 1276 over a hundred people belonging to the sect known as "Paterani" were brought from the castle at Sirmione and executed in the Arena by the order of Alberto della Scala.

Through the ages the Arena was used regularly for jousts, tournaments and acrobatic displays; theatrical performances were also offered to the public and—what was an innovation for Italy—public bull-fights.

Early in 1800 Napoleon the First sent a donation to Verona of £1200 for repairs to the Arena, and in July 1805 he visited the town and witnessed a bull-fight; returning in November 1807 he again attended one of these disgusting exhibitions, and it is said watched with great excitement and pleasure charming sight of unfortunate dogs being gored by the bull. It was probably about this time, his interest in the city of Verona being aroused, that he transported several of the best pictures from the great church of San Zeno to Paris!

Then followed a time when the Arena was given over to touring companies of players, and it is worth noting that both Adelaide Ristori[1] and Ernesto Rossi made their first appearances here about 1824.

In July 1866, when Italy was engaged in her struggle against the Austrians, the Arena became a camp for the prisoners taken by the enemy. Imagine it—the age-old Arena turned into a camp for men who had committed no crime but that of fighting for the freedom of their country! But the tide turned and the victory of Sadowa was followed by the restoration of "Veneto", and the return of Verona to Italy quickly followed. In the October of 1866 this was accomplished, and in the November Victor Emmanuel I came to Verona as the King. Accompanied by his two sons, the King showed himself to the loyal people of Verona in the Arena, accompanied by the Bishop of Verona, a member of the historic house of Canossa.

It is perhaps of interest to record that the Arena was visited by the famous Colonel Cody with his "Buffalo Bill" spectacle, a presentation which delighted the people of Verona.

Now, except for the occasional exhibition, meetings or the like, the great arena lies untenanted and deserted until the summer of every year. Then the old place wakes to life; the whole of the Piazza Bra, where the Arena stands, rings with the sounds of hammers, there is movement where there was solitude. The huge stage is being built, a segment of the great floor space is cut off and there is the stage ready to receive the scenery which will offer to the patrons such a splendid spectacle.

Let me try to take you back with me to one evening before the war, when it seemed that the whole of Italy was flocking to Verona to hear what to me, at least, is possibly the greatest of all the operas of Puccini—*Turandot*.

We drove there from Sirmione, along that road which Michael Kelly traversed, which was then "filled with brigands"; on this night it was peaceful except for the never-ending stream of traffic bound for Verona. The car park was a staggering sight, here was every kind of automobile—the latest models, streamlined Fiats, elegant Lancias, old cars which had rattled over the Italian roads for years, even small trucks which had brought there a group of people—but all waiting while their owners listened to opera.

The stream of people grew more dense with each moment, people

---

[1] I have often wondered if Adelaide Ristori could be an ancestress of Harry Ristori, the well-known British variety artist, whose wife, Marjorie Ristori, is such an excellent producer of cabaret and other forms of music-hall entertainment.—N. J.

were swarming like flies to the topmost tiers, the whole of the floor of the Arena was filled with chairs, men were walking up and down crying "*Il libretto dell' opera*", others were selling cushions—or rather offering them for hire, for if you have ever experienced the acute discomfort of the chairs in the Arena you will realize the necessity for hiring a cushion. And even they grow terribly hard and insufficient at the end of three hours!

Between the audience and the stage is a row of particularly bright arcs which serve to "cut off the stage" as a curtain might do. There is the orchestra entering—over a hundred of them and all picked musicians. Dimly, staring past the great arcs, you may see the figures of carpenters, stage hands and stage managers; you may discern the towers and spires of the City of Pekin rising, towering towards the starlit sky.

A gong sounds. You see the figures of the people on the stage all scampering away, then the lights go out and for a brief second or two the great Arena of Verona is in darkness. That is the signal for one of those delightful and charming customs to which Italians cling. Years ago there was a great fair given at the Arena, and everyone entering was presented with a wax taper, the effect of 20,000 of these was charming and fairy-like. Now, wax tapers are not handed out, but when the lights go out everyone in the audience strikes one of the little wax matches, known as *cerini*, and the effect of them, like thousands of glow-worms, is delightful. They flicker and die, there is a stir, some applause and the conductor— on the occasion of which I am writing, Vittorio Gui—enters; he raises his baton, the lights flare out on the stage, and you are watching the City of Pekin.

Towers, turrets, palaces! There is the long terrace where the last of Turandot's unfortunate lovers—the Persian Prince—will walk to execution; the executioners, stripped to their waists wait for him, grim, repellent and terrible. The crowd moves and sways, the music is wild, even savage. The Unknown Prince enters with his old father and the faithful Lui; Turandot appears upon the balcony of her palace, surrounded by her ladies-in-waiting. The unhappy Persian Prince walks slowly along the terrace, turning to send one imploring last glance at Turandot; he holds out his hands, imploring her clemency. She watches him, smiles that dreadful, secret smile, then turns and disappears, her ladies following her.

Again the crowds pass and re-pass, the headsman opens the door of the prison and hangs the head of the Persian Prince among the other heads of the lovers of the cruel Turandot. The Unknown Prince stands there transfixed. He has seen the face of Turandot—he is determined to try to win her. His old father and little Lui do their utmost to dissuade him; he rushes forward and raising the mallet strikes the great bronze gong, which signifies that he has entered the lists for the hand of the Princess.

The lights flare round, almost blinding the audience—the first act is

F

over. Everyone talks, criticizing, praising; argument is loved by Italians and they all talk at the top of their voices. Those who are "old hands" leave the Arena and visit some nearby *caffe* where you may obtain cold drinks and escape the noise.

The second act, and the music surging forward, ascending to the topmost tiers; for the acoustics of the Arena are perfect. The sudden complete silence which falls everywhere the moment the conductor takes his place is almost uncanny. At one moment the whole great place is filled with the sound of voices, the next—you can hear the "tap" of Gui's baton quite clearly.

At this particular performance of which I am writing the celebrated "Verona incident" occurred, of which I say more later; the matter was the question of "Encore" or "No encore". Gui disliked encores, the Veronese wanted one, for the tenor was of their own city and they wanted to listen to him again in the famous aria of the third act.

In vain did Gui decide that the music should continue; the applause was insistent, the tenor merely stood there making apologetic movement with his hands, implying, "I am ready to sing again, but the conductor will not permit it." The place was pandemonium. Finally Vittorio Gui gave a sign to his violins and they all followed him out of the orchestra. Gui was finally persuaded to come back, the audience quietened down, Turandot was furious, and—the tenor gave his encore! It caused great attention in the Press, and even though he "lost the fight", I maintain that Vittorio Gui emerged with great dignity and immense credit.

Let us suppose that, after the second act, you go round "back stage". There is an army of scene-shifters, busy bearing off the towers and palaces of Pekin. The dressing-rooms are small and uncomfortable; they may have been sufficiently good for the gladiators of ancient Rome, but for modern artists they appear to be devoid of any comfort whatever. It is strange to see Turandot standing in all the magnificence of her Chinese robes heavy with gold and silver embroidery—for the particular *prima donna* of whom I am thinking has a splendid collection of robes which are all authentic, not merely stage props—with her three-inch-long scarlet nails, her huge head-dress—waiting to make her entrance where gladiators stood to make theirs hundreds of years ago.

The warning bell rings and we race back, narrowly escaping death from some huge piece of scenery which is being carried past. Again the noise surges, again it dies as Gui taps the music stand with his baton. The music begins and seems to mount to the skies where the stars look down in such serenity, as they did when they watched the Roman games, as they will continue to look down when even the superb music of *Turandot* is forgotten.

BOBOLI GARDENS, FLORENCE

(Open-air)

THE Arena at Verona is grander, more vast, possibly the acoustics are better, the Baths of Caracalla are unique in their ancient setting, but the Boboli Gardens at Florence are unquestionably the most beautiful open-air "opera house" ever dreamed of.

They are situated on the hillside behind the Pitti Palace, that magnificent palace which was first the property of one of the greatest and richest Florentine families, and later one of the palaces of the Kings of Italy.

The Pitti Palace was planned with its beautiful gardens in the 16th century. The Boboli Gardens are considered to be the most wonderful park in Italy, with their cypresses, laurels, oleanders, with charmingly designed flower-beds ablaze with colour, and the artificial lakes from which seem to rise splendid marble fountains.

The Boboli Gardens were the work of two architects, Tribilo and Bountalenti, at the order of the great family of Medici. They form the ideal setting for both operas and also spoken drama.

During the past *Maggio Musicale* in Florence many operas have been given in the Boboli Gardens. The acoustics are not perfect, but the charm of the setting and the beauty of the music were unforgettable. Here Claudio Monteverdi's *Coronation of Poppea* was given, with very fine scenic effects. Also Gluck's *Alceste* was given here, when Vittorio Gui conducted and Cigna sang the soprano rôle. She refers to this occasion as "the most precious memory of my career".

Aïda (Verdi)

IT must be remembered that in this present volume I have only been able to deal with such opera houses as I knew and visited before the war. At the moment, in this unfortunate country, which was promised —and I believe had circumstances and powers not changed as they have done, might have had—conditions which made travel possible. Unfortunately the journey, for example from North Italy to Bari, would be a very expensive undertaking. Catania and Palermo are out of the question, and although my Italian friends and the authorites at many opera houses have been most kind, generous and helpful, I have not been able to include as many opera houses as I should have wished.

Sicily is rich in opera houses, the most magnificent being that at Palermo. The town itself is beautiful with its long stretch of promenade, and the theatre is in keeping with it. The operas presented there are excellently done, and the finest artists go there for the various seasons.

There is an amusing and slightly scandalous story told of the great *prima donna*, La Gabrielli, who was famous in the middle of the 18th century. She was appearing at the San Carlo at Naples but went over for a season at Palermo. This *prima donna*, like many others of a later date, was exceedingly temperamental, and when she was "ordered" by the Viceroy to appear in a new opera before him and his court, she sent word that she had a headache and could not appear. The Viceroy was furious, messages were sent again and again, expostulations made, orders given. Gabrielli remained obdurate—she would not sing. She was consequently arrested and put in prison, which punishment she accepted with complete coolness, saying to the Captain of the Guard, "Your Viceroy may make me cry, but he cannot make me sing!" She remained in prison for two days, where she made a great *festa* for the other prisoners, having immense and costly meals sent into the prison at her own expense. This *prima donna* was famous for the number of her lovers, and while in Naples, appearing at the San Carlo, was living in tremendous luxury with a certain count. The manager of the opera house at Palermo wrote to her to enquire her terms for singing for a season in Sicily. She replied, "If you will build a bridge from Naples to Palermo I will sing for you, not else."

He replied, "Madame, if you can recollect and give me a list of *all* those on whom you have bestowed your favours, I will build your bridge, not else!"

His free style pleased Gabrielli, who agreed to go to Palermo, though it is not recorded that she supplied the complete list of her lovers as had been requested. What *is* recorded is that she added the manager at Palermo to the list!

Catania, the birthplace of Bellini, has a splendid opera house, named after the master. It is probably about the same date as the majority of Italy's great opera houses, the middle of the 18th or early 19th century, I should imagine. Very magnificent it is, too, with much decoration in gold and scarlet, the usual tiers of boxes and swinging chandeliers. I remember being very much impressed by it, to the great satisfaction of the custodian who, of course, assured me that it was "second only to La Scala".

Bari, that unfortunate town which not only suffered badly in December 1943, when the Germans bombed the harbour where a great number of ships carrying ammunition were lying; and later when a large mine was washed up by the sea and exploded against the sea wall; and yet again much later when other ships were blown up—this time owing to an accident and not enemy action. On the occasion of the first disaster the old theatre—the Margherita—was badly damaged, and was out of action for a considerable time. I do not know if it has been completely restored or not. It was of no great dignity or beauty, but the Petrezelli is a splendid place. There is a fine entrance-hall, the auditorium is large and the acoustics good. The decorations are lavish, and the boxes rising in tiers are commodious and comfortable. The scheme is gold and red, the date, I should imagine, is the early 19th century. It was obviously built for large productions of opera, for the stage is immense, the lighting good, and the dressing-room accommodation ample. There are also innumerable offices, workshops and the like. Not perhaps a very distinguished theatre, but a very good one.

Bari possesses another rather smaller opera house, the Puccini, which, I imagine, is of a rather later date than the Petrezelli. Both these theatres were used for entertainment purposes by the Allies.

At the Royal Palace at Caserta there is a charming little theatre, where performances were given and even opera staged in a miniature form for the Royal Family when in residence. It is a very "doll's house" of a theatre, but conforming in every way to the traditional form. The stage is minute but well equipped, and the decorations are charming.

Pisa had a fine opera house, which was badly damaged, as was so much of that lovely town during the war. It was less ornate than many other opera houses, but it was large, and the acoustics were good. The drop-curtain was, I remember, particularly well painted.

Desenzano, which stands at the extreme end of Lago di Garda, has what was at one time an opera house. The exterior is very simple and not inspiring, but inside are the remains—for the place is now given over to films, dances and variety entertainments—of what was once an opera house of considerable size. I remember going over it once, and noting how each box had the name of the owner painted on the door. Obviously these owners were regular subscribers to the opera when it came to Desenzano.

Como has a fine opera house modelled on the Scala, and I was assured that it held as many people—which statement I should doubt. It is dignified and beautifully constructed, with a good entrance-hall and staircase. The stage is large and well equipped.

Novara has a dignified opera house; in appearance the style, if it were in England, would be called Georgian. There is a fine entrance-hall, and though the auditorium is not very impressive it is commodious enough. The stage is not particularly good. The chief interest is the small private museum attached to the theatre, where there is an astonishing collection of relics of opera. There is a letter of Mozart's in his own handwriting with his photograph; a piece of manuscript in Verdi's own hand; other letters and signed photographs of Duse, Toscanini, Caruso and other famous stars. But most interesting of all are the model "sets" for the original production of *Aïda*. They are a joy to see, and made with the greatest care and attention to detail.

Merano, which was of course Austrian before 1918, has an opera house, and although it is a poorish place of little or no importance, very good artists used to appear there. The place was always packed, but it is without distinction, and the stage is a very indifferent affair.

It is fairly safe to say that eighty per cent of the towns in Italy have opera houses, and many of them well worth seeing and inspecting, for their "back stage" mechanical arrangements are excellent. Very few do not possess a panoramic "back cloth", which is worked from a huge drum. They have good lighting in nearly all cases, and their scenery is frequently painted in perspective, as we discovered in Milano when we had a set painted for the Excelsior Theatre by an Italian scene-painter. There was to be a gallery and staircase, and when Bernard Goodman began to have it "set up" he could not understand what was wrong until he realized that in his "setting up" he was not allowing for this perspective in the scene painting. Once he discovered this all was well, and the set was most effective.

Italians like to "nail" their scenery when they put up a set, and where we should use ropes and hooks they use nails. This is one of the reasons for the exceedingly long waits between the acts, particularly in opera. They stage magnificent spectacles, nothing is too difficult for them, nothing too elaborate; but to tear down for example the first act of *La Gioconda*, and in its place set up the "ship scene", takes time, and requires a good deal of hammering!

In Rome I used to pass the Teatro dell' Opera every morning on my way to my office, and, like any child, I would stand wide-eyed and watch the scenery being taken in through the big open doors as it was unloaded from the great lorries, and marvel at its size and intricacy.

In smaller opera houses, for productions which are not of the standard of the Rome house, La Scala, or the Fenice, strong paper is used instead of canvas for the scenery. The effect is very good while it is new, but when it begins to look shabby—well, it looks *very* shabby.

There is a very splendid opera house at Trieste. I have never seen such excellent dressing-rooms as those provided for the star artists. They are charmingly furnished and upholstered, and each one has its own bathroom. Trieste has also another opera house, the Verdi, not so luxurious, but the acoustics are better, and this is where opera is usually given.

One day I promise myself a long tour of this beautiful country, so that I may visit every place where an opera house stands—and revive my memories of the ones which I have already seen. That, however, must remain a dream until petrol ceases to cost what it does at the moment!

BALLET IN ITALY

THANKS to the kindness of my friend, Geoffrey Handley-Taylor, I am able to include certain facts regarding Italian Ballet. I include this not because I wish to deal with ballet as ballet, but because in many of the finest Italian operatic productions it has played an important part. Ballet is, as Handley-Taylor says, "an organic part of the opera", and although the history of ballet in Italy begins much later than that of ballet in France it has been developed tremendously.

In Italy, of course, the art of miming and what later developed into "pantomime" was born, but there was no actual school for training artists for the ballet until one was opened in Milan in 1837. Now the great opera houses have their schools of training built adjoining the opera house, and giving opportunity for those finely trained dancers who have so often claimed our admiration as we watched *Aïda*, *Faust*, *Loreley*, *La Gioconda*, *La Wally* and, to a much lesser degree, *La Traviata* and even *Carmen*.

Until the State took over the Royal Opera House Ballet there was no systematic training to be had, and it has been a long struggle to equip fully the State group of dancers.

Originally, in the formation of a State-owned ballet, dancers were drawn from existing private companies, and the ranks were later filled by the younger dancers from the Opera House School of Ballet. The pupils in the majority of cases were obliged to study and make good progress for eight years in the ballet school in the systems of Blasis and Cecchetti before they were passed on to the Opera House Ballet.

Blasis, in addition to knowing all there was to know regarding ballet, was a writer and a student of universal art, also a keen debater of matters politican.

His rules for training have been accepted by practically every dancing institution of any standing. Pupils were not admitted before the age of eight years, or after they had passed the age of twelve, though in the case of boys this rule was sometimes waived and they were admitted as old as fourteen years.

Each pupil was medically examined before formal admission, and had to show that they came of healthy stock. Their training was carefully arranged for them. They studied ballet for three hours a day and "mime" for one. They were attached to the school for eight years, after which time—had their progress been sufficiently good—they received a salary on a slowly ascending scale.

It is worth recording that Blasis was the originator of the use of the *barre*, that rod which runs round the walls of dance studios for students to support themselves when they begin their exercises. The pupil of Blasis—or one of them—was Giovanni Lepri, who gave instruction to Enrico Cecchetti, master of the Russian ballet.

The actual renaissance of ballet in Italy did not begin on any great scale until 1938. In this year Aurel Milloss, a Hungarian choreographer and former *maître de ballet* at the Royal Opera House in Budapest, came to Rome. It must be remembered clearly that although Aurel Milloss brought new life and vitality to ballet in Italy, the Ballet School attached to the opera had been existing for many years, and he arrived to find the soil, as it were, already prepared for him to embark on ballet as divorced from opera.

In addition to the students already in training at the Opera House itself, there was the State Dance Academy under the direction of the energetic and capable Theresa Bataggi, and from this school a number of new recruits were drawn.

His company grew in art and progress, and in addition to the various ballets given at the Opera House—whether they were included at the opera or given as individual performances—he arranged the splendid ballet for *Faust* when that opera was given at the Baths of Caracalla, when over 20,000 spectators were present at each performance.

Nothing could have been more magnificent or more perfectly staged than the visit of Mephistopheles and Faust to hell, to watch the sensual pleasures of that infernal place. The whole theatre of old Roman red brick served, in the light of the setting sun, to provide a scene which was almost incredible in its splendour and reality.

In *La Liara* (*The Jar*) Milloss designed and conceived a ballet which should serve to show the art and characteristics of his ballet company in a series of Sicilian folk dances; later he arranged most admirably *Salome*, to give ample opportunities to the *Prima Ballerina Assoluta* of the Opera House Ballet—Attilia Radice, using the famous music of Strauss for the *Seven Veil Dance*.

Milloss is an artist who shares the versatility of this lady, Attilia Radice, and Handley-Taylor records that his "natural swagger on the stage is one of the highlights of discussion, but this swagger of Milloss is as important to ballet as Gigli's sly smile is to opera".

A younger artist, at present not possessing the depth or maturity of Milloss, is Ugo dell' Ara. He is generally partnered by his sister Lia, whose technicalities are superb. Of Attilia Radice there can be no question that she is a great artist. Formally *Prima Ballerina Assoluta* at the Scala Milan, she came to Rome at the special request of the authorities of the Opera House.

Alberto Felici and his understudy Giulio Perugini are both obviously destined to take a great place in the Italian ballet.

These principals with ten other star artists stand at the head of a company of sixty-two members of both sexes, and at times when the necessity arises this number may be increased to 120. Since writing these brief notes I hear that in December 1946 Milloss was called from Rome to assume the position of *maître de ballet* at La Scala. He has a large programme of ballets arranged, but as they are "independent ballets" and not playing an essential part in opera—except in one or two exceptions —it is not necessary to mention them here.

During the war years the ballet suffered greatly from lack of the necessary shoes—the prices of these increased enormously, and even if money were there the shoes were not to be found. I remember going all over Milan to find some place where they were still to be had. I found them at last in a small workroom, where the proprietress had made ballet shoes for years and years. She almost shed tears when she showed me the inferior material, and declared that she was ashamed to have to offer such indifferent stuff and yet charge such a much greater price.

It is worth noticing that the great Giuseppina Bozzacchi, who appeared in the original production of *Coppélia* in Paris on May 25, 1870, was a native of Milan. The part had been given originally to Adela Grantsova, who during rehearsals had the misfortune to fall and sprain her ankle; when she was well on the way to recovery she contracted typhoid fever. Delibes was sent to Italy to see if he could find a suitable ballerina. In the dancing school of Signora Dominique, in Paris, after his return in despair from Italy, Perrin took him to see a dark-haired little girl with beautiful and intelligent eyes—Giuseppina Bozzacchi.

She was born in Milan in 1853. Her parents were humble people but they struggled to pay for her dancing lessons. She was then sent to Paris to study, as we have read, under Signora Dominique. Her progress was rapid, and after she had been noticed by Perrin, Delibes and Saint-Léon they were so impressed with her attainments that they supervised her lessons every day.

In 1869 she was rehearsing every day with Saint-Léon, and so well did she advance that by August the choreographer was able to run through the whole ballet.

She was an immediate success. The whole house applauded her, and she was presented to the Emperor Napoleon the Third and the Empress Eugénie. She was given a new contract, with a considerable rise of salary, and this was a great help to her for she was practically the sole support of her now widowed mother and several small brothers and sisters. It is recorded that in order to save money she invariably refused to take a cab to drive her home after the performance; also she was intent upon repaying various loans which had been made to her, including one to the Italian Benevolent Society.

War broke out, and on July 19th, 1870, the Emperor left Paris to join his troops. In November Giuseppina fell ill. She was found to be suffering from undernourishment caused by the food restrictions owing to the siege. She died on the morning of her seventeenth birthday, November 23, 1870. She was buried in the cemetery at Montmartre.

Looking through many old programmes of various opera houses, I find references again and again to various ballets which, although the artists may not have been trained in any particular school, appear to have been exceedingly popular.

There remain many operas in Italian where ballet is introduced with great effect, and which never fails to gain great applause. Possibly the most notable of all is the "Dance of the Hours" with its exquisite music, given very beautifully in *La Gioconda*. Ballet introduced by the great composers into their work serves—as in *La Gioconda*—to lighten for a few moments the impending tragedy, and to bring essential beauty of movement, as well as music, into stories which are often heavy with drama.

Also is notable the ballet in *Aïda*, the beautiful waltz in *La Wally* and—though it scarcely attains to the dignity of a ballet proper—the chorus and dance in *La Traviata*.

To show that ballet is very active in Italy, Geoffrey Handley-Taylor has sent to me a few additional notes regarding the present season in Rome.

A new company called *Ballets Modernes de Roma* was formed last March under the direction of Padraic O'Brine, the brother of the well-known film actor, John Mills. Dania Manning, who at the age of twenty has already thirteen years of theatrical experience, is the *prima ballerina*.

The choreographer is Giovanni Brinati, from La Scala, Milano, and formerly with the Royal Opera House Company in Rome.

The repertoire has included *Polka Dot* (Johann Strauss), *La Giara* (Casella), *Danza del Fuoco* (Falla), *Sogno Romantico* (Chopin), *L'après Midi d'un Faune* (Debussy), *Festa del Czardas* (traditional), *Prince Igor Dances* (Borodin), *Le Spectre de la Rose*, and extracts from *Coppélia*, *Les Sylphides*, *Casse-Noisette*, *Prodigal Son* (Prokofiev) and *La Boutique Fantasque* (Rossini-Respighi).

The company has had great success in Italy and Austria, and hopes to tour the continent of Europe and also South America during the present year, and to come to England in 1948.

At the Rome Opera House a new ballet, *Carillon Magico*, to music by Pick-Mangia-galli was staged recently by Theresa Battagia, mistress of the school in Rome.

Should these plans for a visit to England materialize, it will give British admirers of ballet an opportunity to see the strides which have been made by ballet in Italy during the recent and difficult years.

SHOULD OPERATIC SINGERS LEARN TO ACT?

Aïda (Verdi)

IT appears to me that this question can only be answered by a definition of what opera is. I find the meaning given in a dictionary of repute to be: A musical drama, a dramatic composition set to music and sung and acted on the stage.

Mark that—*sung and acted*.

I have more than once been rebuked for objecting to bad acting on the operatic stage. I have been told that the quality of the voices, the orchestra and the music of the composer are the salient points to look and listen to and for. If this is so, then surely opera might be given to all intents and purposes just as satisfactorily by the singers merely walking on to an empty stage, in their ordinary costumes, and singing to the orchestra.

Admittedly the music is "the thing", and I confess that I have listened to many, and one in particular, singers with superb voices who could not or did not act, but who by their sheer musical artistry have delighted me. That, however, is not the point. "Sung and acted" is the meaning of opera, and if it is to be "acted" then it might as well be done in the best possible manner.

There is, of course, the old argument that certain singers have voices which are admirably suited to certain rôles, but whose physical attributes are totally incompatible. One of the classic examples is the late Dame Nellie Melba in *La Bohème*. The unfortunate Mimi is dying of consumption, and Dame Nellie Melba appeared to be in robust health. I only heard her once in this opera mentioned, and even then I was "shocked" at her complete inability to act in the slightest; more, I could not feel that she wanted to act even if she had ever learned to do so. It would be nonsense to say that I felt no pleasure in the opera, that the singing of the famous *diva* did not impress me, but I could not resist comparing her performance with the one given by the late Mrs. Patrick Campbell, many years later, whenever I remembered Melba's performance of Mimi.

Mrs. Campbell was touring Greater London and the provinces with *Hedda Gabler*. I saw her at the King's Theatre, Hammersmith, and the production was not particularly inspiring. The scenery was not very good, the stage furniture was ugly and "cheap" and everyone assured me that "Mrs. Pat was far too old, far too fat to play Hedda".

Those of you who know the play will remember how Hedda's entrance is "built up" for her by the scene which precedes it; she is referred to as being young, beautiful and possessing every imaginable charm. I believe that I am right in saying that even her age is referred to as being "twenty-six".

I cannot be certain, but I imagine that at that time Mrs. Campbell must have been about sixty (though that she ever "grew old" I cannot deny too strongly—she was one of those whom the gods loved, and she "died young"). She had grown stout, possibly too stout for the part of Hedda, but such was her consummate artistry that after she entered and seated herself on the remarkably uncomfortable-looking sofa, had anyone after watching her for five minutes said to me, "Where is this lovely young woman of twenty-six?" I should have answered with complete conviction, "There, you damned fool, sitting on that sofa!"

I quote that example to show that if operatic artists—male or female—would study the art of acting as well as the art of singing, they would succeed in making their characters, at least, credible, and to some extent mitigating their physical limitations.

Knowing something of the stage itself, and having learnt something of the art of acting, I admit freely that to act in opera must almost inevitably be more difficult than to act in legitimate drama. There are other things to be considered in addition to the acting—particularly the music and the baton of the conductor—but it can be done, and it ought to be done. The fact that Chaliapine was a magnificent singer was not lessened by the fact that he was also a superb actor; the one art enhanced the other. There, on the other hand, is Gigli, who possesses what is undoubtedly the finest tenor voice since Caruso; Gigli has never "acted" in his life so far as I have seen, heard or read. Whether this is sheer inability to comprehend dramatic art, or because he has never attempted to learn, I cannot say. It would be impossible to derive more pleasure from a voice than one derives from Gigli's, but if only he had learnt to act!

There is a good deal of nonsense talked about "immense sopranos" and "mountains of flesh"; only the other day I read the words "these eighteen-stone sopranos". Of course there are no such things as "eighteen-stone sopranos", certainly not in these days, and I very much doubt if in any others either. I can remember that some of the *prima donnas* in the German operas used to be fairly massive, but I question if any of them turned the scale at more than fourteen stone at the most.

Certainly no sopranos or mezzo-sopranos in Italian opera at the present time or the time immediately before the war, with one exception, were barely even "massive". Many of them act, and a few of them act

93

with remarkable talent. The same may be said of the men. I have seen Malipiero act excellently. Stabile is, of course, admitted to be a fine actor.

Ebe Stignani acts well when she has a part which gives her any scope, also Mafalda Favero; I know that it is customary to declare that Toti dal Monte cannot act, that she relies on her voice and her really excellent clothes to "pull her through", but I have seen this artist when she gave performances which were most moving, one of which was Violetta in Verona (at the opera house, not at the arena) with a lamentably poor supporting cast. She was excellent, perhaps a little too robust for a consumptive, but not to rouse the amusement, indignation and general hilarity of the audience as did Donatelli when she appeared at the *première* of this same opera at La Fenice, Venice, in March 1853. That failure has been accounted for in many different ways, one of them being that the robust soprano, Donatelli, was totally unsuited to the part of the stricken girl. Surely here is another proof that the audience do expect something more than merely singing, scenery and orchestral music, or why should they object to a robust and obviously completely healthy Violetta?

Again it is held that Graziani the tenor was in bad voice and very hoarse, and that Felice Varesi (Germont) made no attempt to exert himself in the part.

Then again the audience were unaccustomed to an opera in what was then "modern" dress, and for this reason when the opera was re-staged the costumes were those of Louis XIII. It is history now that the success at the second presentation was great and immediate.

I know that I am digressing here, but it is a habit of mine. This opera, *La Traviata,* was condemned as being highly immoral; in London in 1850 the newspapers thundered against it, and various well-known preachers denounced it from their puplits. *The Times* even entered the lists against it, stigmatizing the libretto as being filled with "foul and hideous horrors". As a consequence crowds rushed to what was then "Her Majesty's" to witness this monument of immorality! The opera—in which it would be difficult to find the hideous immorality—was a tremendous success.

Melchior used to act well; I have not seen him since 1937; Armando Borgiolo gives performances which from the acting point of view are apt to vary. Pasero, the terrific Italian bass, rarely gets much acting opportunity, but I have seen him give very good performances of Mephistopheles, and during the somewhat long ballet he is capable of keeping still, and yet appearing to take an actual interest in what is going on around him. Cigna is almost outstandingly good as an actress, but she takes trouble over her characterization not only in singing but in the actual acting. I watched about eighteen months ago this artist in the process of studying Giordano's *Fedora* and saw the character gradually built up and "filled in" with the greatest interest. The result was that when she appeared in Bologna, and through some mistake or reluctance to spend the money on the part of the impresario there was no dress rehearsal, she was able on the second night—for the first was obviously for all the artists a "dress rehearsal"—to give a performance which was not only magnificently sung but as well acted as anything I have ever seen *on any stage*.

I have seen various *prima donnas* do terrible things. I can remember one—and she is justly celebrated as a singer—in *Tosca*, when Tosca flings herself down on the sofa in Scarpia's room and bursts into tears. The sofa cushion was not as comfortably placed as the singer wished; she ceased to be the distraught Floria Tosca, and "coming right out of the part" sat up, punched the cushion into the shape she wished, put it back and—again burst into tears!

I have seen the soprano in that celebrated "sleep-walking scene" which occurs in the opera derived from one of Shakespeare's plays, and which no well-brought-up and properly superstitious actor or actress really likes to name, wash her hands in a manner which was reminiscent of someone playing "pat-a-cake"!

Drinking and eating scenes are productive of bad acting, when, after having goblets "filled" with wine, the holders, carried away by their singing, let the goblets hang downwards, and later raise them to their lips to drink! This is usually a chorus fault, and as such the blame lies with the producer.

There have been occasions when one of the leading characters has to fall—whether dying, being shot or what will you—where the stage has been so heavily padded to soften their fall that the sight of the wrinkles in the stage cloth have been noticeable from the audience. Very few people enjoy falling on the stage, but "falls" can be learnt, and it is quite possible to know exactly how and where to drop without inflicting the slightest pain or hurt to yourself. But it must be learnt!

I have seen various Turandots both in photographs and on the stage—they alternated between looking so charming, so utterly delightful, that they might have been Evelyn Laye in a new Hylton production; others have looked like someone from the back row of the chorus of a very cheap provincial pantomime. Only one has succeeded in looking like a very cold, inhuman Chinese princess.

Transporting bodies in sacks, the presentation of small children on the stage—how quickly that infant of Butterfly's grew up, if you remember—boats and the like are fine ground for difficulties of all kinds.

I think that it was Ina Suez who told me that she was playing in Puccini's *Madame Butterfly*, and I fancy at Covent Garden, though I am not sure. The "child" was rehearsing with her, and she felt that she

95

was acting well—as indeed she can do—and embracing the "child" with real passion. Suddenly it whispered hoarsely in her ear, "Give over, fer Gawd's sake, I'm older'n what you are!"

I remember once at a performance of *La Traviata* at the Teatro Puccini in Milano, where for a short season the management used to engage one or two star artists, and the rest—well, I imagine that they were chosen haphazard in the Galleria. A certain tenor, who has always held himself in considerable esteem, in the middle of a long and tense scene burst his collar-stud. The rather high collar flapped about his neck, while he made continual and completely unsuccessful attempts to fasten it. Had that man possessed any knowledge of acting he would have ripped the collar off and played the scene without it, trusting to the beautiful music and his own unconcern to have carried him through. As it was, his perpetual fidgetings completely ruined the credibility of the scene.

So then if opera is music and acting, let us have both. The music will be enhanced, and the often rather improbable "story" made more real to us if the protagonists have studied the art of acting.

Let them study the art of make-up, let them have their wigs well and carefully dressed—few things are more revolting than long-haired wigs which look as if they had not been dressed for months. Let women who have to play the characters of young men, as in *Faust*; pages, as in *Un Ballo in Maschera*; women who are supposed to be "impersonating" men, as in *Forza del Destino*, wear shoes with heels which are not two and a half inches high. They may look elegant when worn with skirts; they don't "go well" with male clothes. Let all Floria Toscas ask themselves if they really believe that a woman who has just murdered a man to save her honour, and is longing to reach her lover to assure him that he is not going to be shot, would rush home and change her dress.

The stories of the operas, though many of them may be unreal and improbable, are nearly all fine, full-blooded stuff which lend themselves to acting ability. La Gioconda is not merely a woman with a long fair wig and a soprano voice; she is—or should be—a real person capable of love, passion and suffering. Norma is not merely a statue in the style of Boadicea on the Embankment, Carmen, Fedora, Violetta, Amelia—all real people; as are Rodolfo, Scarpia, Faust, Rigoletto and Rhadames. To make them real is to give opera its real and full due, to remove one of those rather silly—if frequently justifiable—criticisms that "opera is so unconvincing".

"Sung and acted"—sung beautifully, acted finely!

Part Two

COMMENT AND CRITICISM ON ITALIAN OPERA
By James C. Robertson

JAMES CONSTABLE ROBERTSON

Ca - - - sta Di - va.

Norma

IT is with great pride and pleasure that I have obtained permission to use some of the work of "Jimmy" Robertson on Italian opera.

This young man, taken from us in the early days of the Second World War, had joined the Navy the day before war actually broke out. There could have been nothing less likely to appeal to him than a life in the Navy. He was by profession an accountant, working in his father's business in Dundee. But by inclination he was first a lover of opera, and particularly dear to him was Italian opera, and Italian music of all kinds.

I once told him that he only went back to Scotland so that he might have the pleasure of travelling out to Italy again to listen to opera. He took every available opportunity, and it was nothing for him to travel to Milan, and without sleep rush immediately to La Scala and immerse himself in whatever opera was being presented. As some people travel in order to "follow the sun", "Jimmy" Robertson travelled to "follow opera".

His collection of gramophone records, the data which he gathered, the books which he read, all went to give him the power to "speak with authority". He was a constant contributor to *The Gramophone, The Music Lover* and various other journals of a like kind. His work was characterized by not only great and real knowledge of his subject, but by a sensitive and generous appreciation.

The reason for our meeting originally was a letter of mine in *World Radio* when I had the temerity to express the opinion that Vittorio Gui —for whom I have a great and profound admiration—had tended to "drag" the music in a certain opera which was being performed at the Fenice in Venice. Now, Jimmy Robertson's affection and admiration for this brilliant conductor were unbounded; in addition they were great and intimate friends. After Jimmy's death, Vittorio Gui wrote to me, saying, "Poor Jimmy, I loved him like a son."

G

It was natural that my remarks should call down Jimmy's wrath, and the result was a letter in *World Radio*.

"*... Indeed*" (he wrote), "*in Venice only the other day, Gina Cigna of whom Miss Jacob is, I know, an ardent admirer, stated that the most precious memory of her distinguished career was the occasion on which she sang Gluck's Alceste in the wonderful setting of the Boboli Gardens at Florence, under Gui's direction.*"

I replied to that letter, not to *World Radio* but to Jimmy's private address, and he sent me conclusive proof—because he used to "time" each act of an opera with a stop-watch—that Gui did not conduct in an over-deliberate manner. One letter led to another, and we discovered that we had a common love of Italian opera. That correspondence developed into a constant exchange of letters, and when I was standing in the entrance to Covent Garden in 1938, the last Italian Season given before the war, a tall young man—a very immaculate young man too, I remember—came up to me and said: "I am sure that you are Naomi Jacob. My name is Jimmy Robertson."

How exciting it was to talk "Italian Opera" with someone who loved it, as I did! We must have been to the opera several times that season. I remember, too, a luncheon at the Savoy one Sunday when Jimmy rode one of his favourite "hobby horses" with great success. He detested the *Rosenkavalier* of Strauss, as I detest the music of Wagner. One night in Edinburgh I recall a discussion concerning this opera with Dan Munro,[1] who loved it dearly. Jimmy brought up all his heavy guns and opened fire on poor Dan, speaking to him firmly, "more in sorrow than in anger".

His criticisms were always fair, and he was always open to conviction. For example, a certain soprano for whom I have a real and great admiration had never made any appeal to him; and although he refrained from using words which might possibly have either hurt or offended me —for she happens to be a great personal friend of mine—it was obvious to me that she was not among "the stars" as far as Jimmy was concerned.

He heard her in *Turandot* and thought that she never really "got into the skin" of the character. To a certain extent he was right, and if he were here now I could give him arguments and reasons, for it has become one of her finest rôles. He heard her, with some apprehension, at La Scala in *La Gioconda* and *Aïda*.[2] Immediately his dislike vanished, and the generosity of his criticism could not have been more clearly expressed.

The same attitude existed with regard to various conductors—again

[1] Died in Germany with the Army of Occupation, 1947.
[2] Also in *Isabeau*.

in a long argument concerning the rival merits of Vittorio Gui and Marinuzzi. Jimmy was adamant, so was I. Later, I read his notes and find him giving unstinted praise to Marinuzzi! Had he been spared, there is no doubt that he would have had a great future as an authority on opera, particularly the Italian school. He not only had natural taste, a fine ear, great artistic appreciation and a clear style of expression, but he was always ready to learn, to enlarge his outlook and to make opera-going not only his great personal joy, but to use it for actual study.

I hope, indeed I am sure, that readers will find his notes and criticisms, his articles on Italian opera and the seasons of various opera houses, not only of great interest, but of the greatest value to them in the study of opera. They are not intended to be merely for the *specialist*, or for the extensively educated musician, they are for the average opera lover who wants to know more about it.

I have used two bars of the lovely music of "Casta diva" as a heading for these notes on Jimmy Robertson, because it was a melody which made a great appeal to him. I remember his quoting to me a remark made by some Italian musician—whose name I have forgotten, and all Jimmy's letters to me were destroyed during the war—"This melody should be listened to on your knees—it is divine."

I have to thank sincerely Jimmy's father and mother, his brother Lewis, and my niece Audrie—who was engaged to Jimmy—for all the kind and great help which they have given me, and their generosity in allowing me to use this material.

NAOMI JACOB.

THE LAST FROM JAMES C. ROBERTSON

(Paymaster-Lieutenant, R.N.V.R., Lost in H.M.S. *Barham*, November 25, 1941. Aged 27)

(Reprinted by kind permission of *The Gramophone*, March 1942)

La Sonnambula (Bellini)

"We always knew when Jimmy Robertson was spending his holidays abroad. He never failed to send news of his musical adventures to *The Gramophone*; and I, 'F♯', whom he knew shared his passion for Italy, delighted in his long letters lively with critical enthusiasm. When war broke out I thought they would cease. He would have no more news of Italian opera to send, and he would be in some war job which would not kill his love of music and Italy, even after Mussolini declared war on us, but might starve it.

"He volunteered for the R.N.V.R. the day before the war with Germany was declared. I do not know how soon he was in the Mediterranean, but in June 1941 he wrote his article 'Thoughts From My 31,000-ton Tub', and sent it with another of his long amusing letters, in which he said that he and others had listened-in at sea to the opera at Genoa the night after his ship had taken part in the bombardment of that city. The article was written 'during a four-hour cypher watch when there wasn't much coming in—between the hours of 4 a.m. and 8 a.m.' There was opera from Italy most nights to listen to from his 'Tub'. Before I come to his article I am going to quote from another letter—his last—written on November 6, 1941. I think it gives us a sense not only of his fine sensitive character, but of the spirit of his friends afloat and ashore.

" 'I know so many people who know that war between Italy and England is all wrong, and nobody feels more strongly than my many dear Italian friends. Some of the letters I got just before Italy entered the war made me weep. It is a horrible business—damn Mussolini! I have many Italian friends ashore here; they like my company and I like theirs. It is rather splendid that I do not have to conceal my sympathy for the Italians from my fellow officers in the service. What would happen to a German who declared that he loved the English in his mess? It makes one feel one is fighting for tolerance and kindliness and the other things that make life worth living. The other evening I was at a *festa* in the house of one of these families I know. I brought a *fiasco* of authentic Grignolino, there was delicious *pasta* (*al dente*, not sloppy and horrible!) and we all got a little *brilli* and sang lustily such songs as the one that begins, *"Evviva la Torre di Pisa che pende, che pende, che pende, e mai non va giu"*. (*Viva* the Tower of Pisa, which leans . . . and never falls!)

" 'My host was a liaison officer with a regiment of the Royal Garrison Artillery on the Po in the last war, when he was still in his teens, and he showed me a silver cigarette-case presented "to our blue-eyed boy" engraved with the signatures of all the officers. As he remarked, such gifts will be rare indeed between the Italians and their allies of 1941.

" 'I send so many good wishes and *auguri per la pace* in 1942, and I hope *The Gramophone* will soon be settled again in a peaceful London and that I may come and see you there sometime.

" 'P.S. We have the first visit for the season of the Palestine Symphony Orchestra next week—three concerts and a feast of good things in the programme. If they send us to sea . . . ! Surely the war can wait a few days before it warms up again out here?'

"But it did warm up and H.M.S. *Barham* went to sea. . . . Here are some of the Thoughts from his 'Tub':

" '. . . I have not been so completely starved of music as I had feared. I have been in four ships out here already—for I am attached to a Flag, which has a habit of moving on just when we have all got nicely settled down in a ship and made some good friends—and in every ship I have found a gramophone and a small band of enthusiasts. Moreover, on shore we have had several visits from the Palestine Symphony Orchestra. I would compare this band's present level of accomplishment with that of the Scottish Orchestra, which means that it is a competent body of musicians; its chief merit lies in a rather small but excellent string section. There have been several recitals of various merits—here Cairo has been better served than us. Of opera, my own special passion, there has, of course, been none at all. To anyone who loves opera as I do, it will not seem strange that I inspected the opera house before I even thought of visiting the Pyramids, Sphinx, tombs and mosques when I had a week's sick leave in Cairo. It was at this house that *Aïda* had its world *première* in 1871, and by the courtesy of the present director I saw all over the theatre and was able to inspect many of the original costumes worn on that memorable night seventy years ago.

" '*Gramophone* readers know what a great bond of love music is. I have met nearly all my closest and dearest friends—and my *fiancée* too!—either directly or indirectly because I love music. Inevitably I have made friends ashore in Alexandria in the same way.

" 'A fortunate contact I made ashore occurred at one of the Palestine Orchestra's concerts. During the interval I saw a young man in a lance corporal's uniform whose face was familiar.

" ' "You're Harry Beard, aren't you?" I said.

" 'We had met at the Florence Festival in 1939—at the dress-rehearsal of Vito Frazzi's *King Lear*. Mr. Beard is a baritone who studied in Rome under Mo Cecchini, and whose career has been mainly unfolded abroad. He gave a successful series of recitals in many Italian cities in 1940 after the outbreak of war, but of course before the tragic event of Italy's entry into the field. Now he is here on very different business, but still keeps his hand in by singing to the troops and incidentally proving that they like "good stuff" if it is well sung, and do not appreciate being "played down to". His repertory embraces modern English and Italian songs; but what has made an unforgettable impression on me is his singing of Handel and, above all, the old Italian songs. Caccini, Caldara, Alessandro Scarlatti—these were all names of more or less historical interest to me. But to hear these *arie antiche* sung by Harry Beard is one of the most exquisite musical experiences I have ever had.

" 'Heaven knows my admiration of the best Italian singers—in opera—is so unbounded as to be, no doubt, somewhat biased, but this young Englishman can give the Italians a lesson in the lost art of singing their old songs. What a splendid thing it would be if some day when this is all over, we could have an album of the *arie antiche* recorded by Mr. Beard!

" 'How interesting, for example, to contrast "Amarilli" with the *aria* "Selve amiche" by Caldara—two songs which he sings super-latively well—or with the *arias* of Alessandro Scarlatti, Caldara's contemporary. Caccini was a member of that "Camerata Fiorentina" to which we owe the birth of opera in—roughly—1600, and there is in "Amarilli" that true pathos which one finds in the great Monteverde (remember the heart-rending lament of Orfeo, "*Rendetemi il mio bene*").

" 'With what art did those composers write for the voice! Basil Maine, discussing the future in *New Paths in Music*, makes the following significant prophecy: "Music, we may expect, will be more simply expressed . . . and since the human voice is the most direct and transparent medium for musical expression, it is possible that composers of the future will be increasingly drawn to vocal forms of composition." And again, "It is the peculiar heresy of the present time that musical tone is conceived with no reference to the voice." Surely Mr. Maine is right, and the greatest hope for music—when it eventually emerges, purified, from the universal unharmonious cataclysm—is that at last there will arise once more a race of com-posers who will revive the lost art of writing for the human voice? Last night I happened to be able to listen-in to a broadcast from Italy of *Norma*. It was this profoundly moving experience which made me feel that I wanted to write this article. The longer I live, the more music I understand, and so, love. But there is a special, very warm and tender affection which will always be reserved for those three composers—Rossini, Bellini and Donizetti.

" 'Vittorio Gui, who is Toscanini's legitimate successor in Italy, was asked to conduct an opera at the San Carlo two years ago as a favour to the Naples management, and was given *carte blanche* as to which opera he cared to perform. He chose *La Sonnambula* and rehearsed it with loving care, as exactingly as he rehearsed at Florence later in the same year the world *première* of *Re Lear*, to which I have already referred.

" 'Listening to *Norma* last night, as one glorious melody followed another, it struck me once more that of all the great composers, Bellini is the one most underrated today, in England anyway. His chaste stream of melody was one of the purest, most spontaneous, most lyrical and most haunting that ever flowed—and entirely his own, though he influenced so many of his contemporaries and successors.

" 'Some day—but not until I feel that I can do it really well— I should like to write at length about Bellini, and about Rossini and Donizetti, too. They mean so very much to me.

" ' "When Chopin lay dying, he asked for "*Ah, Non Credea Mirarti*" to be sung to him. I would ask for no lovelier swan song . . .' "

ITALIAN OPERA IN ITS OWN COUNTRY

(Reprinted by kind permission of *The Gramophone*, April 1935)

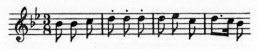

Rigoletto

LAST season a visit to some of the leading opera houses of Italy confirmed my long-standing conviction that the attitude of a certain section of the musical public in this country towards the Italian lyric stage at the present time is entirely unjust. Of recent years we have had unequal productions of Italian opera at Covent Garden; from time to time there may have been a great conductor—there was last season—or several fine singers, but the general atmosphere of Covent Garden does not seem to be the one in which this particular imported plant can thrive. Besides, the repertoire is thirty years behind the times. In its proper environments—not confined to Italy, as our London editor showed in December—Italian opera is healthier than ever. Some readers might like to hear about the most interesting of the seventeen performances I was able to crowd into a short stay.

The evening I arrived in Milan I managed to get one of the seats at the back of the *platea* for the *Mastersingers*. Three nights before I had listened to a broadcast of this identical performance at my own fireside in Scotland. It had been possible to enjoy the splendid singing even then, but this was a thousand times more wonderful. One felt that here opera was no hot-house plant. It is deeply rooted in the soil, an inevitable and important part of everyday life. Karl Elmendorff, who conducts this opera at Bayreuth, was in charge. I gathered from the fascinating "shop" talked during the intervals that my impression of rather unimaginative, precise direction was endorsed by the Milanese; but of course, when *I Maestri Cantori* was last given at La Scala in 1929 the conductor was Toscanini.

The singing was magnificent, Galliano Masini was the most knightly figure imaginable; for once the ideal Walther. He used his voice, fresh and even and ardent, with beautiful taste. His Prize Song was unforgettable. Maria Caniglia, another of the best of the younger generation, was Eva. She is a very gifted soprano of exceptional intelligence and versatility. The rest of the cast was thoroughly satisfactory, especially Ernesto Badini, whose Beckmesser is rightly considered a classic. The staging and production, about which the Italians are very exacting, were of a splendour that clearly did not have to heed expense.

In the enormously popular *Forza del Destino* the one disappointment was Gigli, who did not fit into the scheme of things at all well. At this time of day he is no actor, and even vocally he has developed certain mannerisms in New York. The rest of the cast, with Iva Pacetti a thoroughly convincing Leonora and Tancredi Pasero a sonorous and dignified Father Guardiano, played up well under the excellent direction of Gabriele Santini. I now proceeded to Rome, via San Remo, where I heard Mascagni's own interpretation of his remarkable opera *Iris*. As usual, the sheer inspiration of the introduction (the "Hymn to the Sun") brought the audience to its feet.

The ashes of the old Costanzi have given rise to the new Teatro which fits into the Government's plan to re-establish Rome in its old supremacy. This beautiful theatre is the last word in up-to-date equipment and elegance. I saw an all-star *Rigoletto* there with Giacomo Lauri-Volpi an irresistible Duke of Mantua. He is greater than Gigli, because he is excellent dramatically as well as vocally; and besides having a ravishing *mezzo-voce*, his voice has the genuine heroic ring which enables him to achieve a big effect without having to resort to effort. He murmured, "*E il sol dell' anima*," with the most insidious charm, and brought a unanimous cry of "*bis*" with the *cadenza* in "*La Donna e Mobile*". Toti Dal Monte has the loveliest tone imaginable, but since her serious illness the staccato ending of "*Caro Nome*" gives her some trouble. Benvenuto Franci was a dominating Rigoletto. The next afternoon, the feature of *Aida* was the wonderful Amneris of Ebe Stignani, the finest mezzo-soprano in the world today.

The third performance conducted by the genial Edoardo Vitale was a new opera based on the life of St. Cecilia, which has had an extraordinary success. It is the work of a Catholic priest, Dom Licinio Refice, who was present on this occasion—it was Easter Monday—and had to take part in many of the thirty-odd curtain calls which the newspapers always record with scrupulous accuracy. The "sacred action", as its composer calls it, shows a lofty inspiration. As might have been expected, the religious aspects of the drama show the noblest sincerity; the choral writing in the second episode owes much of its effect to the Gregorian chant. Claudia Muzio gave a hauntingly beautiful performance in the title rôle.

Manon Lescaut introduced me to Gino Marinuzzi, the finest conductor of all; his readings have a sensitive beauty and a vivid quality all their own. It was a memory to treasure for a life-time, and fortunately his collaborators were worthy of him. Claudia Muzio was the protagonist, but young Alessandro Ziliani stole the honours as a delightfully natural

Des Grieux. *"Donna Non Vidi Mai"* sounded more beautiful than ever.

My experiences at the Teatro dell' Opera ended for the time being with Giordano's *La Cena della Beffe*. It is based on a powerful but rather macabre play by Sem Benelli, in the picturesque setting of Florence in the time of Lorenzo the Magnificent. The story deals with the vengeance wrought by Giannetto, who has been the butt of the Chiaramantesi brothers since childhood. Giannetto spreads the story that Neri is mad; and the climax comes when Neri, thinking he has caught Giannetto in his mistress's apartments, slays his own brother and loses his reason in horrible earnest. Gino Marinuzzi, himself a distinguished exponent of the modern school of Italian opera, secured an electrifying performance in conjunction with Lauri-Volpi and Franci (the original Neri at La Scala ten years ago), who caused a genuine Italian furore in parts which gave every scope to their vocal and dramatic powers. Giordano received tributes of enthusiasm and affection.

I am afraid space compels me to confine myself to a bare mention of some of the other outstanding performances I saw: at the San Carlo, Naples, a gala night, the ever popular *Adriana Lecouvreur* in honour of the composer himself, Francesco Cilea, now director of the Naples Conservatoire. It was conducted by the famous Ettore Panizza. Also the immortal *Barbiere* with Mario Basiola a superb Figaro. At La Scala, finally, *La Traviata* with Tito Schipa—still a unique artist—and Mascagni's imaginative *Isabeau*, a work of extraordinary originality and fascination.

OPERA FROM ITALY

(Reprinted by kind permission of *The Gramophone* June, 1936)

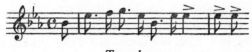

Turandot

JUDGING voices via the microphone is a perilous business. Christopher Stone says so, and he ought to know. The question arose out of the correspondence which followed Mr. H. J. Goodman's views on the younger Italian singers. I had just returned from Italy, and our co-editor, in the casual way which wireless listeners know so well, suggested that I might put my spoke in, for *The Gramophone* has always encouraged a healthy discussion. At first I was only too pleased that the names of the present generation of Italian singers were not entirely unknown in this country; but on reading the letters I felt that too much had been said that ought not to have been said, and incidentally one or two things left unsaid that I should like to say.

As it happens, I have just had an experience of the unreliability of the microphone. A short time ago I heard Boito's *Mefistofele* at the Teatro dell' Opera in Rome—a performance which would have been ideal except for the Faust.[1] He was about five feet tall, and his voice was uneven and lacking in beauty of tone. I heard one of the subsequent performances on the wireless, when this same Faust—not lacking in intelligence, to give him his due—seemed almost worthy to be the companion of the superb Mefistofele of Ezio Pinza. The microphone, which cannot reproduce the timbre of the living voice, does its best to cover up the defects by way of compensation. Personally, I regard the wireless not so much as a means of comparing Signor X and Signor Y as of hearing such a work as Wolf-Ferrari's *Il Campiello* three days after its *première*.

Mr. Andersen professes unbounded admiration for the baritone Armando Borgioli, who sang at Covent Garden until three years ago and is now at his best. He has a voice of dark quality and great power in the middle and upper registers, and he makes most effective use of the *mezza-voce*; but the lower notes, powerful enough on the wireless, are sadly lacking in resonance. To compare him with Mario Basiola is all very well, though he must inevitably come off second best; to declare

[1] Giovanni Malipiero. He improved greatly in '37 and '38.—N. J.

that he is a "much greater artist" is fantastic. Basiola is one of the few singers of whom I can truthfully say I have never been able to find the smallest room for criticism. Every phrase shows the mind of an artist behind a perfectly controlled voice.

Then we have the basses mentioned by Mr. Andersen. Fernando Autori—as we in this country have not had much chance to find out, though we might guess it from his skill with the pencil—is as fine a character actor as there is on the operatic stage; but his vocal equipment is not adequate for such rôles as Ramfis and Filippo in *Don Carlo*, which he sang here in 1933. Then also, Duilio Baronti's beautifully used voice has not the necessary reserves of power.

Mr. Andersen enjoys using our superlatives and applies a few choice ones to Gina Cigna. Opinion is sharply divided as to her merits in Italy, and I confess that after seeing her in a dozen of her favourite parts that I find her a strange mixture. At times I find myself in agreement with those who call her voice "unsympathetic", "uneven", "strident"; yet in certain rôles she is unsurpassed. There can be no two opinions about her Gioconda. I have watched this interpretation improve every season, losing its early irregularities until it is now the finest impersonation of its kind. I agree with Mr. Andersen that she is a splendid Turandot (not Liu please!). A pity she and Lauri-Volpi are not appearing in the opera at Covent Garden this year (1936).

After reproaching Mr. Goodman for mentioning as coming stars certain well-established artists, it was curious to see Mr. Shepherd remark that Gabriella Besanzoni has "made her way to the forefront of Italian opera within the last few years"—for she was singing with Caruso a quarter of a century ago, and has not been heard in Italy since 1934. Mr. Shepherd also mentions Aurelio Marcato, who has certainly made a rapid advance since his début three years ago, when his elementary notions of acting suggested an insufficient preparation. The less said about Mr. Shepherd's "young" baritones the better.

To sum up, I should be sorry to see any of the following artists mentioned by your correspondents engaged at Covent Garden as representative of the present generation of Italian singers: Pauli, Granda, Bruna Rasa, Landi, Sinnone, Paci, Poli.

Now for the singers who should be heard at Covent Garden to restore the sadly depreciated fortunes of Italian opera in this country. First we must dispose of the lament (sometimes not unmixed with malicious satisfaction) that great female singers are no longer to be heard in Italy. That this is false would at once be admitted by the most biased if Maria Caniglia, who made her début in 1930, could be heard, say, as Desdemona for a start.

As it is high time we were hearing an Italian Mimi or Liu again, we ought to have Pia Tassinari and Mafalda Favero—a joy to watch as well as listen to, complete artists with a choice of rôles ranging from *Il Matrimonio Segreto* to Zandonai's *Farsa Amorosa*. Then there is Franca Somigli, who has reached the front rank of Italian sopranos in four years. I suppose one could hardly hope to have her in *Francesca da Rimini*. Augusta Oltrabella as Butterfly or Suor Angelica is almost unbearably moving. Giuseppina Cobelli is perhaps the finest actress on the operatic stage, but as we are hardly likely to have an Italian Kundry (that would be turning the tables with a vengeance), and her talents lie mainly in the direction of the modern repertoire, it is difficult to see where she would fit in at Covent Garden.

Coming to the mezzo-sopranos, it is sad indeed to reflect that we have not heard Ebe Stignani. If I were put to the choice, I should declare that she is the greatest singer in the world. Maria Caniglia is about the only soprano who is not overshadowed by her Amneris or Ortrud. Gianna Pederzini is an admirable artist, though not on the majestic scale of Stignani. She is famous for her *Italiana in Algeri* and such rôles as Carlotta to the Werther of Tito Schipa.

Now for the men. We ought to hear Alessandro Ziliani. He is an ideal Rodolfo, though his best rôle is perhaps Enzo. Ettore Parmeggiani specializes in Wagner and the modern repertoire, so I do not see how we can fit him into our proposed season unless the improbable dream of a revival of *Francesca* were realized. Galliano Masini has one of the finest tenor voices you can hear today. Luigi Fort should have been our Lindoro in *L'Italiana* last season.

With good baritones so plentiful in Italy, it is extraordinary to see a complete lack of them this season at Covent Garden. Mario Basiola *must* be heard; and the huge voice of Ettore Nava would create a sensation in the third act of *Aïda*. Piero Biasini, who has been carefully developed at La Scala, astonished everyone this season with his superbly sung and acted Iago.

Poor Ezio Pinza has been thrown away at Covent Garden—the year *Don Carlo* was done he was at Florence—so I hesitate to advocate the claim of Giacomo Vaghi. This season it seemed to me that he had reached the zenith of his powers when I heard him in *Orseilo*. An artist of a very different calibre is Salvatore Baccaloni, incomparable in *buffo* rôles. I am sure *Don Pasquale* must soon be revived at Covent Garden; and when it is he must be the protagonist. Last time I saw the *Barbiere* he stole the show from an all-star cast as Bartolo.

These artists, though almost all young, are the best in Italy. Time enough to indicate those on the road to success when we have heard the top-notchers. Nor need I enlarge upon such singers as Pinza, Pasero, Lauri-Volpi, Bidu Sayao, and the artful veterans Schipa and De Luca—

they are international figures, as are Gigli, Claudia Muzio and Toti Dal Monte. By the way, I am very sorry that Mr. Poulter is disappointed with the Improperia of Palestrina, which he obtained on my recommendation. I played the record for the first time after a lengthy interval, and I cannot help hoping that he will yet come to regard it as the "treasure he had hoped for".

It would certainly be my desert island record.

OPERA AT LA SCALA

(Reprinted by kind permission of *Musical Opinion*, June 1936)

Otello (Verdi)

APART from the suppression of two operas by way of "counter-sanctions", the war[1] did not interfere with the season at La Scala. The only opera of the twenty-one which was in the repertoire in 1935 was *Otello*—incidentally, one of the best performances of the season. Gino Marinuzzi brings out the full beauty of Verdi's beautiful score. Outstanding in a fine cast was the incomparable Desdemona of Maria Caniglia. The only world-*première* was Wolf-Ferrari's *Il Campiello*, a great success not only for its tunefulness and elegant gaiety, but for the remarkable teamwork of a talented cast. The opera is a short one, and was given together with the inevitable new ballet, which any young Italian composer can turn out. Strauss's *Silent Woman* was new for Italy. The presence of the composer (who had been at Genoa to conduct *Arabella*) helped to secure a *succès d'estime*. Strauss expressed his delight with the "perfect performance" of his opera. The critics, while praising the purple patches to be found in most Strauss operas, found the work as a whole to be a hotch-potch.

Among the important events—still under the direction of Marinuzzi —was the happy reunion of Puccini's three one-act operas forming the Trittico; the revival of *Ernani* with which the season opened on Boxing Day; a radiantly beautiful *Parsifal* during Easter; and two of the most delightful specimens of opera-bouffe—*Il Matrimonio Segreto*, in which many of the interpreters of *Il Campiello* again distinguished themselves; and *Don Pasquale*. Tito Schipa sang in both operas; and it was interesting —and incredible—to recall that Giuseppe de Luca, a model Malatesta, last sang in *Don Pasquale* at La Scala thirty-two years ago.

Ildebrando Oizzetti conducted three performances of *Orseolo*, rendered less static by a few cuts since its *première* at Florence. The performance itself was similar to the earlier one, the Milanese, as ever, showing sympathetic understanding of the ideals of their esteemed fellow-citizen. Pizzetti raised an interesting point in protesting against only three performances being given of *Orseolo*. He was able to cite

[1] In Abyssinia.

several well-known operas which only established themselves at their first appearance after half a dozen performances. Yet there can be no doubt that the repertory system introduced by Toscanini is working better than the old method of producing only a few operas each year, giving a large number of performances, and then shelving the operas for some time. Nevertheless, the system probably accounts for the indifference with which Zandonai's *La Farsa Amorosa* was received in Milan after a triumphant reception in the other leading theatres of Italy; for the opera was given in Lent, always a bad time, especially for a work of this nature. One could not help thinking that the Scala management lost a chance here, for the performance under Giuseppe del Campo was most invigorating.

The Saint-Saëns centenary was the occasion for a spectacular mounting of *Sansone e Dalila*, the only opera conducted by Victor de Sabata, which in itself ensured a popular success. The part of Dalila gave Ebe Stignani a chance to prove once more that hers is the finest voice in the world today.

The Legend of Kitesc, given in Russian in 1934, was to have been sung in Italian this time; but it was one of the forbidden operas, Giordano's *Siberia* being the substitute; a stroke of good fortune this, for it was one of the big successes of the season. Memorable indeed was the enthusiasm after the second act, one of Giordano's most moving achievements. Londoners will know the name of Emilio Cooper, who conducted. The other "sanctioned" opera was replaced by Cilea's *L'Arlesiana*. It was confidently asserted that this was revived because of the *aria* in the second act, which Tito Schipa sings divinely, but the opera—after a spineless first act—has a Massenet-like atmosphere which is rather appealing.

The repertory works performed, roughly in order of merit, were *Lohengrin, Gioconda, Mefistofele, Rigoletto, Lucia* and *Iris*. The season is being wound up by eight concerts, the most eagerly awaited being a Respighi memorial concert conducted by Molinari, and the Verdi Requiem under de Sabata.

This concert is to be repeated at ultra-popular prices.

interior of the restored La Scala, Milan, on a gala night

The interior of the Teatro dell' Opera (formerly the Reale), Rome

Gina Cigna as 'Turandot'

Gina Cigna in *La Gioconda*

Interior of the Teatro San Carlo, Naples, with the drop curtain

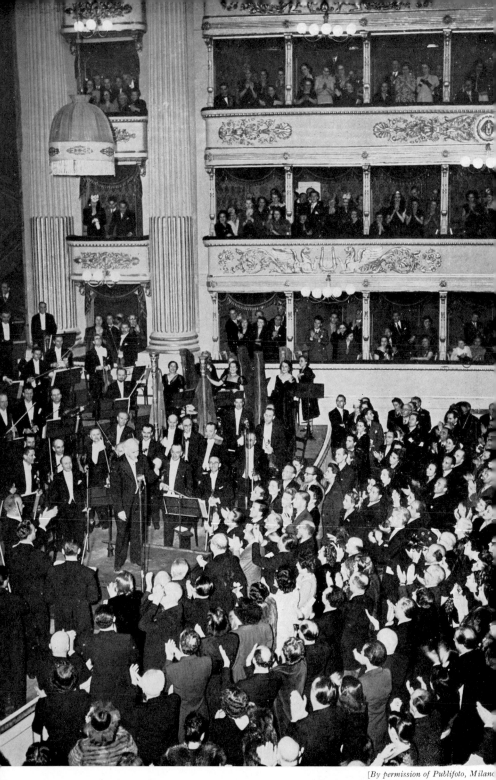

Toscanini returns. Taken at the opening of the restored La Scala when Toscanini
made his first appearance in Milan after his long absence in America

OPERA IN MILAN

(Reprinted by kind permission of *Musical Opinion*, August 1938)

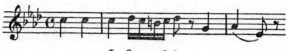

La Sonnambula

ALTHOUGH there has been the usual large number of concerts, organized chiefly by the Conservatorio and the Quartet Society, the musical life of Milan since Boxing Day has centred round the Teatro alla Scala. *Aïda* closed a successful season on May 1. There were ninety-five performances of twenty-one operas, fourteen of which were Italian. Victor De Sabata, making a welcome return to La Scala, inaugurated the season with *The Prodigal Son* for the Ponchielli centenary. The opera—a most spectacular affair—is more unequal in merit than the composer's masterpiece, but the change from the familiar *La Gioconda* was much appreciated.

Other operas conducted by the magnetic De Sabata were the *Valkyrie*, a really exceptional performance; Giordano's fast-moving *Fedora*; and *Falstaff*, which has been performed more often than any other opera at La Scala since the war. In spite of the memory of Toscanini's annual triumphs with this comic masterpiece, De Sabata's spirited leading of the usual team, headed by Stabile, was received with delight. A delightful innovation was the children's matinée—"Old Vic", please note! Judging by the gaiety of the packed house, there must be hundreds of potential opera-goers as a result of the performance of *Gianni Schicchi* and the new ballet *Sunflower*.

On the first day of the year the Bellini centenary was celebrated throughout Italy amidst great enthusiasm, at La Scala by *La Sonnambula*, worthily performed by Tito Schipa and Toti dal Monte under the direction of Antonio Guarnieri, who was also in charge of *Werther*, Charpentier's *Louise*, and *Boris Godunov*, which exercises a particular fascination over the Scala audience—another inheritance from the Toscanini régime.

The great event of the season was, of course, the eagerly awaited *première* of Mascagni's *Nerone* on January 16. The spectacular and historic attraction of the subject, the typical force of so much of the music ensured a clamorous success for the opera, magnificently performed under the composer's baton.

H

February 3 was the date fixed for the last performance of *Nerone*, but two more had to be given to satisfy the enormous demand for seats, and even then the opera had to be put on after a short interval, so it was not till a month after the anticipated date that Mascagni was allowed to leave La Scala.

Gino Marinuzzi proceeded to Milan after conducting all the Bellini operas at Catania. In order to give expression to his devotion to the greatest Sicilian composer, Marinuzzi—the greatest Sicilian conductor—left the Teatro dell' Opera in Rome, which he had inaugurated in 1928, and which now rivals La Scala itself. He opened with Respighi's *La Fiamma*, first performed the year before at the Teatro dell' Opera. Respighi has declared that his aim was a return to 19th-century ideals —that is, he meant to make the voice the chief means of expression; but the chief impression made was by the overpowering virtuosity of the orchestral writing. *La Fiamma* is an intensely dramatic adaption of G. Wiers Jenssen's *The Witch*.

Respighi was also responsible for a free transcription of Monteverdi's *Orfeo*, which masterpiece was also presented at Rome earlier in the season in the arrangement by Benvenuti. Respighi took more liberties with the original in presenting the work to a modern audience; his success was testified by the interest and genuine emotion of all who were present at this important artistic event. In addition to another Bellini opera *La Straniera*, chiefly noteworthy for a remarkable object lesson in the art of *bel canto* by the baritone Basiola, Marinuzzi conducted excellent performances of *Faust*, *Aïda* and *Turandot* with the tenor Lauri-Volpi.

Splendid editions of *Carmen* and *The Bartered Bride* were prepared by Franco Ghione, a born leader who always achieves thrilling results. *Carmen* for one reason or another has not been adequately presented at La Scala for some years, and so it had one of the warmest successes of the season.

Gianna Pederzini sang and acted splendidly in the title-rôle without any of the too common exaggerations to spoil the artistic effect. *The Bartered Bride* had never been given at La Scala. Ghione was responsible for the Italian version, and the invigorating performance of this pleasing opera was greatly to the liking of the Milan audience. The event was considered of national importance in Czecho-Slovakia, and one performance was relayed by Prague. Such golden opinions were won that Ghione is to conduct the work at the State Opera House there.

During Lent an important event was the complete cycle of Beethoven's symphonies, conducted by Otto Klemperer. Perhaps owing to this, the governing body of La Scala decided to abandon the usual series of Philharmonic concerts after the close of the operatic season. A body of practical-minded enthusiasts approached Ildebrando Pizzetti, always willing to co-operate in a good cause, even though on this occasion the first performance of his eagerly awaited opera *Orseolo* was imminent at the Florence Festival. The public response was immediate and now the Milan season is being rounded off with eight exceedingly attractive concerts under distinguished Italian and foreign conductors. Vladimir Horowitz took part in no less than three concertos at the first of these.

OPERA IN MILAN

(Reprinted by kind permission of *Musical Opinion*, August 1938)

Otello (Verdi)

(This pathetic "Willow Song" sung by Desdemona is
said to be a genuine Italian folk tune, many centuries old.)

BOITO'S *Mefistofele* was chosen for the inauguration of the 1937–38
season at La Scala in a new and striking production, as the old scenes
had been in use since the first post-war season. Victor de Sabata conducted a very successful performance in his usual dynamic way, the
protagonist being Tancredi Pasero, who for some years has sung the
leading bass rôles. Unfortunately, however, the great difficulty of the
season at once manifested itself. Giuseppe Lugo, who was a big draw last
year in *Bohème* and *Tosca*, was never really fit this season and could not
reproduce his best form in *Mefistofele*.

The first novelty of the season was Granado's *Goyescas*, which made
little impression, but served to introduce a new conductor, Franco
Capuana, who in the course of an arduous season met with some criticism
(especially for some of his *tempi* in the familiar operas), but who is very
musicianly and maintains an admirably discreet relationship between
stage and orchestra.

There were two world *premières*, but it is not likely that there will
be much competition among the other theatres for the honour of the
second performances. Don Licinio Refice's *Margherita da Cortona* was
looked forward to with some curiosity, as his first opera, *Cecilia*, is one
of the few post-war operas which has had a real success; but unfortunately, the inspiration which is abundant in parts of *Cecilia* is sadly
lacking in the new opera. The less said about the other world *première*,
Renzo Bianchi's *Proserpina*, the better. One wondered how such an
opera came to be produced at La Scala, just as one questioned the
opportuneness of reviving Mascagni's *Silvano* and Giordano's *Marcella*.
Mascagni and Giordano are responsible for several masterpieces in what
in the early years of the century was called the vein of the "younger
school"; but no conceivable purpose is served by resuscitating operas
which deservedly failed at their first appearance and have lain in merciful
oblivion for some thirty years.

After being outspoken about some of the less happy episodes of the season, it is pleasant to pass on to two other operas new to La Scala. The first was Massenet's *Jongleur de Notre-Dame*. Here I must frankly be subjective: this was for me the event of the season. The opera has the composer's typical defect of inequality, but it contains pages of such exquisite beauty as I cannot find in *Manon*. The subject, moreover, has a pleasing quality of originality; it is enough to say that there is no "love interest" whatsoever.

It may be that this is not an opera that can ever become universally popular, but it is worth recording that it had seven performances at La Scala. The interpretation contributed not a little to the success, under the exquisite handling of Gino Marinuzzi, one of the best of the several great operatic conductors whom Italy is fortunate enough to possess. The production was full of inspired touches, and among an admirable group of interpreters the baritone Carmelo Maugeri was outstanding. Unforgettable was his performace as the lovable Friar who sings the "Legend of the Sage Bush", which is one of the most delicately lovely and moving passages in all opera.

Ezio Camussi, whose one-act opera *Il Volto della Vergine* was performed, is one of the few contemporary composers in Italy who has resisted the charlatan current of spurious 20th centuryism, and who believes that the public will still respond to a genuine melodic vein allied to apparent simplicity of expression as emphatically as it rejects lack of inspiration thinly veiled by a would-be dazzling display of technical virtuosity. *Il Volto* has moments of poetic beauty which inspire genuine emotion, and the public appreciated, almost as if unable to believe the evidence of its senses, that here at last was an attempt to follow the best traditions of Italian opera which since the war seemed almost deliberately to have been forgotten.

It is certainly too late to expect from Mascagni at seventy-five another masterpiece; we have waited in vain for Cilea to give us another *Adriana*, for Giordano to write an opera of the appeal of *Fedora* and *Chenier*, for Montemezzi to follow up his only masterpiece *L'Amore dei Tre Re*, and for Zandonai to find again the vein that produced, for example, *Francesca da Rimini*. The public is learning to shudder like a confirmed collector of antiques at the mere mention of anything "modern", and the time is most certainly ripe for Puccini's successor to make his appearance. In the meantime, it was a pleasure to hear Camussi's unpretentious little opera, even if it lacks the stamp of geniality which makes a universal appeal.

The Russian opera this season was Rimsky-Korsakov's *Sadko*, which was very well done and above all was a feast for the eye. Musically the chief interest is in the orchestral pit. The opera has an unfortunate defect in that the last act is by far the weakest. For the centenary of Bizet's birth, the occasion was taken to present *The Pearl Fishers*, as well as *Carmen*. In the latter, the new tenor "discovery" Jussi Bjorling was engaged, but had to be substituted by another artist. In the former, Lugo sang the first performance when gravely indisposed, and did not appear again at La Scala in the course of the season. In these circumstances, it was not to be wondered at if expectations were not realized.

The Ring was given by the entire organization of the State Theatre of Munich in exchange for the Scala's visit to Germany last summer. This was a most interesting event for the Milanese, and the theatre was sold out three months in advance for all performances. The audience were sincerely appreciative of this sample of the authentic Wagner, and there is no doubt that this *Ring* will be discussed for a long time to come; but it must be admitted that in Italy Wagner will always be more acceptable when performed in Italian by Italians. And before looking down their noses at this, I would ask readers of *Musical Opinion* to ponder the significance of the fact that where opera is deeply rooted in the hearts of a people, the works of every nationality are given in the vernacular. Clemens Krauss gave an uncut version which, particularly in the *Gotterdammerung*, caused the public visibly to wilt. Among the singers a particularly favourable impression was made by Gertrude Runger, Hans Herman Nissen and Max Lorenz, who is to learn Italian and sing again at La Scala next year.

Dealing lastly with the repertory operas, it may be said that where the performances fell short of the traditions of La Scala it was more often than not due to the shortcomings of the tenor. For example, Gigli, after an exacting tour in England and after singing in five of the first seven operas of the season at the Teatro dell' Opera in Rome, revealed at La Scala a voice which seemed in need of a period of health-giving repose. Quite apart from the shortcomings of the tenors, however (which, it must be admitted, could not be foreseen by those responsible for the administration of the Scala), the absence of several of the best singers in Italy was rendered conspicuous by the dubious qualifications of certain of their colleagues who filled the gap.

After this preamble, it may be recorded that the happiest performances of the repertory operas were perhaps *Otello*, conducted by de Sabata, with the veteran Francesco Merli (protagonist), Maria Caniglia and Piero Biasini; *Butterfly*, an enormous success with a trio new for La Scala in this opera: Iris Adami-Corradetti, Lugo and Enrico de Franceschi; Wolf-Ferrari's charming *Quatro Rusteghi*, to a libretto in Venetian dialect after Goldoni, in which Salvatore Baccaloni gave an inimitable character study; *Le Nozze di Figaro*, memorable vocally for

Maria Caniglia's "*Dove Sono*"; and *Tosca*, which concluded the season with Gina Cigna as protagonist. Giovanni Malipiero, substituting for Lugo as Cavaradossi, sang very pleasantly at the opening performance, so that we were enabled to forget some of the uneasiness caused us by his colleagues during the preceeding four months.

If artistically the season had its ups and downs, financially it was a great success; and such is the enthusiasm of the Italian public these days (judiciously nurtured by the Italian Government with its work of propaganda) that the catch-phrase "crisis of the theatre" which was current some years ago has dropped out of circulation. Instead one finds preoccupation about the "crisis of tenors"!

OPERA AT LA SCALA

(Reprinted by kind permission of *Musical Opinion*, July 1939)

Nerone (Boito)

THE 1938–39 season was not altogether a happy one. There were, it is true, several performances which were fully in keeping with the traditions of the theatre, but far too many fell a long way short of the standard to which La Scala had accustomed itself. In his statement summarizing the satisfactory financial results of the season, the superintendent of the theatre tacitly acknowledged the criticism levelled at some of the less-fortunate performances when he said: "Great difficulties were encountered by reason of the scarcity of first class artists available, more particularly on account of the engagements abroad of some of our singers of international renown. Apart from this, the insistent ravages of the epidemic of influenza necessitated recourse to understudies on no less than forty-two occasions." The declaration does not throw any light on the mysterious absence from La Scala of certain first class artists who *were* available.

An urgent requirement is the engagement of a really capable conductor to assist Gino Marinuzzi; what a pity Franco Ghione has been lured away (temporarily, one hopes) to America! Victor de Sabata's activities at La Scala this season were confined to four performances of *Tristan* with the cast he will have at Bayreuth this summer, and Franco Capuana conducted a successful edition of *Werther*; apart from these two operas, it is significant that such of the performances as bore the hall-mark of La Scala were in the hands of Marinuzzi. A matter which caused concern was the deterioration in the work of the chorus, which traditionally has been one of the special glories of La Scala. At the beginning of the season, to the profound regret of all those who love the great Milanese institution, Vittore Veneziani[1]—for racial reasons—had to vacate the post of chorus master to which, loved and respected by all, he had

---

[1] Formerly at Teatro dell' Opera, Rome.

devoted seventeen years of unstinting service, a worthy assistant to Toscanini and other distinguished conductors with whom he had collaborated.

The season opened with Verdi's *Macbeth*. Apart from an appearance at the Teatro dell' Opera in Rome, the popularity of the opera in Germany of recent years had not had any repercussions in Italy; and indeed the Scala audience did not hail the revival with the enthusiasm which marked its attitude towards *Nabucco* in 1934, for example. There are, of course, effective and imaginative passages here and there, but in 1847 Verdi was by no means ready to do justice to such a formidable subject, and the opera is mainly interesting as a document in the evolution of the composer in his gradual throwing off of the shackles of the conventional early 19th-century operatic formula, of which in *Macbeth* he is still too often the slave rather than the master.

Those who have seen *Macbeth* skilfully produced as a chamber opera by Ebert at Glyndebourne would have found it interesting to institute comparisons. As far as the performance was concerned, the indisposition and consequent withdrawal of the artist who was to have taken the part of Lady Macbeth presented the management with a difficulty which they were unable satisfactorily to surmount; but Alexander de Sved—who is immeasurably improved since his undistinguished appearance at Covent Garden three years ago—was an excellent protagonist, and made the deepest impression of all the newcomers to La Scala during the season.

Another revival was the *Barbiere di Siviglia* of Giovanni Paisiello, which may be mannered and faded in parts, but contains some delicious music. Formidable comparisons with Rossini's masterpiece were inevitable, since the unfolding of the plot follows almost identical lines; but Paisiello frequently sparkled or charmed in his own rights. The performance was excellent. The attentuated orchestra (conducted by Marinuzzi seated at the *cembalo*, on which he accompanied the recitatives) played with rare delicacy and appreciation of the true essence of the music, the settings on the diminished stage showed admirable taste, indeed "taste" was the keynote of the evening, and the *ensemble* was a model of precision while at the same time achieving a wholly successful suggestion of spontaneity. The individual performance which must be mentioned was Baccaloni's Bartolo—well worthy to rank with his unique impersonation of the same character in *Le Nozze di Figaro* (familiar at Glyndebourne) and in the other *Barbiere*.

Another opera which might be classed among the revivals was Boito's *Nerone*, which had languished somewhat after its famous *première* —after fifty years of expectant speculation—in 1924 under Toscanini. On this occasion the whole resources of La Scala were called into play;

as a spectacle, and as a triumph of organization, the results were most impressive. For a composer to labour with self-torturing insatiability for fifty years on his second opera and then to leave it unfinished at his death must be unique in the annals of the lyric stage; *Nerone*, then, inevitably exemplifies in many places the recalcitrant inventive powers of Boito as a musician in comparison with the positively luxuriant fertility of his imagination as a poet (it is probably unnecessary to state that he wrote the libretto himself), but it is work which compels respect if only for the grandeur of its conception.

Space compels me to resist the temptation to write at length about an opera which possesses a peculiar interest for me, but in general it may be said that it symbolizes the conflict between material and spiritual values; on the one hand, the pagan and decadent splendour of the temporal domination of the Caesars, on the other, the birth of a new eternal Kingdom, the "voice of Christ lifted up in a cry of hope and victory to a needy world". The music associated with the later aspect of the drama is full of sincerity and genuine emotion. The performance of *Nerone*, which presents enormous difficulties, was in all respects memorable.

Another revival was Rabaud's *Marouf*. Very colourful as a spectacle, it shows the hand of a master of orchestral technique; but on the whole it is not an opera one would care to sit through again, the fragmentary music seems to be the precursor of the type we associate with "background music" for the films.

The only world *première* of the season was Wolf-Ferrari's *La Dama Boba*, which unfortunately proved to be an uninspired and mannered *rechauffe* of the composer's own more successful operas. A *succès d'estime* was barely achieved. Indeed, the examples of contemporary operatic output—accorded a generous place in the programme in accordance with departmental instructions—met with a uniform fate; Mule's *Dafni*, Pizzetti's *Fedra*, and Ghedini's *Maria d'Alessandria* were received with varying degrees of indifference and even hostility.

It seems unnecessary to chronicle in detail the repertory operas, some of which (e.g. *La Sonnambula* and *La Traviata*, which had eleven performances) were well done, while others (e.g. *Adriana Lecouvreur* and Catalani's *Loreley*) were, as the critic of the *Corriere della Sera* put it, "murdered".

For the opening of the 1939–40 season, the happy choice is announced of *Guglielmo Tell* in the identical performance which was one of the outstanding events of this year's Florence Festival.

AN ITALIAN *DIVA*

(Reprinted by kind permission of *The Gramophone*, December 1939)

Andante mosso

pp

Aïda (Verdi)

WHY is it, I wonder, that we so often as a nation descend to rudeness when we are trying to be clever? The question is prompted in this instance by some of the cheap and contemptible abuse of Gina Cigna that has appeared in print within the last few months. Here is the bald and ungarnished testimony of three choice examples:

1. "We have had to put up with this artist in the past at Covent Garden, and if we are not careful we may have to do so again."

2. "*Alla cantata ancor manca la diva.*" Here, of course, the highly respected critic in question was dealing with the performance of *Tosca* at Covent Garden, and so choice was this specimen of fourth-form wit esteemed to be that it was given the further prominence of a heading in heavy type to preface and adorn the paragraph in which it occurred.

3. This one is from the article on the Opera Seasons in the August number of *The Gramophone*, and the italics are mine: "She was at times *two or three beats* behind the conductor, and *either a semitone sharp or flat*".

It beats me how anyone could pen such an extraordinary statement as that without foreseeing the devastating effect it was bound to have in rendering suspect the whole article as the concoction of a man talking through his hat.

My aim in claiming the indulgence of your correspondence columns to participate for the first time in a discussion as to the merits or demerits of a particular artist—which is, after all, so largely a matter of taste—is not so much to hold a brief for Signora Cigna, for she has plenty of sincere admirers familiar with her work in Italy who can be relied upon to do that much more effectively than I could. Instead, I should like to ask these "critics" if they have any sense of responsibility whatsoever. I know these gentlemen have a sense of their own omniscience which borders on the sublime; but do they ever pause, while engaged on the congenial self-imposed task of bringing discredit to the gentle (!) art of criticism by couching their remarks in as insulting and insensitive a shape as possible, to consider what the reaction is on those distinguished foreign artists to whom we "condescend" to offer our hospitality. It may interest them—and perhaps even feed their colossal self-satisfaction, though that hardly seems possible—to know that the Italian artists went back to their own country at the close of the last season firmly convinced that departmental instructions must have been issued to the effect that the Press was to lose no opportunity of being as nasty as it could be to them.

This misapprehension, unhappily, was not one that any sensitive person could wonder at, but that it should have been allowed to arise must be particularly deplored by anyone who has spent any length of time in Italy, and has thus been able to experience the invariable courtesy and sincere friendliness of the Italians towards all English visitors to the country—even in the face, not infrequently, of an uncompromising lack of the most elementary principles of good breeding on the part of the latter.

No one objects to honest criticism—it was the bad taste of the methods employed to "have a dig" at Signora Cigna that has aroused this protest. It really does seem that there are people in this country who derive a spiteful pleasure from slating this artist on all possible occasions. I have even heard her performance of Tosca at Covent Garden in 1938 described as "unspeakably vile"; but Cigna did not sing at all in London last year—so it seems that even the alleged shortcomings of other artists are sometimes laid at her door!

Lest it should be gathered from my remarks that I have a bias in favour of Signora Cigna, I should like to set out briefly my personal estimate of the artist. There are two main criticisms that can fairly be levelled at her, the one dependent on the other: she sings far too often and she is the most inconsistent artist I know.

The deplorable shortage of Italian dramatic sopranos at the moment induces a tendency on the part of the leading theatres to take advantage of Cigna's amenability; but it is a thousand pities that she did not place herself long ago in the hands of a wiser adviser.

I remember an occasion at La Scala in 1935 when in the course of eight days she sang twice in *Turandot*, twice in Bellini's very exacting opera *La Straniera*, and once in *Aïda*, with rehearsals into the bargain, and this unfortunately is all too typical an example of the impossible demands she makes on her voice which an intelligent adviser would never dream of countenancing. I have heard Cigna sing many times in each of the last seven seasons, and I can recall too many occasions when her performance has been that of a very tired woman, and all the signs of an overworked voice have been palpably evident: faulty intonation, inequality, strain, unsteadiness. On the other hand, there have been several evenings when her singing has been of the temper we have a right to expect from one who is, after all, acknowledged to be the foremost Italian dramatic soprano, now that Ponselle and Arangi-Lombaird have withdrawn. I heard all the performances Mr. Bailey refers to in your last issue; and as it happens, the month of April, when he was in Italy, was the peak period of Cigna's activity in 1938. . . .

It is a pity that Mr. Bailey did not hear the first performance of *Gioconda* at La Scala, which took place in February. It was Cigna's first appearance after returning from America, and her voice had had the unusual and very salutary experience of a short period of complete rest. That night she always had something in reserve; a sense of security was engendered which, Mr. Bailey will agree, was entirely lacking two months later. Then in May, what an amazing contrast was provided by her performance on the first night of *Aïda* at the Florence Festival compared with those at La Scala a few short weeks before. Cigna's *Aïda* at the Florence Festival that night was a revelation to me, who had heard it many times before. Her confidence grew with the realization of the fact that she was in form, and so complete was her control by the time the third act was reached that her singing in that most exacting scene was a memorable experience. Her *mezza-voce* throughout the Nile Scene was perfectly managed, the B flats in the first part of the duet with Rhadames really were sung *pianissimo*, and I have never heard *"O Patria Mia"* sung more finely.

One could not help regretting that an artist with such potentialities should so seldom do justice to herself; certainly when she has come to Covent Garden, after four months of continuous overwork, she has never done so. Of course, Cigna has largely herself (or her advisers) to blame for the fact that opera-goers in this country have formed an unfavourable estimate of her work, but that does not excuse in the least the deliberate discourtesy which has marked the attitude of so many of her critics.

In conclusion, I should like to say that it seems to me curious that Mr. Bailey, after saying that Cigna seems incapable of holding a note steady, should spoil the effect at once by proceeding, "After hearing Eva Turner sing *Turandot* at Covent Garden it was an effort to sit through a performance of the same opera with Cigna singing." All I can say is, Mr. Bailey evidently did not hear *Turandot* at Covent Garden this season!

Part Three

INDIVIDUAL OPERAS

By James C. Robertson

LA SCALA

"La Wally" (Catalani)

(Heard at La Scala, Milan, April 14, 1936)

NO need to say how much I appreciated this unexpected opportunity of hearing Catalani's masterpiece—an extra performance having been decided upon during the intensified activity of the Milan Fair. *La Wally* is an especial favourite of mine, and I was delighted to find that seeing it on the stage increased my opinion of the opera's worth.

Poor Catalani, to die so young, with so much music in his heart! *La Wally* contains a few pages which have dated a little—as usual, the fault lies mainly with the librettists—but what an abundance of lovely music is in this work, of an individual stamp too! Illica's book may leave something to be desired here and there, but the subject was one exactly suited to Catalani's romantic and melancholy spirit. His music, intensely romantic in essence, seems to breathe the atmosphere of this Tyrolese Canton in the early years of the last century. There is an extraordinary fascination about this work, it is full of lovely melody, certain of its pages are amongst the finest to be found in any opera, particularly the famous soprano *aria "Ebben Ne Andro Lontano"*, and the unutterably sad prelude to the third act, which is of breathless beauty.

The prelude to the fourth act is diffused with an atmosphere of hopeless desolation, like the scene which meets our eyes when the curtain rises. Wally herself is the central figure, and by far the best characterization of the musician, who excelled in atmosphere and melody rather than in profound characterization. The other characters are conventionally effective.

The drama of *Wally* has a certain affinity with that of *Loreley*, but the opera is more intimate in its appeal and certainly better "theatre".

126

Giuseppe del Campo is something of a specialist in Catalani, he was in charge of the revival of *Loreley* some years ago at La Scala. Marinuzzi is to my mind his ideal interpreter, but Del Campo caught the atmosphere admirably and took special care that the phrasing of many exquisite or celestial passages would leave nothing to be desired.

On the stage we had competent performers. It is a difficult opera to present, but well worth the trouble to create the "atmosphere", which I keep referring to. Gina Cigna's Wally contained much that was admirable; her voice is not always of a sympathetic timbre, but it is a fine one and particularly well used in the middle register. She has a well-developed dramatic instinct, but her characterization lacked a certain "something" which one would find it difficult to name exactly. Who would be the ideal Wally, I wonder? Cobelli, Paccetti, Ponselle, Caniglia? It is very difficult to say.

The only change in the cast from the earlier performances—the first one was broadcast on March 18—was far the better. Ettore Parmeggiani replaced Merli, who was later singing in *Otello*. Parmeggiani did not seem to be in his best form at first, but he sang finely in the last act, the only place where he has any really distinguished music to sing. In this part the splendid timbre of his voice had its proper effect.

Armando Borgioli was a very efficient Gellner. His is a splendid voice, and its dark and powerful quality was very effective in such passages as "*L' Amo Ben Io*" and the outburst in the third act. Both were considerably applauded. Only after having heard Basiola the night before one could not help noticing in Borgioli a certain lack of body in the lower register, and an occasional *vibrato*.

Margherita Carosio was a convincing Wally and sang her rather undistinguished part with a nice tone; while the minor characters were in safe hands—Zaccarini, Baracchi and Vittoria Palombini.

The scenes were in keeping with the spirit of the work, only a little moonlight would have been appropriate in the last act. The costumes were extremely picturesque.

LA SCALA

Sunday, April 8 and Friday, April 13, 1934

FOR a considerable time I have considered this the most powerful of all Verdi's works, apart from *Aïda*. It may not be such a work of art as *Otello* or *Falstaff*, or perhaps even *Rigoletto* or *Don Carlo*; but it has a compelling strength that is possessed by none of these. The book has many flaws; the long arm of coincidence is stretched to inconceivable lengths, and the figures are the conventional characters of the blood-and-thunder romance of last century. Yet Verdi was not at fault in choosing it as a vehicle for his matchless genius; for it has a tremendous power. The title of the opera exactly describes it; we are made to feel the relentless destiny that drives on the three leading characters towards final tragedy. And Verdi was quick to realize that many of the situations were of the kind to draw out the very best that was in him. Never, save in *Aïda* itself, was he so overwhelmingly lavish with his incomparable gift of melody. Such is the force of it that Guerrz's romantic figures come to life in the most amazing fashion; and not only the three leading characters live before our eyes but, as never before, Verdi created genuine characters in the secondary rôles—the noble priest Guardiano, whose music is so sonorously beautiful, the comic priest Melitore, to whom we owe the successful "comic relief" which lightens this long tale of the inexorability of fate, and even the momentary appearance of an old tinker.

The overture rightly played is an excellent piece of work. It is not a masterpiece of construction, but its appeal is irresistible. It employs the main *motifs* of the opera, and works up to a thrilling climax.

The music of the short first act is not distinguished. This scene merely paves the way for what follows. Neither does the first scene of the second act, in the tavern, contain anything memorable. It is put in largely to avoid monotony and enhance the effect of the scene that follows, and it succeeds admirably. The music depicts the scene; and in that scene there was nothing to arouse the hidden fires in the composer. We have Don Carlo's rollicking *ballata* "*Son Pereda, son Rico d'Onore*".

The second scene, outside the monastery in the majestic setting of a moonlit spot among huge rocks, is a masterpiece. First comes Leonora's great *scena* and *aria "Madre Pitosa Vergine"* which, mingling with the chanting from within, seems indeed to reach to *"Dio Sui Finnamenti"*. Then a little comic relief with the first appearance of Melitore, and the Padre comes on the scene. The conversation which follows is set with extreme simplicity, and is all the more touching. But when the scene changes, and we are in the chapel where Guardiano explains to the assembled monks that the "youth" is to enter the hermit's cave, and they all invoke the Virgin's protection, we find one of the mightiest monuments to Verdi's genius. What could be more impressive, more gripping, than the solemn address of Guardiano, the powerful *"Maledizione"*, and the heavenly *"La Vergina Degli Angeli"*, one of the simplest and most moving, most sublime melodies that even Verdi ever conceived? This is perhaps the finest scene in the opera.

The first scene of the third act contains the lovely introduction and *scena* for Don Alvaro, which I consider the greatest tenor *aria* ever written—*"O in Che in Seno Agli Angeli"*—in which he laments the implacable fate that has snatched everything worth living for from him and implores his Leonora to look down from heaven and pity his terrible distress. After the superb intensity of this appeal, the succeeding passage in which he and the disguised Don Carlo swear eternal friendship is bathos indeed.

In the second scene the best number is *"Solenore in Quest'Ore"*, so absolutely appropriate that it is worthy to stand beside *"La Virgina Degli Angeli"*. Then follows Don Carlo's conventional but distinctly effective *scena*—difficult to make convincing on the stage.

The third scene in this act is successful in avoiding that excess of intensity which Verdi carefully guarded against. In it the best things are the quaint ballet, or rather country dance, and Melitore's famous punning exhortation. It is here that the tinker makes his effective appearance. The Rat-a-plan chorus is not worthy of the composer, though ingenious enough.

The last act opens with the excellent scene where Melitore dispenses charity, and the succeeding duologue between him and Guardiano. Then the *Forza del Destino* gets going again, and we have that famous duet between Alvaro and Don Carlo in which Don Carlo in the end triumphs over Alvaro's resolution that he will not shed the blood of a Vargas again. Here one may inquire if it is not a mistake to cut out the important duet in the preceding scene, which is excellent music and explains exactly what has happened? This duet, however, is powerful in the extreme, and ends in thrilling fashion.

The last scene of all opens with the marvellous *aria "Pace, Mio Dio"*, the sheer genius of which leaves one prostrate with devotion. There only remains the final trio, which winds the opera off in the only possible way.

Gabriele Santini has the lion's share of the direction at La Scala this year, and he is worthy of the honour. His rendering of the overture was praiseworthy in the extreme, simply could not be bettered. Indeed, I could not find a single fault in his direction all through.

Of the artists engaged, Iva Pacetti is due the most praise for the success with which she portrayed the tragic figure of Leonora di Vargas. From the second act, where her part really begins, she was superb. Her vocal equipment is by no means flawless; some of her high notes do not fall easily on the ear, and she does not sing very consistently; but she has an individual quality of her own, and her beautiful personality and excellent stage movements greatly enhanced her performance. Beautiful indeed was her rendering of *"La Virgina Degli Angeli"*—especially at the second performance—sung throughout in a faultless and touching *mezza-voce*. Best of all was her singing and unobtrusive acting in *"Pace Mio Dio"*. This indeed was the high light of the performance, and she took a lovely B flat here—indeed, some of her high notes are quite unexceptionable. Only occasionally do we get a certain harshness. A sincere and highly praiseworthy performance for one whose vocal equipment is perhaps better suited to Puccini than to Verdi.

Beside her was the much-fêted Gigli. The Italians have always been willing to meet the owner of a heaven-sent voice half-way, and Gigli's voice is certainly superb.

Carlo Moulli revealed a superb baritone voice, and if he lacked the ferocity that Franci would have been able to reveal, he was certainly an acceptable exponent of his part. His singing of the *scena* in act Act 3 was excellent, his acting a little less convincing.

Tancredi Pasero made a most dignified Superior and sang with great sonority, although, once you have noticed it, his frequent trick of singing out of the right-hand side of his mouth is disconcerting.

Lione Paci has not a great voice, but he made a real "hit" with his impersonation of the comic friar, especially in the last act.

Granna Redezini was sprightly in her usual rôle of Preziosilla.

Giuseppe Nessi was excellent as the tinker—he is one of the best "small part" artists and very versatile.

Duilio Baconti sang with power the small part of the Marchese.

The chorus, important in this opera, was admirable, specially in the monastery scene, and the country dance was really excellent.

There are no less than nine scenes. For the sake of a quick change while the orchestra plays a few bars of descriptive music, the scene preceding the bringing back of the wounded Alvaro, in which occurs his big *aria*, seemed to me to be a poor setting for such a *scena*. But for the rest, the scenes were, as usual, perfect, and the last scene before the hermit's cave was majestic, with the canyon between the huge rocks and the waterfall as large as life.

Although this is the fourth time the opera has been given at La Scala in six years, it has had the honour of six performances—more than any other opera this year—and always to a theatre sold out and boundless in their admiration and enthusiasm.

LA SCALA

"ISABEAU"

Saturday, April 14, 1934

AS with *La Una delle Beffe* this was specially interesting in that I had not previously heard a note of the music. I discovered the opera to be a most unusual and engrossing affair. The Milan Press, after relating the extraordinary story of the conflict between La Scala on the one hand and the Fenice of Venzia and Mascagni on the other, over the first performance in Italy in 1911, went on to illustrate at some length that this was not "pure" Mascagni, but in some respects to be regarded as an experiment. I agree. The action is long-drawn and the libretto imaginatively legendary; Illica was given full play in his somewhat fanciful poetic instincts which Puccini wisely gave a sort of check in conjunction with the more prosaic Giacosa.

To some extent, then, the opera is almost in the "Wagnerian" line. Yet it is entirely Italian in execution, if not in conception. Isabeau is a thoroughly believable personage; and even Filco commands some measure of understanding. In his case, perhaps, there is an abundance of the Wagnerian tendency towards difficulties in the way of gesturing, etc., to fill in time and make him seem a natural character.

But to return to the music. Its chief interest is more intellectual than emotional. Seldom indeed are we irresistibly thrilled by the characteristic Mascagnian surge; instead, we have a constant and fascinating ingenuity and mastery of exotic harmonical effects that captures and holds the attention.

Some of the descriptive writing in what might be called scenes of pageant was most arresting. I should like to hear the opera again. There were times when pure Mascagni popped out, as in the final duet, when Isabeau's, *"Non Sai Tu la Tua Morte!"* had the old supercharged effect. Filco's famous passages were in the way of intense declamation in a sort of Italianized Wagner-cum-Mascagni vein. This is emphatically music that grows on one—an acquired taste, as with most music that is not in the patent line of a genius such as Verdi or Puccini. It demands a sympathetic listener. I see that, in company with *Iris*, this opera is to represent Mascagni in the mammoth EIAR season beginning on the last day of May; so I shall have a welcome opportunity of getting to know the work thoroughly. I shall therefore pass on to the performance.

Gabriele Santini is certainly one of the best Italian conductors. He deals equally well with the old and new in opera, and he obtained an excellent orchestral playing of Mascagni's fine score; this was a thoroughly intelligent director who gave a reading which it would be impossible to improve upon. His *tempi* seemed to me to strike a very happy medium. In an unostentatious way he contrived to appear the leading factor in the success of the revival.

Gina Cigna took the title rôle, which dominates the opera as far as the stage is concerned. I have now seen this artist in four rôles and heard her in another half-dozen or so, and I can safely say that this is the rôle to which she is most suited. Indeed, I have a new angle on her importance after this. Nearly all the familiar blemishes disappeared, entirely in the case of her noisy breathing and forcing of high notes with a resultant piercing effect, to a great extent in her tendency to get a little sharp at times! Her acting was excellent in this difficult part; she was thoroughly convincing. Her singing showed real sympathy and understanding of her character, and was unusually finely graded. She was excellent in the last act. Cigna's art is more aloof than intimate or appealing; she should, on the strength of this performance, make an exceedingly good Turandot.

Next in importance was Ettore Parmeggiani, who revealed a splendid voice, rich and even. Folco is a difficult part, bearing a certain similarity to the naïve Wagnerian heroes such as the young Siegfried. Parmeggiani has a voice well suited to Wagner's music, as the Milan Press pointed out; but his acting was too conventional to fill the somewhat exacting demands of this part. Vocally, his *"Canzone del Folco"*, his *scena* in the second act and his share of the final duet were admirable.

Ettore Nava was Isabeau's royal father; the part is undistinguished, but he filled it with credit, revealing a well-balanced baritone voice free from any mannerisms.

Quilio Baronti as the scheming Cornelius gave his usual admirable performance. The scenes were striking and effective—though the colouring seemed bizarre at times.

CASINO, SAN REMO

"Un Ballo in Maschera"

Wednesday, March 28, 1934

THE performance of *Un Ballo* was chiefly notable for the appearance
of Pertile in one of his best parts. The chief character of this performance can be summed up in one word—*vitality*. The enormous, vibrating
sincerity and vitality of Verdi found a worthy protagonist in the celebrated
tenor, and in the work of both there were serious blemishes, more than
compensated for in the long run. In Verdi's case, the truth is that the
book of *Un Ballo* is poor stuff, and although the plot, especially if considered in its true setting, has a certain crude power, which would be
enormously enhanced by really great staging and acting, the fact remains
that in the end the libretto was just a tag on which to hang some of Verdi's
most vivid and pulsating melody. And what melody! The opera may be
just a collection of numbers, but they are marvellous examples of the
genius of the "Lion of Busseto".

And Pertile? It is unjust to write about him the day after the performance. At the time one is irresistibly swept away by the way in which he
throws himself into it heart and soul—he obviously believes in it, and in
himself, so completely. True, in spite of his excellent stage movements
and his charming smile, he cannot overcome the handicap of his middle-
aged "top-heaviness" in appearance; true, also, that he offends the taste
frequently in his vocal mannerisms—although here once more they are
not nearly so obvious in the theatre as on the radio; his *vibrato*, for
example, turns out to be simply the natural vibrant quality of his extraordinary voice. But what matter these criticisms when he is thrilling us
with the lyricism and passion of *"La Rivedra Nell' Estesi"* and the two
parts of the love-duet, or captivating us with his wonderful rendering of
the fisherman's song or his delicious *"E scherzo od e Follia"*? Those who
accuse him of shouting are not doing him justice. It is second nature to
him to allow his voice—securely grounded as a rock—to sweep to a
climax of the most thrilling intensity. It is no effort to him. His quieter
moments are of extreme beauty.

Having paid homage to Pertile—and I am very glad to have heard him, since he is growing older—I want to say that it is time for him to quit. He has written an ineffaceable page in the history of Italian opera by his many triumphs at the Scala during Toscanini's régime, notably as the protagonist in *Nerone*; but now he ought to make way for the rising generation who are bringing new spirit into Italian opera.

The soprano was Maria Canena. She revealed a voice of great natural resource, but, my God, what noises issued forth! Her day is of course over, and she has only herself to blame. I never in all my life heard anything so unpleasant as those top notes of hers, which begin without exception with a breathy reediness and end in an acid shriek. Every now and then she produced a lovely tone, and the wireless had not revealed what an enormous organ she possessed, but she is a thoroughly bad singer. I heard Mascagni say some nasty things about her after the performance, when I just happened to spot him and secured his autograph. As an actress she was one of the old school—capable enough in a purely conventional way. *Basta!*

Cesare Formichi sang unevenly as Renato. The best part of his voice is the lowest register—he has none of the flexibility of the typical Italian baritone. He produced some big tones from his enormous frame, but on the whole he was only an average Renato—rather a "ranter".

Maria Falliani revealed a powerful organ as Ulrica and sang her invocation effectively enough, without by any means getting the most out of it. She has trouble with her change of registers. As a matter of fact, this particular scene was rather spoilt by the extraordinarily unimaginative stage setting.

Elisa Farroni was a sprightly, chubby little page and revealed a very charming soprano *leggiero* which did full justice to the graceful, vivacious music accorded her.

The minor characters were moderately good. Giacomo Armani made some good points, but on the whole his conducting lacked equilibrium—it came and went like the waves of an incoming tide.

The large audience was unsparing in its enthusiasm for Pertile, but the "star" refused to take a personal call.

One last word. Behind me were three English people whom I could willingly have brained. They were a damned nuisance—chattering, laughing, making irritating remarks and obviously did not know the first thing about opera.

"*Avei diavoli d'Inglesi*," as the old lady next to me remarked with feeling!

Additional Notes

Some note on the original production of *Un Ballo in Maschera* may be of interest here. I have read a great many comments on this opera, and among them the truly astounding statement that this opera is presented very seldom. However, one lives and learns, as also in reading that Verdi only wrote for immediate and popular successes. I also read in another "study" of this great master the amusing remark that "Verdi has a distinct ability for melodic writing". This for stupendous impertinence cannot be beaten!

However, to return to *Un Ballo in Maschera*. The scenes were originally set in some unidentified European city, but this was objected to by the government censors—who were always ready to make difficulties for Verdi, and who were at this time very active indeed. The *venue* was changed to Boston, in America, a city which at that time, 1859, was strictly Puritanical, and quite improbable as the scene of *Un Ballo in Maschera*. However, the censors admitted that Boston was a long way from Italy—and allowed the setting. In these days the scenes are sometimes laid in Naples, though when I last saw this splendid opera it still retained the original Boston scenery.

Verdi composed this work for the San Carlo at Naples, where it was to have been produced for Carnevale in 1858. During the rehearsals Felice Orsini, an Italian revolutionary, made his attempt on the life of Napoleon III. In consequence, the authorities forbade the production of any opera or theatrical performance which dealt with the assassination of a king. The authorities suggested that Verdi should adapt his work to a completely new libretto, which he refused—somewhat indignantly—to do. The opera was therefore ordered to be cancelled and not produced. This action caused a kind of minor revolution in Naples, where people marched about the streets bearing banners inscribed "*Viva Verdi*"—the initials V. V. having a second significance—*Viva Vittorio Emmanuele*, and showing the determination of the people for a united Italy.

The opera had been originally named *Gustavo the Third* and was written round the assassination of that monarch while attending a masked ball at Stockholm. The authorities, who were nervous at the idea of the assassination of a king on the stage, had no compunction in allowing the assassination of an English governor in far-away America. The title was changed to *Un Ballo in Maschera*. The opera was produced in Rome at the Apollo Theatre in February 1859.

When I heard this opera at La Fenice—which I did three times in one week, and admiring it more with every performance—the conductor was Vittorio Gui, who performed miracles with his orchestra, and brought beautiful light and shade into the music. Bagnariol was the Governor, and Armando Borgioli the Renato. His performance was admirable, sung with restraint and deep feeling. Gilda Alfano sang Ulrica; and Cigna sang Amelia, which is surely one of the most touching rôles—as well as one of the most exacting—in all Verdi's operas. I have written elsewhere of Cigna's performance in this opera.—N. J.

LA SCALA

"OTELLO"

1936

I WENT to *Otello* expecting an enjoyable evening but hardly a revelation, seeing that I have heard the opera so often, and saw it recently
at Covent Garden. Instead, this was one of the greatest experiences
I have had in the theatre; never before did I realize the mighty genius
of Verdi's penultimate opera. The reason for this revaluation was the
performance, perhaps the best I have seen at La Scala of any opera; as
perfect an *Otello* as was Toscanini's *Falstaff*. From the tempestuous
opening I had the keyed-up feeling that every operatic enthusiast will
recognize; and it was only during part of the third act that I inevitably
lost this tense excitement—inevitable, because Verdi's genius is here
temporarily under a cloud. As for the fourth act—its exquisite beauty,
unique in all Verdi's opera, sent me out of the theatre walking on air.

Gino Marinuzzi takes chief credit for his magnificent conception and
execution of the composer's intentions. What shattering dynamics in
the storm music, what exquisite handling of the incredible last act! But
all through his share of the success—the lion's share—could not con-
ceivably have been bettered. It is significant, by the way, that *Otello* is
the only opera in the repertoire this season that was done in 1935.
Marinuzzi has revealed *Otello* in its full glory to the Milan audience for
the first time. One of the greatest achievements of his luminous career.

The standard on the stage was exceptionally high, even for La
Scala. Maria Caniglia I have long considered the finest living soprano,
yet I was not prepared for such an exquisite Desdemona. How fortunate
that such a wonderful voice should be allied to such impeccable artistry!
This was the finest soprano singing I have ever heard; since I last heard
her in 1934 as Eva her art seems even more refined and moving. Never
shall I forget the "*Ave Maria*" as she and Marinuzzi realized it.

Francesco Merli's Otello was another surprise. Could this really
be Merli, one wondered, remembering the banality of some of his past
characterizations? This is by far his best part; and it is all the more

gratifying in that he is the only adequate interpreter in the world today of this most exacting of tenor rôles, which Caruso knew better than to attempt. His voice rang out triumphantly in the arduous passages such as *"Esultate"* and the *"Ora e Per Sempre"*; and on the other side of the picture there was his moving interpretation of the Monologue, and above all the Death scene, where he reached real tragedy. It was his acting, however, which was so extraordinary. He deserves great credit for identifying this part so completely with his name, for it has not been done without a great deal of painstaking effort from one whose acting is usually so conventional.

Piero Biasini, too, exceeded all expectations, and on his showing as Iago must now be admitted to the select company of No. 1 baritones. Particularly in the second act was his interpretation appreciated; for his Iago was admirably acted, without exaggeration, always showing a keen intelligence which was reflected in his singing. His fine baritone voice, of excellent quality and perfectly trained, was used every minute with a purpose. He was not just singing; the inflections of his voice were part of his admirably conceived characterization.

The minor characters were in capable hands—particularly Gino Del Signore and Giulio Borronti distinguished themselves. The chorus was outstandingly good, even for La Scala, and I for one would have liked to see Vittore Veneziani share in the curtain-calls. The scenes were admirable—particularly the storm in Act I, with the tempestuous sea and the vaguely discerned ship, half submerged. The production, too, was a credit to the diligent Frigerio.[1]

[1] Frigerio was the *regista* Vittore Veneziani the chorus master.

TEATRO DELL' OPERA, ROME

"MANON LESCAUT"

Saturday, April 7, Tuesday, April 10, 1934

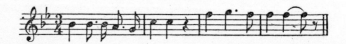

GINO MARINUZZI has presumably a partiality for this work, as it is the second time in four years that he has lavished all his skill on the preparation of an adequate edition of it.

The first time I saw it, the impression was not wholly favourable. For some reason or other I was not in a receptive mood. The second time I was roused to great enthusiasm, and there may be some significance in the fact that on this occasion the audience were also more enthusiastic and there were innumerable calls.

The opera was Puccini's first great success; it was in 1934 exactly the same age as the protagonist—forty-two—yet it retains its freshness to a comparable degree. It is really divided into two parts. The atmosphere of the first two acts is all youth and freshness and elegance —and, of course, in the painting of such an atmosphere Puccini stands alone. We have here the same sure, spontaneous touch that flowers out in all its incomparable beauty in *Bohème*; examples are easy to quote. In the first act we have the light-hearted *aria* of De Grieux, "*Ma Voi Belle, Breve e Bionde*", which is effectively murmured by the chorus at the end of the act in derision at the discomfited old roué; as might be expected, the passage[1] when Manon and De Grieux meet for the first time is simply exquisite in its tender youthful sentiment; then follows De Grieux's lovely and very famous lyric, "*Donna Non Vidi Mai*". The second passage between the young lovers, in which we are made to feel a rising passion, is hardly so successful, although effective enough; and through all this runs Puccini's superb orchestration, always delighting us with felicitous and appropriate passages that are sometimes gone almost before we savour them to the full, only to return again with heightened effect.

The second act in Manon's boudoir in old Geronte's house is delightful. Here all the characters are again painted with unerring skill. Incidentally, the libretto, to which so many pens contributed their quota, turned

[1] "*Vedete! Io son fedele alla parola mia.*"

out in the end to be a surprisingly good unity. In this act the gems are Manon's famous *"In Quelle Trine Morbide"*, in which she wistfully remembers love in a cottage with De Grieux as compared with the stifling elegance all round her; the exquisite music which accompanies the Madrigal and lesson in dancing, and of course the famous duet when De Grieux comes on the scene.[1] The *finale* of the act shows signs of the immaturity of the composer.

Now we enter on the second part of the opera. The transition is helped by the famous *intermezzo*, which, like most of Puccini's efforts in this line, owes its effect to the poignant parading before us of many of the motives already employed, but painted now with the harmonization of which Puccini was a master, rather than to any continuous working out that would make a genuine symphonic poem of the thing, such as we get from Mascagni or Catalani.

We are now ready for what follows, and while the music is faithful to the situations, we cannot but confess that the second half is not nearly so pleasing as the first. In the third act, De Grieux's plea to be allowed to accompany Manon into exile is very effective, full of genuine, almost distracted, passion and despair.

One has a feeling that the Opera should have ended with the reunion of the lovers at the end of this act. The last act is needlessly harrowing. True, Puccini has found music that is as sad as the scene itself—and as formless—but on the whole this savours too much of the conventional unhappy ending of Grand Opera.

On this occasion we had a positively magnificent rendering of the score under Marinuzzi. Someone has said that there is a pulse, a breath of life itself, in Puccini's scores, and they remain dead except in the hands of a director who senses this pulse. Marinuzzi can truly be said to have brought the score to life. Criticism is utterly impossible. He plays on the orchestra with a touch that is now gentle and caressing, now majestic and thrilling. They say he is shy and nervous, but when on the conductor's platform he is a very god.

Claudia Muzio's seasoned art was brought to bear on the title rôle, which has always been a speciality of hers. As with Violetta, it gives her a chance to display her famous physical attractions to the full. And a very pretty picture she made in the first two acts. In the last two the music was less distinguished and so her performance was the less memorable. She sang *"In Quelle Trine"* beautifully, and all through displayed her well-known lovely quality—specially in the *mezza-voce* passages.

But on the whole it must be said that Alessandro Tiliani put her somewhat in the shade. He has one of the finest tenor voices in existence

[1] *"Vieni! Colle tue braccia stringi Manon che t'ama."*

—youthful and robust, with a beautiful, even quality, thrilling in his perfect high notes and beautiful in his excellent *mezza-voce*. He moved well on the stage, and experience will bring even better results here, for he is a young artist who improves every season. He was specially good as the ardent De Grieux of the first act. Disillusionment brought a certain lack of restraint, specially in the third act—where he was very effective, however. In the last act he was admirable. Altogether a joy to see and hear such youthful sincerity. He sang his *"Ma Voi Belle"* very nicely, and was beautifully lyric in *"Donna Non Vidi Mai"*. In the more impassioned music of the second and third acts, as I have said, a few of his gestures were a little exaggerated, but he was very effective for all that. An excellent young man.

Gino Vanelli was Lescaut to the life. He was an amusing drunkard in the first act, and made a genuine character of the self-satisfied brother in the second. He has a superb voice and a rare sense of the stage.

Giulio Cirino is one of the best character actors on the rostrum, and gave an excellent impersonation of Geronte. He has the faculty of making a genuine creation of every rôle he undertakes.

All the minor parts were excellently played, and the chorus was as good vocally, and as well drilled and natural scenically, as usual. The scenes were up to the usual high standard; the difficulty of the departure from Havré was admirably surmounted, but the last scene in a barren part of America definitely detracted from one's appreciation of the score.

TEATRO SAN CARLO, NAPLES

Prima of "Adriana Lecouvreur"

Wednesday, April 4, 1934

THIS performance was a very welcome surprise. I had heard the opera broadcast from La Scala in the past two years and from Torino, but without the score; so I listened a trifle perfunctorily. On a closer inspection it is clear that this opera is one of the finest works of the modern Italian school, worthy to stand beside the best work of Mascagni, Puccini, Giordano and Zandonai.

The Teatro San Carlo is clearly not such a flourishing affair as the Rome or Milan theatres; but it was at its best to greet this *prima* of the masterpiece of its Conservatorio Directore, who honoured us with his presence.

The libretto by Colanth is a good piece of work, particularly strong in the drama of the second act, and drawing the various figures very clearly. The music follows the libretto with fidelity and considerable inspiration. In the first act we have the excellent motive which might be labelled *"Commedri Française"*, the motive of Adriana which finds expression in the splendid solo *"Io Son L'Umileancella"*, and the love motive introduced on the entrance of Manrizio with his flowing *"La Dolcissima Effigie"*. Excellent also is the music allotted to the sympathetic figure of Michonnet—throughout the opera very well characterized—and the witty music of the old *roué* and the Abate is equally satisfactory.

The second act, commencing with a conventionally effective solo for the jealous Princess, contains much music of the highest order—specially the passage for Manrizio *"L'Anima Ho Stanca"*. One of the best examples of the modern Italian style at its most effective, and the perfectly lovely orchestral passage that accompanies the touching exit of the ever-faithful Michonnet.

In the third act there is not a great deal of interest apart from the phrasing and original ballet music, but the drama moves along in good style.

Before the last act we have the lovely *Intermezzo*, which has a certain amount in common with similar passages in *Wally* or *Traviata*. It is worked out of the motive, hinted at in the first act and widely used as the drama draws to a close, of *"Poveri Fiori"*, and there is much poignant harmonic beauty. The last act itself requires very delicate handling by the protagonist if it is not to seem rather laboured. In the hands of a Cobelli it can be made as effective as the last act of *Traviata*. The main musical interest lies in the passage already mentioned, *"Poveri Fiori"*.

All in all, then, an excellent piece of work on the traditional Italian lines of distinguished and irresistible melody.

On this occasion, as the Neapolitan Press pointed out, we owed everything to the magnificent preparation and execution of Panizza. I am inclined to say that he is the best director I have yet seen. It was a treat to see him at work. In his hands the beauties of the score were all brought out in the most favourable light. I understand this is his farewell to the San Carlo for the season, and he could not have made a more portentous exit. He is a most inspiring musician.

Adelaide Saraceni was the protagonist, and she did her best, making quite a presentable figure of the unfortunate actress. But her performance fell a long way short of what we might have had from Favero, Caniglia, or above all Giuseppina Cobelli. Her voice lacks power in moments when it is required, and she strives to make up for this by a continual *sforzando* at the close of every sustained note. She was not equal to the considerable histrionic demands of the last act.

Galliano Masini, whom I admired so much in *I Maestri Cantoni*, sang superbly as Manrizio Conte di Sassonia. His voice, as I had occasion to observe, is perfectly placed and produced, and one hardly knows whether to admire most his effortless high notes or his lovely *mezza-voce* effects. He excelled last night in *"L'Anima Ho Stanco"*, where he seemed to "feel" the character most. At other times, there was a certain mechanical effect in his gestures which one hardly expected after the beauty of his representation of Walter di Stolzing. This was his first appearance at the San Carlo and he made a most favourable impression by the beauty of his voice and bearing. A little more study of the dramatic exigencies of the part would leave nothing to be desired in his interpretation, for vocally he has only the slightest of blemishes—a tendency to "slide" up to certain of his notes.

Emilio Glinardini, the most experienced of the artists on view, was also the most irreproachable. His presentation of the figure of Michonnet was touching and thoroughly convincing. In appearance and action he relived the character, and his singing of the part was perfect. The music is not very distinguished, but as sung by Glinardini it exactly fitted the part. He has a very beautiful and even baritone which he uses with the most exquisite taste. This season I have already had occasion to admire him enormously in *La Maschera* and *Don Pasquale*, in the latter opera in association with Baccaloni, who appeared in the small part of the Principe and was as artistic as ever. One of the delights of the first act was the "patter" duet and following quartet, sung with excellent assurance and effect by Baccaloni and Giuseppe Marchesi, who made a very droll Abate.

Miny Giani was also something of a revelation. After hearing her at Covent Garden in *Aïda* and *Don Carlo* last year I formed the opinion that although she had genuine intentions the execution left a lot to be desired. Last night as the Principessa she was greatly admired; indeed, she made such a beautiful figure, noble in mien and bearing, that one secretly thought Manrizio rather blind in turning to his Adriana. Her voice revealed itself as much better; whether she has improved in the ten months or so, or whether it was just the effect of being on her native soil, I cannot tell; but it rang forth with the utmost assurance and dramatic effect; and the only blemish now (and even that is improving) is that she still tucks her chin in to obtain certain full-throated tones, thus preventing the flow of full, even tone that she is presumably striving for. She is a young artist with very great possibilities.

The rest of the cast were not very conspicuous, and the ballet by no means absorbing.

The performance was greeted with much enthusiasm, particularly at the close of the second act, and the composer, both alone and in company with Panizza and the artists, was accorded tumultuous evidences of approval.

IL TEATRO DELL' OPERA

"RIGOLETTO"

Saturday, March 31, 1934

THE Teatro dell' Opera is an unbelievably sumptuous affair; it is indeed more dazzling in its splendour than La Scala. The entrance is most imposing, and the appointments inside—the vast halls for perambulation in the intervals, the liveried attendants, the awe-inspiring perfection of the lay-out of the theatre itself—make it clear that the State has spared no efforts to give the Teatro dell' Opera a position of world supremacy. The staging and lighting, the choice of *maestri* and artists, the important *primas*, bear this out. Only one thing is missing that makes all the difference—the indescribable atmosphere that tradition lends to La Scala. There you are, as it were, on sacred ground.

This performance of *Rigoletto* was nothing short of perfection. I had no idea that this opera could be made so gripping dramatically. Frequent hearings on the wireless seemed to indicate that it was wearing a little, yet with such a production as this, the opera stood revealed as a masterpiece untouched by the passage of eighty years and more.

Such a trio of principal artists has perhaps never been equalled. The director was Edoardo Vitale, the senior *maestro* in Italy now that Toscanini has gone. He has been associated with great operatic productions in Rome for nigh on forty years, but never has he accomplished such feats as this year. He stood revealed last night as a director of intense power, to whom years of experience have given absolute mastery over his material. At times, perhaps, he allowed the orchestra, and especially the overpowering brass, to assert itself too much; but on the whole it was principally due to the "vitality" of the illustrous *maestro* that the score was presented in such a fresh and favourable aspect.

Of the singers, the first to be mentioned is Giacomo Lauri-Volpi, assuredly one of the most fulgent of Italy's glorious line of *divos*—a true descendant of Mario, of Rubini, not since their time has there been a voice of such miraculous flexibility. The sheer beauty of his *mezza-voce*, the thrill of his high notes—the most perfect in living memory—secure for him a place at the head of present-day attractions. Nor is he only a virtuoso, as one might call Gigli. He is a consummate artist. Allied to his excellent stage bearing, his lyric art presented to us a Duke of Mantova in whom we had no option but to believe utterly. What girl, we asked, could have resisted the positively unearthly beauty of his tones as he murmured in her ear, "*E Il Sol Dell'Anima*"? Here was a piece of singing which will linger in my mind as long as I live. Once more I realized what an imperfect impression the wireless is able to give us of an operatic performance. Yet how much I owe it! Lauri-Volpi's "*Quest'o Quella*' was nothing to make a song about, but his singing in the second and last acts was a wonderful privilege to hear.

Allied to him was another singer whose vocal art was also in the tradition of *bel canto* in a precious sense which is dying out. Only in her case the sheer virtuosity of her singing is not matched to the same extent by the essentially modern mastery of the dramatic side displayed by Lauri-Volpi. I allude, of course, to Toti dal Monte. Here the difference between hearing her on the wireless and in the flesh is very striking. The wireless quite fails to convey the ethereal beauty of her tones. She may not possess a very efficient staccato, and her highest register may lack a little of its one-time security—and if it is true that she is dying of consumption,[1] which I can hardly credit, one can hardly wonder at these minor slips—but there is an irresistible beauty in her unforced, bird-like tones. She sang in this pure, unforced style all through and was particularly admirable in the third act. I expect Bider Sayao is, physically and dramatically, a more appealing Gilda, and her voice is more artistically produced; but I doubt if she has that peculiar quality in her voice that Dal Monte derives from Melba, Tetrazzini and other *divas* of a bygone age.

Rigoletto was Benvenuto Franci, who poured out volumes of sound and gave a thoroughly impressive, dramatic representation of his character. I wonder if he was perhaps not quite in his best voice. If he was, then one must admit that there are certain traces of unevenness here and there—a bit of breathiness in certain soft passages, and a lack of natural power in his top notes compensate for his colossal middle and lower tones. He is undoubtedly one of the most dominant baritones in the world today, and in certain operas, such as *Andrea Chenier*, quite unrivalled.

The minor characters did not get their words over too well, but fitted well into the scenic effect. The Sparafucile of Giulio Cinno was a good piece of characterization, and Gilda Alfano was an attractive Maddalena. Melchiorre Luise was not a sufficiently impressive Monterone.

[1] His information was incorrect. Today Toti dal Monte is singing magnificently (April 1947).—N. J.

The chorus was well drilled and succeeded admirably in avoiding the stiffness sometimes attendant on choruses in a work of this nature. As I have said, the staging was excellent, particularly of Rigoletto's house and of the sinister spot in the last act, when the storm was done in extraordinarily realistic style.

LA SCALA

"LA GIOCONDA" (PONCHIELI)

VERDI always held, with a complacency which lesser men must envy, that the judgment of the public is the real indication of an opera's merits; not the judgment of the *prima*, which can hardly be anything but fortuitous, but the test of Time. On this basis, *La Gioconda* is a masterpiece; and one realized last night that, let the critics fulminate as they will (what would Newman say about this opera?), the public is justified in its affection for this work. An affection which assumed spectacular proportions; a theatre completely sold out, seats being hawked outside at a fabulous premium, a discomfort cheerfully borne in the overcrowded galleries. One would have thought this was a particularly important world *première*!

In all this vast crowd, it would have been difficult to find a single one who did not know *La Gioconda* off by heart. A melodrama *par excellence* this "twopence coloured", as Herman Klein used to say; no subtleties must be expected. The music is perfectly in keeping; sweeping melody that overpowers one even as does, say, *Un Ballo in Maschera*; together with *Mefistofele*, this opera is the only one of its epoch which could stand up to the dazzling blaze of Verdi's genius.

As in *Mefistofele*, the episodes, highly coloured in themselves, make an admirable contrast. The best is the fourth in which one feels only that the farewell between Gioconda and the united lovers is unduly protracted. The weakest is the third; which, however, contains the "Dance of the Hours", never failing in its effect. The other two acts have their highlights and their less-successful pages, but *Gioconda* is like *Lucia*: after hearing it so often as to know it by heart, we accept it *en bloc* and would not stand for any of it being cut.

The reason for the enormous attraction at La Scala lay partly in the exceptional promise of the new edition—largely similar, indeed, to the last in 1934. In fact, four out of the five were re-engaged; but, Tiliani having withdrawn from a part which is indubitably one of his best, the management made the best of it by engaging Galliano Masini. Masini returned to La Scala with an enhanced reputation; but in spite of the fact that his voice was inevitably recognized as one of the finest of its type, he did not give complete satisfaction. It may have been nerves, as one critic suggested, which account for the strange inequality of his performance, it may simply have been that the older operas are not so suited to his style. So much of his singing was of really great quality that one could not but hope that by Thursday, when the third performance is to be broadcast, he will have complete control of his resources.

Of those who were heard in 1934, Gina Cigna and Ebe Stignani seemed even finer than before, and won the greatest applause of the evening for their "*L'Amo Come Il Fulgor*". It was a positive duel between the two, with the honours triumphantly even. Heaven knows the part of Laura contains conventional enough material; but, like the whole of the opera, it is singable, and Ebe Stignani is the greatest singer in the world. The splendour of her resources seemed to be heightened by the poverty of the material.

As for Cigna's Gioconda, it was a revelation, even although I have long suspected that this was her best rôle. I first heard her in it in 1933; then in the Scala performance of 1934. This was the seventh time I have heard her in the rôle, and each time her interpretation has deepened. Without losing anything of dramatic force, her vocal splendour is now judiciously restrained. Thus in "*Suicidio*", magnificently sung, she seems to have something in reserve, whereas previously she was singing all out. The inequalities, rough edges, cold quality sometimes noticed in her work disappear in *La Gioconda*; vocally and dramatically, it is a magnificent study gathering force until in the fourth act it reaches great heights. She even looked like a different person!

Mario Basiola, so polished in, say, *La Favorita*, was a superb villain in *La Gioconda*. Not a trace of exaggeration, but a suitably stylized interpretation. His magnificent voice had plenty of opportunity and he made the most of every one without ever usurping more than his fair share of attention or for a moment descending to the over-emphasis often heard in such a part. "*O Monumento*", "*Enzo Grimaldo*", "*Pescator*", "*Ebbezza Delicio*"—these are the four opportunities, every one of which won him applause *a scena aperta*.

Fernando Antori, as in 1934, was Alvise. He acted the part well but as usual his voice sounded "hollow".

Vittoria Palombini was an admirable Cieca, though formidable indeed was her task with Stignani on the same stage!

Chorus and production, perfectly drilled. A most picturesque set of cenes, especially, of course, the second act with the ship, the moon, the laguna, Venice in the distance . . .

Last, but not least, Giuseppe Del Campo was an admirable

conductor, not striving to make any new points, but allowing nothing to escape.

I wonder if he is left-handed.

(Note. N. J.)

I heard this magnificent opera in Venice in the summer—open-air season—of 1945, when Tagliabue, Cigna and Cloe Elmo were the protagonists. I have always found the Venice open-air theatre unsympathetic, and how the "stars" contrive to dress in the wretched little improvised rooms at the side of the stage passes my comprehension.

Jimmy Robertson has criticized the singing of Cigna, and it only remains to speak of Tagliabue. I heard this artist in America; I thought then that his fine baritone was of excellent quality, and time has, I feel, enriched it, and given him even more complete control over it.

His acting is above the average, and his lightness of movement is a joy to watch; he moves "like a dancer", as someone once said of the English actor, Claude Rains.

I heard *La Gioconda* in 1946 at the open-air theatre in Trieste where it is situated very finely in the old Castello high up above the town. No setting could have been more delightful.

Here again I heard Tagliabue—and, as good as ever, Cloe Elmo was singing magnificently and making the most of what is, after all, a rather dull part; Signora Grandi, who is, I believe, by birth an Australian, and who sang at Glyndebourne in *Macbeth* with Valentino and Franklin, and again in *Tosca* at the Cambridge with Stabile, appeared as La Gioconda. The latter I did not hear as I was out of England, the former I heard in company with Jimmy Robertson, and we were neither of us much impressed.

On the night when I heard her at Trieste I am ready to admit that her voice was good, though not outstandingly so, but she has a trick of "squirming" about when she takes a top note which is irritating in the extreme. Her duet with Laura was not appealing, but in the last act, both in the farewell scene with the two lovers, and her scene when she is left alone debating as to whether she shall kill herself, was increasingly good; it lost in both tone and conviction after the exit of the lovers, and the bedecking of herself with the mock jewelry was, from an acting point of view, untidy. Her last outburst, however, was very fine.

I have forgotten the name of the young tenor, but he was excellent and his "*Cielo! e Mar!*" was applauded to the echo.

La Cieca, unless I am mistaken, was played and sung by the same artist I had heard in Venice, and very good her singing was too; but here is a part which needs very careful characterization and must be very attentively studied—in the way of having had a great deal of "study" devoted to it, and also needs a "make-up" which is credible. Surely there is no real need to make this unfortunate o d lady quite so desperately feeble and so dreadfully "tottery", and in order to get the effect of age it is not necessary to cover the face with lines, making it look like a drawing of Clapham Junction!

I longed to say, "Will you let me show you what can be done with careful *shading*, and throw away that pencil you have used much too generously?"

The ballet in this production was very good, the chorus well trained, and the orchestra most ably handled by the conductor.

IL TEATRO DELL' OPERA

"AIDA"

Saturday, April 1, 1934

THERE were three principal memories to take away from this performance. First, the wonderful singing of Ebe Stignani as Amneris.
Stignani is one of Italy's very greatest singers. She has a heaven-sent
voice of a lovely quality, even throughout an exceptionally big compass,
capable of endless degrees of expression and without any changes of
registers to worry about. The secret lies probably in a sound training. She
made a magnificent Amneris. In the second act she revealed the plenitude
of her powers, but it was naturally in her big scene in the last act that she
was able to make the biggest effect. Without ever departing for a moment
from a pure, unforced Cantilena that would have delighted Verdi himself,
she made an unforgettable impression. Her head notes are magnificent,
and she is incapable of uttering an unmusical sound. Little wonder that
she has practically a monopoly in her own line at La Scala.

Next falls to be mentioned the inspiring direction of Edoardo Vitale,
who even excelled his efforts of other presentations. The vigour of his
beat in the second act was irresistible, but equally fine was his beautiful
phrasing of the Prelude and his tone-painting in the Nile scene. He had
a great ovation.

Thirdly, the *messa in sena* was magnificent. All the scenes were
excellent, but for sheer perfection we must mention the Temple Scene,
the Nile Scene—greeted with applause—and the splendid effect of the
last scene of all. Undoubtedly the Teatro dell' Opera has an expert
group of stage technicians.[1]

To come back to the artists, Giacomo Vaghi made a most impressive
High Priest and sang well, though he is lacking in the vocal solidity of a
Pasero or a Pinza. Gaetano Viviani made an effective Amonasro, having a
powerful baritone voice which is apt to be a little irregular.

Zara Pacetti, bless her, having departed to La Scala, we had Mina
Horne. Artists like the delicious Zara are not found on trees, but surely
they could have replaced her more worthily than this? Mina Horne looked

[1] And in addition the finest mechanical equipment I have ever seen.—N. J.

the part—but there it ended. As a singer she was a washout. The subject needs no elaboration. She never got within a mile of her top C in "*O Patria Mia*", and her breathing is pitiful.

Francesso Merli was an adequate Rhadames, doing some things well, producing a fair round tone on the whole but also some poor notes.

The chorus was excellent, and the three ballets all splendid executed.

The difference between a *popolare* and an *alboramento* performance was easily seen. I infinitely prefer the latter. On this occasion the audience was well-meaning but not very discriminating.

"LA TOSCA" (PUCCINI)

(Heard at La Scala, 1936, Covent Garden in the last Italian season before the war, at the Arena Verona during two different seasons, at San Carlo, Naples, 1945, also at Bologna)

THIS opera, as has been said elsewhere, was the combined effort of Puccini, Giacosa and Illica (these two the librettists); the work was adapted from the play of Sardou. As usual, Puccini worked himself into a frenzy over the dramatic as also over the musical side of the play. His knowledge of what was "good theatre" was never more clearly evinced, and the following anecdote is illuminating:

Puccini went in January 1899 to visit Sardou in Paris; he writes to Giulio Ricordi:

"This morning I spent an hour with Sardou, who told me of various things in the *finale* that he does not like. He wants that poor woman dead at any cost. . . . Sardou has introduced an enormous flag on the Castel Sant' Angelo, which flying and flashing (so he says) will make a magnificent effect; go in for the flag, he is keener about that than about the play at the moment. . . . in sketching the panorama for me, Sardou wished the course of the Tiber to pass between St. Peter's and the Castello! I pointed to him that the *flumen* flows past on the other side, just under the Castello, and he, as calm as a fish, answered, 'Oh, that's nothing'!"

One has only to read another of the composer's letters—this time to a friend living in Rome, one Don Pietro Panichelli, to realize how very strongly developed was this astonishing dramatic sense of his.

He is writing of the first act of *Tosca*, and says:

"Now I wish you to do me a kindness. At the end of the first act in the church of S. Andrea della Valle there is sung a solemn *Te Deum* of rejoicing for a victory. Here is the scene: from the sacristy enter the abbot in his mitre, the chapter and all the rest, while the people watch the procession on either side. In front of the stage one of the characters (the baritone) soliloquises independently, or very nearly so, as to what is happening in the background. Now for the sake of the phonic effect, I want some prayers recited during the procession of the abbot and the chapter. Whether it be by the chapter, or the people I need some murmuring of prayers in subdued and natural voices, without intoning, precisely as real prayers are said.

"The *Ecce Sacerdos* is too imposing to be murmured. I know that it is not usual to sing or say anything before the solemn *Te Deum*, which is sung as soon as they reach the High Altar, but I repeat (whether it be right or wrong) that I should like to find something to be murmured during the passage from the sacristy to the altar, either by the people or the chapter; preferably by the latter, because they are more numerous and therefore more effective musically."

The opera was produced in Rome on January 14, 1900, before an acutely nervous audience and company of singers, nervous owing to the various threats that a bomb would be thrown during the performance. However, the number of calls taken in all were twenty-one, and there were five *encores*. The opera was also produced in Paris and New York, where Scotti played Scarpia and is still acclaimed as the finest Scarpia ever seen or heard. Caruso played Cavaradossi, and for one season the soprano was Jeritza, who insisted playing Tosca in a *fair wig*[1]—thus robbing the quarrel scene in Act 1 of much of its credibility. She also sang the famous "*Vissi d'Arte*" lying flat on the stage, so I have been assured by people who saw the production.

The opera has been accused of being "brutal", "decadent", "melo-dramatic"—which last it frankly admits itself to be—and various other epithets; but it remains one of the finest dramatic works ever produced. The three characters who sustain our interest throughout are, of course, Floria Tosca, Cavaradossi and Scarpia—and, indisputably, with the exception of "*Vissi d'Arte*", the second act "belongs to Scarpia".

As in *Turandot* there is no overture. *Tosca* opens with three sharp, rather brutal chords, effective and sinister, suggesting the character of the dominating Scarpia, the dreaded Chief of the Police. There is a photograph existing of the famous Scotti, and what a Scarpia he must have been—in looks to say nothing of his vocal powers! There is the harsh, dominating face of a man who is utterly ruthless, completely without pity.

The music changes for the entrance of the Sacristan; this music is a comedy in itself, and it is obvious that the writing of it gave Puccini great pleasure, for he went to the trouble to "design" a special sign to indicate where the Sacristan shall twitch his shoulders.

Cavaradossi enters, and taking from his pocket a miniature of Tosca, he compares her beauty with that of the woman he has painted as the

[1] I have read that this was not a wig but "her own fair hair".—N.J.

Virgin. His *aria* here, "*Reconsita Armonia*", is very beautiful and essentially lyrical. The plot is too well known to need a detailed account here, sufficient to say that the characterization of Floria Tosca with her tempestuous nature—alternating between passion, jealous rage, tenderness and gentle piety—is as fine and complete as anything which Puccini ever conceived. Her beautiful *aria* sung to Cavaradossi, "*Non La Sospiri La Nostra Casetta*", is a miracle of tenderness.

After her exit, the Sacristan enters again and the orchestration becomes lively once more, until Scarpia appears on the stage accompanied by his "police hound" the horrible Spoletta. The music which marks his entrance is again harsh, and immediately we sense the approach of tragedy. In fact, all through this opera phrases occur again and again denoting that the tragedy is coming nearer. The effect is at once exciting and terrible. It is the same in Scarpia's room at the Farnese Palace, where Scarpia like a great spider sits weaving his web, while the clear, pure voice of Tosca ascends from the Palace where she is singing in a cantata. The purity of her voice as opposed to the air of sinister malevolence in Scarpia's room is very effective. The scene which follows is tense in the extreme. Cavaradossi is brought in, and threatened with torture if he will not divulge the hiding-place of the unfortunate Angelotti. Tosca enters, tempestuous and crazy with grief at the sight of her lover in the hands of the police.

The scene between her and Scarpia is admirable, both musically and dramatically. Scarpia begins by treating her with respectful courtesy, and she answers his questions quietly but guardedly; it is only when she hears the cry of agony from Cavaradossi, who is being tortured to make him speak, that Scarpia's manner changes, and becomes coldly furious, while she changes from the slightly defiant woman to a very frightened and apprehensive one.

With Cavaradossi's exit, with the order that he is to be killed, and his final outburst, "Tremble, Scarpia, butcherly hypocrite!" her last remnants of control give way. Here is Scarpia's great acting opportunity —he is cool, calculating and suave; he polishes a wine-glass carefully, he seats himself and begins to eat "my poor supper", he begins to tell Tosca that no doubt together they can concoct some plan to save her lover. She flings back at him a question, "What is your price?"

He sings that fine *aria*, "*Già Mi Struggea L'Amor Della Diva*", and then, longing to embrace her, rushes towards her. They are interrupted by that sinister drum roll—which the audience come to know so well, and to dread. It is then that she sings her magnificent *aria*, "*Vissi d'Arte*", which has so often been so cruelly murdered by shrieking sopranos, who too often forget that this is a woman in a state of desperate fear, not a harridan screaming defiance!

The scene draws to its close. Tosca will sell herself to Scarpia, and her lover will have only a "mock execution"—"as was done in the case of Count Palmieri, you understand" is the order which Scarpia gives to his loathsome henchman. He goes to his desk to write the permit which will enable Tosca and Cavaradossi to leave Rome for Civitavecchia. She leans, almost exhausted, against the table; her fingers feel the cold touch of steel, she takes the knife. Scarpia comes towards her. "Mine—at last!" he sings. Her reply comes, "At last! Here is the kiss of Tosca," and kills him.

She sets candles at either side of his head, places a crucifix on his breast, and steals out—while drawing nearer comes the *motif* which might be called "the doom *motif*".

The Castello of S. Angelo is one of the most beautiful scenes produced in Italian opera, and when this work is seen at such opera houses as the Teatro dell' Opera at Rome, the San Carlo at Naples, or La Scala at Milan, with all the magnificent potentialities of lighting and scenic effects it is almost breathtaking. There is the early morning, with the great statue of the angel towering above the platform on the roof of the Castello. In the distance, faint and dim, is the dome of St. Peter's. The change from the stormy atmosphere of Scarpia's room is wonderfully done, for here is a dim light, and complete tranquillity, silence only broken by the sound of sheep-bells and the music of a shepherd's pipe playing some old tune, the voice of the shepherd rises clear and pure.

Cavaradossi is brought in, and begins to write his last letter to Tosca; it is here that he sings that heavenly melody, "*E Lucevan Le Stelle*", which ends with the splendid closing words, "*e muoio disperato*". Tosca enters and the great duet follows, in which again the drums are heard and the orchestration becomes more elaborate; later comes their *aria* filled with hope for the future which they will spend together, "*Trionfal Di Nova Speme*". The mock execution which takes place while Tosca watches in admiration her lover's "acting" is quickly over; she waits until they march off, then rushes to where Cavaradossi lies covered with the cloak which Spoletta has flung over him. "Mario! Up quickly! Up—up, Mario!" Then, realizing that he is dead, that the soldiers are rushing back because they have discovered the dead body of Scarpia, Tosca leaps upon the battlements and flings herself over to certain death.

It will be seen that this part offers tremendous scope for dramatic talent; even in that closing scene, "Mario! Up quickly!" an actress can throw shades of tone into her voice ranging from exultation to fear, and fear to agony.

The finest Cavaradossi I have ever listened to is Gigli—there is a tenderness in that splendid voice which cannot be equalled; Lugo sang well, and acted tolerably; Malipiero, handicapped by his lack of inches, both sang and acted very excellently indeed. Curiously enough, I cannot recall the name of a single Scarpia, though one at least was admirable.

I have seen various Toscas. Caniglia's voice is excellent, even though like many other sopranos she tends to grow a little "hard", and when I saw her her acting in Act 2 left much to be desired. I never believed that she was in the least frightened, or that she cared a great deal what happened to the unfortunate Caravadossi. I cannot recall the name of the soprano who appeared with Gigli in Naples, I only remember that she changed her dress between Acts 2 and 3—which I have always felt to be "out of character". Cigna has always moved me deeply in this rôle, and while her *"Vissi d'Arte"* is always applauded tremendously, I find her voice at its best in some of the other *arias*—in the first act particularly.

The orchestration is masterly, and unforgettable.

LA SCALA

"LA TRAVIATA"
(First Produced at the Fenice Theatre, Venice, March 6, 1853)

Thursday, April 12, 1934

LA SCALA can always be counted on to avoid any tendency for a work of this period to seem faded, as is only too easy in less exalted surroundings. *La Traviata* was my first love; I've known every note of it for years, and although I am no longer blind to its shortcomings I love it still. What is more, as staged at La Scala some of the shortcomings surprisingly disappeared. For example, the scenes of gaiety—as usual with Verdi before *Falstaff*—are not to be compared with the emotional parts of the score; specially trite seemed the matadors, etc., in the second scene of Act 2. But this was avoided by the diverting dance set to three measures. Nothing could take away from the conventionalism of the *finale* that follows, however. The last act contains some of Verdi's most moving music. On the whole, *La Traviata* may be the least admirable of the great trio which it forms with *Rigoletto* and *Il Trovatore*, but it is still worth while as the greatest monument to the romanticism of the last century, as well as for the sake of the abundance of true Verdian melody it contains.

Particularly lovely are the Preludes—specially that to the last act—Violetta's exquisitely pathetic *"Addio del Passato"*, the beautifully simple *"Parigi, O Cara, Noi Lasceremo"*, the scene between Germont and Violetta, and in the first act the little duet, *"Un di Felice"*, and the famous but still fresh scene for Violetta.

On this occasion Giuseppina Cobelli, a charming and gifted artist, was to have been the protagonist. For one reason or other—some say 'flu, others are not so complimentary—she was substituted by Gina Cigna, and I must say the result was not as bad as I expected. Save for her uproarious breathing, La Cigna sang with a delicacy and restraint that I hadn't expected of her. It is no wonder she is a favourite at La Scala, for in that theatre her voice is revealed as a splendid organ, and those acid and sometimes rather sharp high notes are soothed into quite thrilling trumpet tones. She threw herself into the part with any amount

160

of abandon, and deserved her warm reception for her very creditable effort. But—she is not a great Violetta. With memories of Muzio and dalla Rizza, she must be definitely the least *traviata* Violetta the Scala has had since the war. If they had to find a substitute quickly, did they not have Iva Pacetti and Mafalda Favero at hand?

Tito Schipa's art is a delight to behold—just as art connoisseurs revel in the work of an old master. His vocal equipment is not on a par with that of Gigli or Lauri-Volpi—or, indeed, many other contemporary Italian tenors. He is rather tremulous at times, and his lower notes are only just there. But his floating *mezza-voce* ravishes the ear, just as we are ravished by the artistry with which he vocalizes his *"Un di Felice"*, his *aria* in the second act, or—above all—*"Parigi, O Cara"*. He is unique. As an actor, he had unconvincing moments, but on the whole he was polished.

Giuseppe Danise is also an exponent of *bel canto*. I must say his voice is not so fine as I had expected after hearing it on the radio in *Favorita*. His art belongs to another generation. He was cradled in the school of Battistini. He met with some disapproval from the gallery; but I must say that, if his art lacks the vividness of the modern school, it seemed to me eminently suited to this work, and a joy to the connoisseur of studied *bel canto*. I am glad I heard him before he quits.

The chorus behaved as only the Scala chorus knows how to. Sergio Failoni—looking very nice—gave a very sympathetic reading of the score. His *tempi* were excellent, his phrasing of the Preludes, beautifully played, worthy of Toscanini himself. The only criticism was that occasionally—both Danise and Schipa were sinners here—the orchestra got on ahead before the soloist finished some *rallentando* or other.

The staging was elegant in the extreme.

It was gala night and the theatre was crammed in all sections. The love for Verdi's opera was as genuine as ever—rapt attention followed the opera all through. There were sixteen calls, and applause at appropriate points throughout the opera.

LA FANCIULLA DEL WEST
(THE GIRL OF THE GOLDEN WEST) (Puccini)

(Heard at the Teatro dell' Opera at Rome in February 1937, and also in Brescia in early 1939)

Andante molto lento

Ch'ella mi cred-a   liber-o e lon-tan-o

*L*A *Fanciulla del West* was derived from a play by David Belasco. In the year 1906 Puccini was staying in Paris on his way to New York; he met his friend, Antinori, who urged him to see a play which was running with immense success at the Belasco Theatre in New York. Puccini saw the production and was much impressed by its possibilities. He immediately began negotiations with Belasco, and on Puccini's return to Italy arranged for Carlo Zangarini to compose the libretto. Later Guelfo Civvinini was taken on to give additional help, owing to his sound theatrical instinct, and the beauty of his poetry.

The first presentation was given at the Metropolitan Opera House, New York, where Toscanini was then acting as artistic director. The rehearsals went smoothly. Toscanini, Tito Ricordi (who had travelled from Italy with Puccini) and Belasco attended them, as well as Gatti Casazza who was anxious to collaborate with Puccini in every possible way.

On December 10, 1910, the opera was produced at the Metropolitan, and was one of the greatest successes imaginable. So great indeed was the enthusiasm that the prices of all seats were raised for the second performance.

The first performance given in Italy was at the Costanzi (now the Teatro dell' Opera) at Rome. Again nothing but praise was given to the new work. The soprano was Burzio, Bassi the tenor and Amato the baritone. The whole of the Press declared that in this work Puccini had "vindicated his right to be included among the greatest Italian composers of opera". Toscanini conducted at the Costanzi.

The music is possibly less melodious than other operas by Puccini, and there is, admittedly, a good deal of recitative which tends to drag a little. The real highlight is the tenor's solo in the last act, "*Ch'Ella Me Creda Libero e Lontano*". This is sheer beauty as Puccini loved to write it, an exquisite melody and, when sung by Francesco Merli as I heard

162

it at the Teatro dell' Opera, it gave him every opportunity to use his fine voice to its best. The Minnie was sung by Corbelli, and not only sung beautifully but acted with discrimination; but to me the part is not attractive. This very sensible young woman in a miner's shirt and top-boots, so slick at her gambling, seems too "commonsensicle" to be the heroine of an opera. Franci was a good sheriff, his voice being clear and powerful without ever degenerating into mere heavy-sounding "noise". De Fabritiis conducted admirably, giving colour and light to some of the heavier passages without, one felt, taking any liberties with the score. The chorus was, as is usual at the Rome house, beautifully drilled and excellently dressed.

The performance as Brescia was, of course, a less impressive affair, as was only to be expected, but it was an excellent production. The conductor was Podesta, who, if he was less brilliant than De Fabritiis, certainly got the best out of his orchestra and never allowed them to play with such vigour that the artists were in danger of not being heard, as is regrettably what happens in some of the smaller Italian opera houses.

The opening chorus of miners and cowboys went with a great deal of *verve*. Mario Bianchi, although his voice had not perhaps the smooth quality for which one looks, had excellent control, and many of his tones were most pleasing; his solo in the last act was sung with real feeling. Gilda della Rizza gave a good piece of characterization in the soprano part of Minnie, coupled with the right degree of hardness and fire, while many of her notes in the lower register were very full and pure. I was told that Viglione Borghese had been singing the part of the sheriff for a very long time, and that his voice was no longer in the full flush of its beauty. It was the first time I had heard him, and I admit that while there were traces of the years he had left behind, his acting ability, the knowledgeable manner in which he handled his part, filled me with admiration. I should have liked to have heard his Scarpia when his voice was at its best.

The rest of the cast, while not being particularly outstanding, were just a little more than merely adequate.

ARENA DI VERONA

"Giulietta é Romeo"

August 10, 1939

"*Paolo, datemi pace*"
Francesca da Rimini (Zandonai)

FIRST of all let us get a few facts straight. Riccardo Zandonai was born in 1883. *Conchita* (1911) showed that he had great talent, and suggested that he was only waiting for a subject which would really fire his imagination before giving us the measure of his latent possibilities: then in 1914 came *Francesca da Rimini*. If you count up the number of operas written in the current century which have shown themselves to be possessed of lasting vitality, I'm very much afraid you will have difficulty in reaching a round dozen—even if you take for granted the operas of Puccini! *Francesca da Rimini* is certainly one of the few. It was an achievement all the more remarkable in that Zandonai, in setting himself the task of turning a D'Annunzio drama into an opera, succeeded brilliantly where Mascagni, Montemezzi, Franchetti, Pizzetti (to name the most outstanding) had failed: nobly in the case of Pizzetti's *Fedra*, dismally in the case of Mascagni's *Parisina* and Franchetti's *Figlia di Jorio*. It is significant that Puccini, *homme du theatre* to the depths of his soul, in the end gave up the idea of the projected collaboration with D'Annunzio which, we know, seemed several times to be on the point of maturing between 1906 and 1912.

Make no mistake about it, *Francesca*, in spite of the fact that it has its faults, above all in the second act (a weakness inherent in the drama itself, for this was the scene which was largely responsible for turning the first night of the play into a riotous failure), is a masterpiece. It is an opera which gets under your skin, once you have heard it three or four times. My adoration for it borders on the fanatical, and it is remarkable the way I keep finding people all over Italy with whom a mutual sympathy is quickly established by reason of the fact that we are each ready and willing to spend hours on end enthusing over the opera.

However, if I start talking about *Francesca* I may never get on to the subject of *Giulietta* at all, so let us advance beyond 1914 and see what Zandonai did next. Or, rather, next but one, for we shall pass lightly over the appearance at Pesaro in 1919 of a trivial farce entitled *La Via della Finestra* which gives rise only to speculation as to how the composer came to waste his time on such worthless material.

Let us now make one of those whimsical digressions which are the essence of good form in criticism of the theatre in the best Agatian manner. We know how it is in Hollywood: after a smash hit like, say, "The Thin Man", Mr. Solomon Zizzbaum gets the boys together, and in due course their organized travail brings forth "Another Thin Man"—what could be more practical and natural and, above all, profitable?

But it's not just as simple as all that for an operatic composer because, you see, a sequel is impossible: quite frequently it seems to happen that the hero and/or heroine dies a tragic and protracted death at the end of Act 4. So, having sung the immortal passion of Paolo and Francesca, Zandonai looks round for another pair of Great Lovers—one can see Mr. Zizzbaum benignly nodding approval. He writes *La Via della Finestra* to keep his hand in, but his heart is not in his work. Then—he has it! Romeo and Juliet. Of course, Bellini and Morlacchi and Gounod and several others had already had the same idea, but he does not allow a little thing like that to stand in his way any more than Solomon Z. would. Had not Verdi's *Otello* consigned Rossini's to the limbo of historical curiosities?

So—*coraggio*, and to work! Arturo Rossato furnished the libretto, and in case any future listener possessed of more acute sensibility than mine should feel disposed to hold up his hands to high Heaven in pious horror at the non-appearance of seventeen of the twenty-one characters in Shakespeare (among them Mercutio, Friar Lawrence and the Nurse), I shall forthwith confound him and indeed score off him by stating that Rossato based his version on the original *conte* by Da Porta from which Shakespeare cribbed the idea, and further, to absolve himself beyond equivocation of a possible charge of sacrilege towards the memory of our poet, he chose the disarming expedient of calling it *Juliet and Romeo*. (I suppose it is too much to hope that anyone hasn't heard the story of the foreign conductor at Covent Garden in the last century who was asked if he had visited Stratford-on-Avon. "Ah yes, the birthplace of the well known writer of opera librettos," said he brightly.)

One of the first requirements of a good "book" for a composer to get his teeth into is that the plot shall be INTELLIGIBLE, even if the artists' diction is of the ludicrously inefficient standard prevailing, above all, on the English operatic stage. Local colour is all very well, but sub-plots are an encumbrance and a damned nuisance. Tito Ricordi did a very useful job of pruning with the overloaded *Francesca*, cutting out the inevitable D'Annunzian extravagances and exuberant absurdities while preserving all the incomparable poetry which was just crying out to be set to music. Similarly, Rossato may be no Boito, but he knows his stuff and provid a taut, consistently developed and by no means inelegant libretto.

On the evening of February 14, 1922, *Giulietta e Romeo* had its *première* at the old Teatro Costanzi in Rome, conducted by the composer and interpreted by Gilda dalla Rizza, Miguel Fleta, Carmelo Maugeri and Luigi Nardi in the leading rôles. The *chiamate*[1] attained the comforting figure of twenty-eight (let us respect by all means the venerable custom of the Italian critics of accepting the religiously counted number of curtain-calls as the thermometer of the success or otherwise of a *première*).

The consensus of opinion was that Zandonai had presented *Francesca* with a healthy younger sister. Of course, there were those who expressed a less-favourable impression. Puccini, for example, wrote in the following strain to his dear friend Sybil Seligman: "I heard *Romeo* last night —a disaster! Ugly ornamentations in the orchestra and shrieks from the stage—no heart, no feeling. And the libretto—very far from Shakespeare!" Of course, no one is more savage than a composer, even the most good-natured of them, when confronted by an opera by one of his colleagues—not if the colleague has the bad taste to write a successful one, anyway!

As a corollary to the above, it is amusing to find this passage in Zandonai's reminiscences of the first night: "All at once the crowd makes way, respectful and impressed, and Puccini steps forward with out-stretched arms. We embrace in silence, with emotion, while the whole room strains its ears to catch the pearls of wisdom about to fall from the lips of the creator of Mimi, of Manon, of Butterfly. No doubt the judgment he is about to express will become historic—to be telegraphed immediately to all corners of the earth: three-inch headlines perhaps, in tomorrow's *New York Sun*! Puccini smiles affectionately, his eyes very kind, puts an arm round my shoulders, and says: 'Well, young Ricky, and how was the quail shooting last summer in Val di Fiemme?'! I heave a sigh of relief, and we engage in an animated discussion on our mutual passion until the bell warns us that Romeo is ready to set out on the journey to the bier of his beloved."

One likes that story, somehow. Dear Puccini! Much too honest to be hypocritical about it.

But now—enough digressions! It is high time I was tackling the job I set out to do—viz. to co-ordinate my impressions of the opera. Twice

[1] Curtain calls.

before, to amuse myself, I have scribbled a bit about it: once in 1934; that was my first hearing of a Zandonai opera—before I knew *Francesca*, even—and, except for the *Cavalcata*, it bored me. Without a trace of smugness, I must say it amazes me how insensible I was, musically, in those days. In 1936, after a very fine performance conducted by Serafin at the Rome House, I wrote roundly, "This is one of the half-dozen greatest operas ever written"! ! ! These indiscretions belonged to the days when I could at least *tolerate Pagliacci*, and before the miraculous perfection of *Falstaff*, after repeated hearings, had dawned on my grateful perceptions. I am a little wiser now, in spite of having so much still to learn, and I have heard *Giulietta e Romeo* seven times, so there is rather less danger of such very hot air being talked.

To be quite honest, after twenty-five years we must still point to *Francesca* as Zandonai's *chef-d'œuvre*: he has never given us anything to compare with it. Only two of its successors have given proof of inherent vitality: *I Cavalieri di Ekebu* (from Selman Lagerlof's famous novel), which is so often performed at the Royal Opera in Stockholm, and *Giulietta e Romeo*. For—*pace*, Puccini!—*Giulietta* has qualities enough to be well worthy of a more frequent appearance in the *cartelloni* of the leading Italian theatres.

The hand that surrounded the figure of Francesca with a musical atmosphere of such exquisite beauty and sympathy, which made so truly dramatic that scene where Malatestino betrays Paolo to their brother, which penned the charming scenes between Francesca and her hand-maids, the irresistibly touching episode of the parting of Francesca and her little sister and the equally delicate scene in the last act between Francesca and the tenderly solicitous Biancofiore . . . that hand has by no means lost its touch. The musical characterization of Romeo (with one lapse, of which more anon) is consistently convincing and truly poetic, while in the last act the composer has "felt" the drama of Romeo's despair with such genuine emotion that we, too, are deeply moved. The music associated with Romeo is the best in the opera—but a word of warning! (particularly appropriate in connection with this performance at Verona). The rôle demands a tenor who is also a sensitive artist—*rara avis, purtroppo*!

Giulietta is a pale figure by comparison with Francesca, and one wonders greatly that Zandonai did not write the music for a genuinely lyric soprano instead of a *lirico-spinto*—often very decidedly *spinto*. She too has her moments, notably in the duets with Romeo in Acts 1 and 2, but—this is not Shakespeare's Juliet, and if it is Da Porta's, *tant pis*! The character of Tebaldo (Tybalt) is delineated by vigorous and undeniably effective declamation, but here again a comparison with the treatment of the hunchbacked Gianciotto reacts all in favour of the

167

earlier opera: Tebaldo with all his threats and proud recriminations remains a melodramatic puppet, while Gianciotto comes to life before our eyes and is a real figure of tragedy whom we can understand and sympathize with even while he repels us.

A feature of *Francesca* is the talent displayed by Zandonai for passages evocative of "atmosphere", achieved by his mastery of orchestral colour and harmony with an individual and appropriately archaic flavour, and by his very successful descriptive use of the chorus—all of which, of course, would be of little avail if he had not a rich vein of thematic raw material, for fine clothes will not cloak vapidity.

Now, the scene in Act 2 of *Giulietta* between Juliet and her companions is a flagrant and inferior imitation of the corresponding scene in Act 3 of *Francesca*, and so, unacceptable to those who love the earlier opera: but in Act 1 we have several characteristic episodes, such as the snatch of ribald song from the tavern, the passing of the Guard which quickly restores order—curiously impressive, this—and the finely poetic effect of the *finale* of the act as dawn breaks over Verona after a troubled night. An effect legitimately obtained, the ingredients being an ounce of colouring from the wind instruments, celeste and campane, a generous helping of inspiration and a dash of internal female chorus to add flavour.

Zandonai's distinct flair for effective "curtains" is worthy of note, for it is a sure hall-mark of the born operatic composer. Is there, I wonder, in all opera an act that closes more magically than Act 1 of *Francesca*?

The first act, then, is good: there is plenty of action, nothing superfluous, and only one serious defect. The balcony scene was naturally intended to be one of the highlights of the opera, and the first part of it, with the shimmering, ethereal *motif* sung high up by the violins, and with Juliet's fine outburst, "*Ah! Siete bello e mio*", does not deceive our expectations, and is doubly effective after the turbulent scenes at which we have assisted. Alas! Zandonai has written a climax to this duet in the more apoplectic Mascagnian vein, empty and emphatic, noisy enough to constitute a breach of the peace and cause the listener to speculate as to what on earth the Guard can be up to that it does not hurry along to see what all the rumpus is about.

The second act is the weakest, though effective in the theatre, but it improves with the entrance of Tebaldo. Unforgettable is the lacerating exclamation of the orchestra which flares out at each of Tebaldo's increasingly violent taunts of "*Leva la Spada!*"; there is, too, an excellent example when Tebaldo is killed of how eloquent a dramatic silence can be following upon a scene of extreme violence, and there is that touching little duet between Romeo and Juliet—which has an affinity with the lovely "*Lontano, Lontano*" in Act 3 of Boito's *Mefistofele*

—while subsequently the despair of the lovers' hopeless parting is genuinely suggested.

In the third act occurs the gem of the score, when Romeo, exiled in Mantua, learns by chance from the mouth of a troubadour from Verona of the "death" of his beloved. Hearken, O Will of Avon! Zandonai and Rossato have thee whacked to a frazzle in this scene! The troubadour, seated on a table outside a tavern in the *piazza*, intones his melancholy song, accompanying himself on his lute. At the climax of his narration, "*Che e Morta Giulietta Capuleto*", Romeo, who has been sitting a little way off, remote and indifferent, freezes with horror; then he turns ferociously on the troubadour in a vain attempt to cancel the fateful words by forcing them back down his throat. All at once he recovers control of himself. The frightened minstrel says with timid compassion, "Peace, good sir." "Peace I shall find, brother," replies Romeo gently, giving him a purse; "and now sing me the lament again, but softly, in the shadows, that it may seem the distillation of my silent grief." The singer complies, and Romeo sobs, at first restrainedly, but finally breaking down with the abandon of a child. This scene is magnificent theatre, and would melt the stoniest heart to tears.

The famous *Cavalcata*—an orchestral interlude depicting Romeo's dash to Verona—with its pounding rhythm and its abundance of sound and fury, is familiar to everyone in Italy owing to its frequent performance in the concert-hall. It is an irresistible piece of descriptive music— more so in the theatre, when the choral interjections of the words with which Romeo's mind is obsessed ("*Giulietta mia! Giulietta mia! Ah morta! Morta!*") are not omitted. The *bis* is invariably demanded as a matter of course. I shall never forget the electrifying effect on me of hearing this interlude for the first time, when the opera was broadcast from Genova in 1934. Up to this point, as I have already remarked, I was not impressed. But this brought me leaping out of my armchair, beside myself with excitement and roaring, "*Bis!*" in the hope that my cries would carry all the way to Genova and mingle with the frenzied shouts of the audience. Whether they did or not I can't say, but I do know that my father came down in his pyjamas to see what all the noise was about, and we got our *bis*. . . .

The best thing in the final scene is Romeo's beautiful and pathetic invocation, "*Giulietta Son Io, Io, Non Mi Vedi?*" which roused the deepest compassion in the composer. The last duet is peaceful and suggestive, if of no great musical significance. After the *première* it was opportunely pruned of its verbosity, but Zandonai restored the cuts in the present performance, which was a pity. There are no heroics at the end: Giulietta and Romeo lie side by side, hand in hand like two children. The rising sun through the window of the crypt touches the peaceful smile on their

169

lips, and the air is warm with the echoes of the love-song we heard at the close of the first act. At least, that is how it should be, and usually is, but the producer made a mess of it at Verona.

To sum up: perhaps only intermittently, but notably in the scene of the troubadour, does Zandonai reach the exalted heights of *Francesca* while the music of *Giulietta* contains more numerous and graver defects than that of its predecessor. One must agree with the late Alberto Gasco, such an exceedingly reliable and readable critic by the way, when he says that *"Giulietta* would profit immensely from an ulterior examination by the composer with a view to cutting out certain episodes, and revising others so that they might become less an assault on our attention by their sheer emphasis and more eloquent by virtue of truly musical expressiveness." But, especially to those who are grateful to Zandonai for giving us *Francesca*, *Giulietta e Romeo* remains a very interesting work which they, and intelligent opera-goers in general, will always listen to *con buona volontà.*

The performance was good, but by no means beyond criticism. It was an inestimable advantage to be present at the *prova generale.* Apart from giving my companion a chance to get to know the opera (she had never heard a note of Zandonai's music), we were sitting in about the one place in the Arena where the acoustics are fairly satisfactory—i.e. about twelve rows back. I do not want to be misunderstood: I think the open-air theatre is a *grand* institution which does an immense amount of good in Italy, but acoustically these theatres all leave a great deal to be desired. At the first performance itself we were in the "first-come-first-served" section at the back of the *platea* (having "got in on our Wilkies", as a very dear friend of mine who delights in all things theatrical, an old "pro" herself, would put it!), and it was astounding how much we lost: one had almost to strain one's ears to hear the *"Cavalcata"* even, which blasts you out of your seat like dynamite in a closed theatre. The dress rehearsal went right through without a stop, like clockwork, not a single repetition. It was like a sixth performance of the opera, whereas the *première* of *Faust* on the previous Sunday was only too reminiscent of a *prima prova d'insieme.* . . .

So evidently Zandonai had insisted on a very considerable number of rehearsals. It was, of course, rather an important occasion for him— at least 100,000 spectators would be hearing his opera in the course of the four performances allotted, and surely Verona is the inevitable setting for *Giulietta e Romeo* if ever there was one?

Zandonai conducted superbly. He is the only living composer who ought to be allowed to conduct his own works. He has a real talent for the interpretative art, a very unusual gift in a creative artist. Mario Cordone, one of the finest conductors of *Francesca da Rimini*, once remarked to me that Zandonai often passed slips on the part of the orchestra without comment during a rehearsal of the opera which Cordone watched him handling. No doubt Zandonai's rehearsal schedule was not so generously budgeted for at Malta, where this incident took place, and he was probably more concerned in securing eloquent than literally precise playing: in short, a few spelling mistakes were relatively unimportant if the thought was expressed convincingly. At any rate, at the Arena the orchestra played magnificently, and responded to Zandonai's leading in a way which showed how he had fired their imagination and enthusiasm. A funny little man like a monkey he is, with a large head and dome-like brow, but on the rostrum very much the fulcrum of the performance.

On the stage, not such a rosy picture can be painted. The choice of Alessandro Granda as Romeo was an inspired piece of mis-casting. God knows, tenors are a thick-headed, unimaginative, conceited, exasperating race—*bête comme un tenor*, you know!—but there are exceptions, and there was no need to choose this man for the part of Romeo Montecchio. He made the death scene ludicrous, and incited murderous feelings in more than one usually mild enough breast. I need not enlarge on the subject, which is a painful one to me: all I shall add is, I hope next time I see *Giulietta e Romeo* the tenor will be Jose Luccioni, a heaven-sent "natural" for this part. Intelligent, aristocratic, voice exactly right, figure slim and boyish, face sensitive and—yes, beautiful: Zandonai's Romeo.

Giulietta was Gabriella Gatti, who is such a *musician* that conductors love working with her. A singer it is a delight to listen to, so intelligent—and such impeccable taste. Her soft notes are lovely, and carried in these wide-open spaces in a most astonishing manner. Her high notes are not so well produced: too far back, and often coming from a tight throat, lips drawn back and one row of teeth almost touching the other. She sang "*Sono La Vostra Sposa*" like an angel. Physically not the ideal Giulietta—but, as I said before, Zandonai made this difficult by writing the rôle for a *lirico-spinto*. If I were casting the opera I should choose my Giulietta from the following, all of them vocally suited to it, all of them intelligent artists: Maria Carbone, Franca Somigli, Sara Scuderi, Iris Adami-Corradetti, Pia Tassinari.

That superb Zandonai interpreter, Carmel Maugeri, whose name is associated with the part of Gianciotto in *Francesca* in much the same inevitable way in which *Falstaff* makes us think at once of Stabile, created the part of Tebaldo and has remained unapproachable in it ever since, which was a severe handicap for Luigi Borgonuovo from the start. He was adequate: I really don't think there is anything more to be said. The only member of the cast who was thoroughly satisfactory was the excellent Adelio Zagonara in the small but important part of the troubadour. I remembered how he had acted the others off the stage as Malatestino in *Francesca* in Rome in 1937 . . .

So often it happens thus, that the best artistry comes from one of the "small part" players, while the stars with the big names comport themselves with revoltingly complacent insensibility! I feel I owe it to Mafalda Chiorboli to mention the enthusiasm with which she played her minute part in Act 1. She sat next to us at the rehearsal, after her active participation was over, and she had dined—or at any rate wined—very well, and a lively companion she was too, both there and over an *espresso* in the *piazza* later. Zandonai, she told us, is a delightful man, full of faith in his work, and believing firmly that, after he is dead, his operas will be *universally* hailed as masterpieces as Verdi's and Puccini's are. Which is all very satisfactory, because it is not an idle boast but the creed of an artist who knows his worth and is too honest to assume false modesty of the kind which courts flattery.

The producer was Mario Frigerio, expert in the handling of big crowds at the Arena. The first scene of the third act was a grand affair, with sheep, goats, horses, the two huge dogs Zandonai is devoted to— Giosta and Biancofiore—and masses and masses of people. Very animated and colourful and just the thing for a stage like the Arena's. What one missed was the subtle psychological touches of the Frigerio who, rather unexpectedly, produced Massenet's intimate and profoundly moving *Jongleur de Notre Dame* so beautifully at La Scala that I went to see it four times and was brokenhearted at having to leave Milan without seeing the other three performances. But I imagine when he heard he was to have Granda as Romeo he just shrugged his shoulders and said to himself, "*Beh! Lasciamo andare.*"

The scenery—well, I don't profess to be a judge of that. "I knows what I likes and I knows what I doesn't like": in the latter category are included all "arty" and impressionistic settings, except of course when we are in the realms of fantasy, as for example in the operas of Rimsky-Korsakov. Otherwise, I must say I fail to see why a scene should not look more or less like whatever it is supposed to represent. Naturally, the Arena went in for broad effects, and on the whole the results seemed to me to be satisfactory. Nothing that jarred, as several things did in *Faust*. Such a profusion of that colour which I should describe—probably quite erroneously—as russet red would, I feel sure, have induced a sense of monotony in the gentleman who writes in the *Corriere della Sera* with such devastating virtuosity about the production side of the performances at La Scala: an earnest soul whose analysis is unhappily so technical that it is almost on a par as a weariness to the flesh with that school of musical criticism which imagines that it can only sound convincing if it talks about "postludes brought to a close on a pedal of A, the cadence being retarded by four chords forming an *arpeggio* of a diminished seventh, each grade serving as a tonic for an unprepared chromatic inversion".

A grand night to look back on: *chi sa quando si ripetera?*

ENVOI: *Giulietta e Romeo* was the last of the four operas *in programma* for the 1939 season at the Arena: this gives me a convenient excuse for saying a few words about the future which I feel are particularly opportune at the present moment, when the Arena is no longer a unique institution to which tens of thousands of Italians inevitably gravitated every August from all over the peninsula, as if drawn by some irresistible force. Open-air theatres have sprung up like mushrooms within the last three summers, and now there is not a centre in Italy that has not its Castello Sforzesco, its Terme di Caracalla, or its Piazza del Comune. To speak plainly, Verona must look to its laurels. I am one of those who would like to see Verona continue to lead the field, not only for sentimental reasons but because of its splendid pioneer work and its quarter of a century of praiseworthy activity and unchallenged superiority, because Verona is such a lovable town and the Arena is inestimably the finest natural setting for open-air opera, both from the aesthetical and practical points of view. Competition, when it is fair, is a healthy and stimulating thing.

Those responsible for the future destiny of the Arena di Verona have a great responsibility and a great chance, if they can prove themselves worthy of it—if, that is, they are men of vision and resolution. After twenty-seven years, they must be well aware of the fact that open-air opera is a new medium presenting particular problems of its own. They must ask themselves, in the light of a not inconsiderable experience, how far these problems have been studied and resolved, and what are the conclusions to be drawn. In case anyone should consider it uncalled-for presumption on my part to be writing in this strain, I must point out that in the last few seasons it would appear from the actions of the directors themselves that they are capable of a cardinal mistake which must astound Zenatello and his colleagues, who so courageously planned and executed the earlier seasons at the Arena.

The open-air theatre must have a repertoire of its own. It is absurd to imagine that all operas which are recognized as masterpieces, and in which the public of the *teatri chiusi* never tire of hearing, can be transplanted lock, stock and barrel to such a stage and such an auditorium as the Arena. Last year *La Bohème* was performed there. No doubt this monstrous folly was perpetrated so as to give Giuseppe Lugo the chance to exhibit himself to his fellow-citizens in one of his most famous rôles; but that is an explanation, and in no way an extenuating circumstance, while in any case it was not the first time such a thing had happened. It would not surprise me in the least to hear that next year they are contemplating giving *La Traviata*—an opera which has actually been performed at the Castello Sforzesco and other open-air theatres! To perform an intimate work such as *Bohème* or *Traviata* or *L'Elisir d'Amore* on the vastest stage in the world is a manifest absurdity and an artistic crime. In the earlier seasons of the Arena's activities they had more sense: they chose operas like *Aïda* and *Il Figliuol Prodigo* and *Mefistofele*: grand opera in the real sense of that much misused term.

Let the Arena, then, seek inspiration for its own sound tradition, and build up a repertoire which will show the way to, and become the norm for, all the open-air theatres; and let the standards of presentation of that repertoire prevailing at the Arena be such that the most its rivals can hope to do is to approach these standards as closely as possible. 1937 was a peak year in the short operatic history of the amphitheatre: surely the lesson of the new enthusiasm inspired by Vittorio Gui and Carl Ebert, the producers, and the new artistic level attained, will not be allowed to go to seed? The Arena is an exceptional theatre, and demands exceptional artists to realize its immense possibilities. Ebert is *persona non grata* in Italy now: let us hope this is only a temporary misfortune for the Italian operatic stage. In the meantime, the best men available must hold the fort. Gui shook the dust of Verona from his feet after the famous "incident" over the *encore* in *Turandot*[1], but he might well be persuaded to return if he felt that a real artistic satisfaction would ensue.

As these remarks are intended to be in the nature of *constructive* criticism, I shall conclude by giving detailed suggestions for the 1940 season at the Arena, but before I do so I should like to make one last point which incidentally serves the purpose of linking this postscript to the subject matter of the article which precedes it. Last season new ground was broken by the inclusion in the programme of *Giulietta e Romeo*—a work by an eminent living composer. The success of this venture should have suggested to the directors the possibility that there are certain operas of the modern repertoire which are particularly suited to performance in an open-air theatre—which indeed may actually gain by their transference to a more spacious setting than that of the *teatri chiusi*. I have in mind two such operas as I write—Respighi's *La Fiamma* and Pizzetti's *Fra Gherardo*. No doubt there are others which further reflection would discover.

Arena di Verona—1940

GUGLIELMO TELL: Conductor, Gino Marinuzzi; Producer, Koloman Nadasdy.

Cast: Gabriella Gatti, Todor Mazaroff, Alessandro de Sved, Tancredi Pasero.

[1] Referred to elsewhere in this book.—N. J.

LA FIAMMA: Conductor, Gino Marinuzzi; Producer, Gustav de Olah.
Cast: Gina Cigna, Licia Albanese, Ebe Stignani, Angelica Crawcenko, Jose Luccioni, Carlo Tagliabue.

DON CARLO: Conductor, Vittorio Gui; Producer, Guido Salvini.
Cast: Maria Caniglia, Ebe Stignani, Todor Mazaroff, Francesco Merli, Francesco Valentino, Tancredi Pasero, D. Baronti.

LA DANNAZIONE DI FAUST: Conductor, Vittorio Gui; Producer, Piero Scharoff.
Cast: Pia Tassinari, Giovanni Voyer, Alessandro de Sved, Salvatore Baccaloni.

A *cartellone* which would make the eyes of any opera lover pop out of his head! And what of *Prince Igor, Simon Boccanegra, Freischutz, Boris,* Boito's *Nerone, La Wally, The Flying Dutchman, Sansone e Dalila?* It is so easy to think of operas for this "open-air repertoire" that one cannot help believing that, sooner or later, a more enlightened policy will be adopted by Pino Donati and his colleagues at the Arena: who knows but that one day they may even get Max Reinhardt to produce *Oberon?*

Additional Notes

NOTE. One must regard this article on the opera at the Arena as particularly interesting to those who have read the other criticisms of Jimmy Robertson, for it is evident in this that he was really spreading his wings and launching out into a critical study of some length and considerable imagination. This was what he had always planned and hoped to do, but his constant remark was always, "But not until I know more about it." He was not content with merely visiting the opera itself, he definitely studied every opera, made himself conversant with the author's works, and so was able to draw comparisons which are of great value. More than that, they rouse the curiosity of the reader, and fire him—or her—with a wish to know more of the various operas referred to, and other singers who, Jimmy felt, were "ideal" for the various rôles.

I cannot remember why *Giulietta e Romeo* was the only opera at the Arena which he attended that year, for in addition were given *Faust, Rigoletto* and *Tosca.*

In *Rigoletto* the Duke was played by Lugo, Rigoletto by that admirable artist Tagliabue, Gilda, by Margherita Carosio, and the conductor was Franco Capuana, who went to London with the first Italian opera company after the war.

Tosca was sung by Maria Caniglia—who I have never cared for in this rôle, though I admit that in various other operas she is admirable; Lugo sang Cavaradossi, and Antenore Reali, Scarpia. Again Capuana conducted.

In *Faust* we had the great *basso* Tancredi Pasero, who was magnificent, Malipiero, who though his size has always been against him attaining the success which he well deserves, was excellent, and Francesco Valentino —who appeared at Glyndebourne in *Macbeth* with considerable distinction—sang Valentino. The Margherita was Mafalda Favero and beautifully she sang in this rôle. Again Capuana conducted.

Giulietta e Romeo was, as Jimmy has said, under the direction of the author himself. As he has given so complete an account of this opera there is no need for me to add anything to his comments.

There was almost an "incident" during this season, when into the huge box of the *authorita* at the back of the Arena were ushered with great ceremony half a dozen high-ranking German officers. I think that I am right in saying that *Tosca* was the opera for the evening of their illustrious visit. Capuano conducted, and as was always done in those days, the Fascist anthem, "*Giovinezza*", was played and everyone stood. Then again he called his orchestra to attention, and our ears were assailed by "*Deutschland, Deutschland über Alles*". I glanced round the Arena and saw that certainly ten per cent of the Italian audience sat down while this was being played. Then followed—and I could scarcely believe my ears, that the Arena's ancient walls should be so insulted and degraded —the *Horst Wessel*! There was a little ripple of noise which ran through the audience, a stir, and certainly at least fifty per cent of the people present sat down; including a certain Contessa of Verona, who holds a very old, noble and honoured name. She not only sat down herself, but motioned to the long row of guests she had brought with her to do the same. Two stout German tourists who were standing immediately behind me leaned forward, and in true Teutonic style hissed into my ear as I sat there that I must be a Jew! I replied with a statement which is only twenty-five per cent true, "I am."

The horrible music ended, there was no applause, and apart from the fact that the subject is vile and disgusting, why should there be applause for music (save the mark!) which is of so poor a quality as to be unworthy of the name? The Contessa turned to me and said in Italian, very loudly and clearly, "May I be allowed to offer you my sincere apologies—I am ashamed!"

Interior of La Fenice at Venice

The Memorial to Verdi at Parma. (In every niche is a statue of some character from one of the Verdi operas. Happily this memorial was only very slightly damaged during the war.)

My thoughts went flying to Vittorio Gui, who rather than do something which he thought musically wrong, rather than allow anyone to dictate to him when he was conducting—left the chair. I remembered how Toscanini—the greatest of them all—had faced the fury of the whole Fascist Party, had risked his life and had shaken the dust of the country he loved off his feet rather than obey an order which he felt had no right to be given!

The opera that evening was spoilt for me at least; all the time I was conscious of the high-ranking officials sitting smugly in their box, and I could not refrain from wondering if that opera had been a completely wise choice.

Cavaradossi's cry of, "Vittoria! Vittoria!" his splendid defiance of the tyrant Scarpia might, had they been possessed of any imagination, have sounded like a warning. And surely Tosca's cry before she leaps from the battlements of S. Angelo must have rung unpleasantly in their ears: "*O Scarpia, avante a Dio.*"

—N. J.

In 1947 the Arena is to be open again for the opera season. The names of the artists are not yet published; the operas are to be *The Pearl Fishers* (*Les Pêcheurs de Perles* of Bizet), *Carmen* (Bizet) and the *Aïda* of Verdi. Unless this programme is changed, one might ask, "Why two operas by the same author?" It is not a Bizet celebration, for he was born in 1839, and died in 1875!

TURANDOT (Puccini)

Heard at the Arena, Verona (open-air theatre), also La Scala, Milan, both in 1938; again at Novarro at a special gala performance in 1937, also at Rovigo in the same year. Various other performances, including one at Covent Garden and at the Teatro dell'Opera, Rome.

Turandot

UNFORTUNATELY, Jimmy Robertson left no records regarding his impressions of this opera, but both he and I have always held it in great admiration; indeed I would go so far as to hold that it is the finest of all Puccini's operas. Not—and this cannot be sufficiently insisted upon—the most lovable, or possibly the most melodious, but for sheer greatness, and for that unerring sense of the theatre which the master had developed to such an extent, *Turandot* stands alone.

In one of his letters—and what charming letters they are!—Puccini writes, "I believe that God touched me with the tip of His finger and said, 'You can write music, but remember only music for the theatre!'" Again when he visited Sardou in Paris, the author, listening to Puccini's ideas for the opera *La Tosca*, exclaimed, "Ah, you are a man of the theatre!"

And how true that was, and what knowledge of the theatre Puccini possessed, what a realization of dramatic possibilities, what a sense of characterization, and what a judgment of real "situations"! A considerable amount of rubbish has been written regarding this, his last opera, left unfinished at the time of his tragic death in Brussels on Saturday, November 29, 1924. The opera was produced at La Scala, on April 25, 1926, with Toscanini conducting. The Principessa for this performance was Rosa Raisa.

Now, with regard to my statement that a "considerable amount of rubbish" has been written regarding this opera, let me elucidate what I mean precisely.

People talk lightly about "the unfinished opera of Puccini". I have even heard those who declared that they could tell exactly where, as Toscanini said at the first performance, "The Master laid down his pen", and where the music was composed by another hand. That Alfano did

178

his best, and that his best is very good, no one will deny; but was *Turandot* left in such an unfinished state after all?

Turn again to Puccini's own letters, and see what he himself says. This letter is dated January 23, 1924, he is writing from his home at Viareggio. He writes of *Turandot* and the work that he is doing on the score:

"I am certainly not coming to Milan just now. I cannot leave my work on Act 3, which I shall begin to orchestrate today or tomorrow, and in Milan I am incapable of writing a single note."

Again, on February 11, 1924, he writes: "I have almost finished the orchestration of Act 2, and I can assure you that it is going to be beautiful."

In September of the same year he is working at the great duet between the Princess and Calaf, which occurs in Act 2, after the death of Liu. "It must be a great duet. These two almost superhuman beings descend through love to the level of mankind, and this love must in the end take possession of the whole stage in a great orchestral peroration." And lastly, on October 10, 1924, he writes, after having seen the throat specialists: "Is it really true that I am not to work any more? Not to finish *Turandot?* There was so little still to do for the completion of the famous duet." And, "Here I am! Poor me!" for the letter is written from the Institut Chirurgical, Brussels. "They say that I shall have six weeks of it. You can imagine how pleased I am. And *Turandot?*" It is a tragic story.

I have heard this opera many times, and in many places, seen it presented simply—or as simply as is compatible with its subject—on such stages as Novarro and Rovigo. I have seen it at the great Arena at Verona, where on that immense stage wonderful scenic effects were obtained, and I have seen it in the majestic setting of La Scala, where the whole production was splendid and dignified. I have seen it at Covent Garden. Two of these productions stand out in my memory most vividly—La Scala and the Arena.

I notice that in one of his "records" of operas seen Jimmy remarks of Gina Cigna "she should make an excellent Turandot". To me she is the ideal Turandot, not only for the quality of her voice but for the careful characterization which she gives to the part—and it is both difficult and intricate. I turned a few moments ago to an exquisite photograph of Jeritza in the part. She looks magnificent, lovely and completely charming—but she is not Turandot ("Thou who with ice art girded"). I have another photograph of Scacciati in the part, she is slim, beautiful, with a head-dress which appears to be made of stiffened lace, her robes falling softly to her feet. Behind her hangs a Benares brass tray of the type found in "oriental cafés"—which does nothing to enhance the illusion that this is a Princess of Old China!

Cigna not only wears the robes—authentic—of Old China, but her whole make-up, her movements, show a great perception, and tremendous attention to the character with all its intricacies and implications.

Her eyes are made to take on an oriental slant—achieved by a little device which she contrived when she first played the part; her face is pale, the mouth heavily made up, but in no way made to look "soft" and "bow-like"; it is painted to look hard and rather large. Her finger-nails are shields which are slipped on, giving the effect of the elongated nails of Chinese aristocrats.

She looks beautiful, completely cold and inhuman, as Puccini tried to paint her.

There have been many arguments regarding Cigna's voice; I have heard it called hard, unsympathetic and unpleasing; I have heard her accused of "sharpening every note", but I have heard this artist again and again and have to admit that I have always derived great pleasure from her voice, and been filled with admiration for her acting ability.

Her voice has an immense range, her "attack" is faultless. There are not many records of her voice, but those which exist are well worth listening to. There is the complete recording of *Norma* with the divine "*Casta diva*"; a complete *Turandot* which is finely done, and a single record of *Ballo in Maschera* with Cigna singing "*Morro, Ma Prima in Grazia*", which I have heard acclaimed by an authority as one of the finest records ever made.

Turandot is sufficient to strain any soprano to the limits of her endurance, for not only is the music exceedingly difficult, but the transitions are great, and the amount of work which is done on the top register is enormous.

In the first act Turandot makes only one entrance and does not sing a note; she emerges to stand on the balcony of her "pavilion" to watch the Prince of Persia go to execution. She is "static", cold and inhuman. In the second act she shows emotion, but it is merely of annoyance and finally anger when the "unknown one" succeeds in guessing the riddles which she puts to him. Only in the scene overlooking the ceaselessly unsleeping city of Pekin, when the unknown takes her in his arms and kisses her with all the ardour of which he is capable, does the strange, icy creature become human. This is how Puccini devised the character, and that is how La Cigna portrays it.

The tenor who appeared on the night at La Scala was Renato Gigli, the Liu—I have only pencil notes and they have grown indistinct—appears to have been Rachele Radina.

Renato Gigli did not please me as much as Lugo did at the Arena; I found that his voice was not sufficiently impressive in the heavier passages, and not sufficiently tender in his lovely solo "*Nessun Dorma*".

The chorus was admirably trained and drilled, the scenery all that one has come to expect from the Scala, and the orchestra admirable in every way. A memorable production, and worthy of the applause which was lavished upon it by the huge audience.[1]

My other outstanding memory of *Turandot* was at the Arena, when the conductor was the admirable Vittorio Gui, the tenor was young, and something of a local favourite. The whole opera went magnificently, until the tenor's solo, "*Nessun Dorma*", when the audience demanded an *encore*; the tenor standing on the stage made gestures obviously protesting that *he* was willing to oblige them, but Vittorio Gui was adamant. His baton ordered the orchestra to continue! The audience, furious that they could not have a repetition of the *aria* which they adored, and also that they were not allowed to listen again to the voice of their townsman—and a very good voice it was—continued to applaud and shout. Turandot, with a train at least four yards long, began to make her entrance—the noise from the audience was deafening! Lugo continued to make his wordless assurances, Gui continued to order his orchestra to continue the opera, Cigna stood uncertain and nonplussed. Finally Gui, with a superb gesture, signalled to his violins and strings to leave the orchestra and—walked out!

Only after much persuasion from the management and from various high officials did he return, and—the tenor gave his encore! His voice was exceptionally sweet, but it was evident at times that his musical education had been barely sufficient for him to meet the demands made upon his voice; his top and low notes were good, but there was often that fatal unevenness of the middle register.

The conductor was Gino Marinuzzi.—N. J.

MADAME BUTTERFLY (Puccini)

Produced at La Scala with no success on February 17, 1904. Slightly revised, with Act 2 divided into two distinct acts, whereas in the original version there had been two acts only, this opera was reproduced at Brescia, May 28, 1904, with great success. Heard by J. C. Robertson at Teatro dell' Opera, Rome, April 12, 1936.

Un bel di vedremo

NEVER having seen *Butterfly* done in a great theatre, I was quite glad to renounce my proposed visit to San Remo, and to visit the great opera house in Rome.

It was interesting to see how immeasurably more theatrical a composer Puccini was than Wagner, to realize once more that so surely calculated was the effect that the passage of thirty years has not left the slightest mark on the opera that caused Puccini such heartbreaking disappointment at its première.

Above all it was wonderful to renew the experience of being carried off into a world of sounds, to live and breathe with the characters as Puccini lived and breathed with them when creating them. Especially is the second act one of the composer's most moving creations. The calls were endless after the last chorus of that supreme inspiration that ends the act had died away.

The performance was not exceptional, but there was much to admire and no serious flaw. First of all, of course, stands the Butterfly of Rosetta Pampanini, a famous study which is a treat to behold. The change in the Japanese girl's philosophy from act to act is realized with a sincerity of intuition and execution beyond praise, and with really exceptional vocal art. In the second act she not only had a great ovation for her *"Un Bel Di Vedremo"*, but was continuously rewarded by applause at the culminating points of her really extraordinary interpretation.

A competent set of artists revolved round this protagonist. Emilio Ghirardini's Consul was, needless to say, most sympathetic and a wholly lifelike study, though his clear diction could not always atone for his lack of carrying power in the lower register. Augusto Ferranto has a voice of a somewhat unsympathetic timbre, but he has improved greatly, and gave a good account of himself in his ungrateful rôle of Pinkerton.

De Paolis was an admirable Goro, never overdoing the part for a second, and Dubbini contributed greatly to the pathos with a fine performance of Suzuki.

Olivieno De Fabritus gave another proof of his worth by his perfect control of the orchestra, and his exact and by no means exaggerated eye for effect; clearly his idea is that the composer knows best. A most admirable young man!

The scenery was of the Teatro's standard and the production of Marcello Govoni impeccable.

Carabella's Ballet *Volti La Lanterna* followed, but does not call for comment. I have already only a hazy recollection.

NOTE. It may be interesting here to include some extracts from Puccini's letters, as they have a bearing on the disaster when *Madame Butterfly* was so ill received at La Scala on February 17, 1904.

Puccini writes to Rosina Storchio, who was to play Butterfly:

"Dear Rosina, My good wishes are superfluous! So true, so delicate, so moving is your great art that the public must succumb to it. And I hope that through you I am speeding to victory. Tonight then, with sure confidence and much affection, dear child!"

Here is another letter again to Rosina Storchio, after the first performance, when she was on the point of leaving for Buenos Aires, where *Madame Butterfly* was to be produced. Puccini writes:

"And so, my Butterfly, the lovesick little maiden, would leave me. You seem in your departure to be taking away the best, the most poetical part of my work. I think that *Butterfly* without Rosina Storchio becomes a thing without a soul. What a shame! After so many anxious fears, after pouring out such riches of your keen and delicate intelligence, to receive the reward of brutality! What a disgrace it was."

Later, on February 24, he writes to his brother-in-law:

"I am very well—except for a slightly bitter taste in my mouth! But I hope that it will pass into many other mouths, and in a more poisonous form."

From Brescia, the letter is merely dated "Saturday", but it was while rehearsals were in progress for the new version of the opera:

183

"Rehearsals are still going well. The tenor's new passage is good, and fills in a gap which needed filling. Kruceniski sings very well, and is not deficient in grace and feeling for the part. She is less expressive certainly than little Storchio. . . . The Consul is a little 'sausagey', but as such he serves to complete the meal. . . . So that's all the news. I forgot to tell you that the chorus girls are monsters!"

Then comes his letter writing of the Brescia production:

"It went exactly as I had wished, a real and unqualified triumph; the success is greater every evening."

N. J.

Part Four

THE MEN WHO WROTE THE OPERAS

By Naomi Jacob

GIUSEPPE VERDI (1813–1901)

Allegro con brio

"Quan-dé-ro pag-gio del Du-ca de Norfolck."

THERE is something pathetic and almost tragic in the fact that while thousands of people listen to the operas of the great Italian masters of music with appreciation and enjoyment, so few—comparatively—know anything of the lives of these men, of their trials, their despair and often their conviction that they would never attain recognition.

I in no way regard myself as a specialist regarding opera, in fact I might almost use the *cliché*, "I only know what I like"; though this would not be completely true, because so ignorant of the real aims of the masters am I that I do not yet fully comprehend their meaning, and perforce must listen to their works many times before I can hope to attain real appreciation.

Interest in opera must not stop short at merely knowing the opera "by sight", as it were. Take, for example, that delightful work *Le Jongleur de Notre Dame*, which I heard only once at La Scala with Malipiero singing the tenor rôle. I was delighted with it, but on one hearing I do not feel myself in a position to give a real opinion as to its merits. To me it seemed delightful, with real musical value, and this opinion was backed by that given by Jimmy Robertson. If I wish to understand, even in so limited degree as is possible to me, the value of an opera, then I must hear it not once, but several times. Only then shall I—if I *listen*, and this actual *listening* is something which does not come as a natural gift to opera-goers—be able fully to realize the salient points, the whole scheme of the opera and the work which went to make the spectacle which is presented to us—for our delight orally and visually.

So in addition to my attempts to write something of the history of Italian opera houses, and Jimmy Robertson's undoubted gift and critical faculty for commenting on the various operas which he saw, I feel that I want to give some information regarding the kind of men who wrote the operas.

Were their lives easy, or difficult; did they find that composition came easily to them or were they constantly beset by doubts as to their own ability to "give an opera to the world"? Were their works accepted immediately by the public they served, or were they given before audiences who were cold if not actually hostile? I have chosen to deal only with the Italians, because this book concerns Italian opera and opera houses, and Italian opera is the only form—with a few French exceptions —which has ever made an appeal to me. One exception remains— Mozart. Mozart, I believe, belonged to no nation, he was—Mozart, and one of God's gifts to music-loving people.

I have chosen the men whose works I know, and have seen not once but again and again. Verdi must take pride of place for his grandeur and his unmistakable genius (and that is a word which by sensible people is used very rarely) and his numerous successes. There is the lovable Puccini, with his liking for the good things of life, his proclivity for sport, his depressions and despairs, and his triumphs and realizations. Not as the Italians say "*classico*" as was Verdi, but giving us melodies which are surely unsurpassed. Rossetti, Bellini—and Donizetti, to be followed by Verdi's friend for twenty years, Boito, and lastly Mascagni.

There is my choice of the musicians and writers of opera who represent Italian opera. Admitted that there is also Amilcare Ponchielli, who wrote his opera *I Promessi Sposi* when he was only twenty-two years of age and later gave us *La Gioconda*; and Leoncavallo the author of *I Pagliacci*, and an opera named *La Bohème*, in which he was unlucky, for it was produced a short time after the opera of the same name by Puccini, and was also based on Mürger's book *La Vie de Bohème*.

Leoncavallo remains to the average opera-goer as "a man of one opera" and, frankly, that not of the very first rank.

I shall ask you to meet, then—if you have not met already—the great Verdi, the greatest of all Italian writers of opera. After him I shall introduce to you his friend Arrigo Boito.

If you could go to Parma, and study the splendid bust of this great man, you could not help being struck by the essential grandeur of his features. The massive head, with its immense brow and deep-set eyes; there is a certain sternness in his expression, and yet a great kindliness. You feel that he would be intolerant only of meanness, insincerity and affectations. That he would be tolerant of all human failings, sufferings and difficulties.

He was born in the tiny village of Roncole, near Busseto, which was not far from Parma, in the year 1813. His family were poor, modest people, and the child was their greatest joy and their chief preoccupation.

They were difficult days, those early years of the young Giuseppe Verdi, for the Austrian and Russian soldiery were ravaging all north Italy; it was the end of the long struggle of Napoleon to attain supremacy in Europe, and lives of peasant people or small tradesmen in villages were both difficult and dangerous.

The soldiers reached the village of Roncole, and the terrified women with their children rushed to seek sanctuary in the village church, Luigia Verdi among them, carrying in her arms her baby son. The soldiers broke down the doors and slaughtered many of the women; she escaped to the belfry and, hiding behind some piles of wood and sacking which had been stored there, remained unseen until such time as the soldiers had left the village.

The child grew up, dreamy and always deeply affected by music; there are many stories concerning him as a boy. For example, he served at the altar in the village church, became so absorbed in listening to the organ that he slipped and fell on the altar steps, remaining stunned for a long time.

His father recognized the boy's love for music, and although he could ill afford it, bought Giuseppe a little spinet on which he tried to teach himself to play.

He stumbled on, and one can imagine his many difficulties, and often his acute sense of frustration during the time that he tried to learn to play the spinet—alone and untaught.

Finally—and remember that the Verdis were poor people—he was put under instruction with the village organist, one Baistrocchi, who agreed to give him lessons. At the end of a year Baistrocchi went to little Verdi's father saying: "There is nothing more that I can teach him. I shall resign my position as organist—Giuseppe must take my place."

Giuseppe's father was practical, the boy was learning music, but very little else; he was sent to school in Busseto, where he lodged with a family who charged 3d. a day for his keep. Each Sunday he walked backward and forward to Roncole to play the organ in church.

Two men at this time exerted a great influence on young Verdi—the one, Barezzi, was a tradesman with whom the elder Verdi dealt, the other was Provesi, who was conductor of the local Philharmonic Society, and who often gave Giuseppe music to copy for the Society. This gave him a certain amount of knowledge of the first principles of orchestration which stood him in such good stead later. When Provesi resigned young Verdi took his place as conductor of the Philharmonic, and so considerable was his success that he determined to make an application to enter the Milan Conservatory.

Milan! Imagine the excitement to a young man who had scarcely left his home except to visit Roncole. We can imagine his country-made clothes, his bewilderment at the crowded streets and his nervousness at entering the doors of the famous Conservatory. He was given an examination, and the verdict was given. He was refused admission on the grounds that he "showed no special aptitude for music"!

A blow such as this to a young man whose whole soul was filled with the love of music might well have broken an ordinary individual. But Verdi was no ordinary individual, and in him already burned that essential greatness which was to be shown again and again in the music which he wrote.

He had a small amount of money saved—and how small it was we can only conjecture—and he applied to Lavigna—who at that time was one of the most famous teachers in Italy—for lessons in composition and orchestration. With that energy which is still—thank God—typical of the Italian peasant, he set to work.

For two years he studied and worked incessantly, then came the news that the good Provesi was dead, and that Verdi had been appointed director of the Philharmonic and organist at Busseto.

Then followed a stormy period. The church party, having learnt that Verdi had been composing opera and studying with a view to continuing on this road, took an immediate dislike to his association with the church. He resigned the post of organist. The church continued to show its disapproval of the young man, and finally the Philharmonic—his only means of livelihood—was disbanded.

It was at this time that Verdi, now twenty-three, fell in love. She was the daughter of the man who had helped him before he went to Milan—Barezzi, the tradesman. Her name was Margherita and Verdi adored her. They were married in 1836, and in two years had two children. Verdi, tired of the bickerings of the local clergy and musicians, returned to Milan, and with him went his score for his first opera—*Oberto, Conte de San Bonifacio*.

During his previous two years in Milan, Verdi had met and come to know moderately well the Count Borromeo, who was always a patron of the arts, and also Bartolomeo Merelli, an impresario.

Thanks in part to their good efforts the opera was produced at La Scala in the early part of 1839. While not an outstanding success, it was sufficiently well received for Merelli to ask for three more operas. The payment was not large, and even that—so far as the actual profits went—was to be divided between Merelli and Verdi. He began work immediately.

There was the first difficulty of a suitable libretto. Verdi was at this time desperately poor, and there were his much-loved wife and children to provide for. Merelli offered him the libretto for a comic opera—how strange to imagine Verdi setting to work on this type of work!—which was named *Un Giorno di Regno*.

It is recorded that he did not like it, but he was in grave financial straits. However, he had not only boundless energy, but tremendous determination. He began to work on the libretto. His wife sold her jewellery, they managed to live while he worked, full of hope. Then suddenly fate struck at him. One of the children became gravely ill and died, the second passed away immediately afterwards, and within a few weeks Margherita was taken ill and after a few days' illness died also. Verdi was left alone, heartbroken, and with his whole life apparently shattered. Imagine the unfortunate young man, trying to work on this comic opera while his heart was broken. It is a tragic picture.

The opera was a failure—as, after all, was to be expected—and for months Verdi allowed himself to drift into a kind of despondency and state of acute depression. He showed not the slightest wish to write music. And Merelli, while doing everything in his power to rouse the young man, realized that it was better to leave him alone. So Verdi wandered about Milan, terribly poor, desperately unhappy, until one day, entering Merelli's office, listless and uninterested, he turned over the pages of a libretto. The young man's eyes brightened suddenly, his attitude of weary boredom vanished, he was alert, interested, even faintly excited.

He had read the words: *"Va, Pensiero, sull' ali dorate"* ("Rise my thoughts on golden wings"). He forgot that he had declared that he would attempt composition no more, he was excited and eager. Merelli encouraged him, gently—wisely—and with sympathy. The opera *Nabucco* was written. Merelli arranged to produce it at the first possible moment; the work was ready to be given to the public in 1842, and although I am at this moment surrounded by books of reference dealing with music, I cannot trace its first presentation. It was a success, and Verdi as an operatic composer was established.

I have heard this opera at the Arena, Verona, and found the music magnificent and exciting, and the Prayer which is sung by the bass voice—in this case Tancredi Pasero—is a splendid and inspiring piece of music.

Then followed *I Lombardi* (1843), another success, and Verdi then sought for a libretto based upon the drama of Victor Hugo—*Ernani*. The librettist was Piave, a Venetian. The censor did not approve and again and again insisted upon alterations and changes, until the patience of Verdi was almost exhausted. I find that when this opera was finally produced at the Fenice, Venice, on March 9, 1844, it is recorded as having been *un grande successo*.

I heard this opera last in Rome at the Teatro dell' Opera in 1937 or 1938 (many of my notes have been lost during the war), and I was immensely struck by its power, and the great "sweeps" of the melodies. I remember that Gina Cigna sang "Elvira"—a part which Patti sang, as did also Sembrich.

Then came *I Due Foscari* and *Giovanna d'Arco* in 1884 and 1885, neither of which was particularly successful. *Alzira* was a fiasco, but *Attila* attained a certain success—if short-lived—when it was produced at the Fenice on March 17, 1846, and was given a "patriotic demonstration" (*"dimostrazioni patriottiche"*.)

Now came *Macbeth*, with Piave as the librettist, which has been recorded as a complete failure. This is, however, not entirely correct, for I find references to it in the chronicles of La Scala. It is recorded that the first performance was given at Florence, March 14, 1847, and came to La Scala on February 14, 1849, to return on the programme in 1852, 1854 and 1858.

Verdi apparently made certain alterations or "adjustments" to the opera for its Paris production in 1865, and later when it came back to La Scala in 1874. It then appears to have fallen out for some years but is back at La Scala in 1928, and its success has been so great that *"Macbeth est compris dans le répertoire ordinaire de 28 théatres"*.[1] In the season of La Scala in 1938 it was given again, and the words in the official programme issued are as follows: "It is with this glorious voice that we begin the season! The Macbeth of Verdi!"

The production was a magnificent one, in eight scenes under the direction of Nicola Benois with designs by Oskar Walleck. The artists were Cigna and Jacobo, Battaglia, De Sved and Pasero—a wonderful cast, and the whole performance is to me very memorable.

Verdi then wrote *I Mesnadieri* (taken from Schiller's *The Robbers*). The first performance was given in London, with Jenny Lind in the cast, but the opera failed to please. Two more failures followed, one of them being the opera *La Battaglio di Legnano* in 1849. This was the opera that the Austrians renamed to "suit themselves", as may be read in the history of the opera houses in this volume.

It was about this time that, Verdi's financial position having become stable and ample for his needs, he bought the villa of S. Agata near Busseto. A beautiful place, "well furnished with park and farm lands", where he spent much of the rest of his long life, except that in the winters he departed for Genova and Venice.

Verdi now entered into what is known as his "second period" with *Luisa Miller*. The opera was produced at the San Carlo, Naples, in 1859, and its success was immediate. The music shows greater mastery and greater maturity.

In the following year Verdi's opera *Stiffelio* was produced at Trieste, and was not a success, but late in that year Verdi began to write *Rigoletto*, and completed it in under two months. The opera was produced at the Fenice, Venice, and is recorded as a triumph (*Trionfo del Rigoletto*). Once

[1] This refers particularly to German opera houses.

190

again Verdi was taken to task by the censor. The opera was based on the play by Victor Hugo, *Le Roi s'Amuse*. After the stirring times of 1848 and 1849 it was not considered wise to stress the failings and frailties of kings, and so Verdi created a "Duke of Mantua". The success of this opera was immediate; it was produced at Covent Garden in 1853, Caruso made his American début as the Duke at the Metropolitan, New York, in 1903, and Galli Curci as Gilda in 1916.

I saw this opera last in 1946 at the open-air theatre in Trieste, with Tagliabue, Grandi and—I think, though I cannot be certain—Cloe Elmo.

Il Trovatore (1853) followed, produced at the Apollo Theatre at Rome; the libretto by Cammanaro is not completely to blame for the complexities of the story. It is melodramatic, and often, to anyone hearing it for the first time, inexplicable. This is due in a measure to the fact that Ferrando recounts much of the story immediately after the rise of the curtain. The action later is involved, but the whole opera is carried along on the great tide of Verdi's genius, and it remains one of the most popular operas in the repertoire of the opera houses.

Two months later—for the operas must have been finished at almost the same time—*La Traviata* was presented at the Fenice. This is recorded in the annals of this theatre as *Storico Fiasco*. The possible reasons for this terrible fiasco of March 6, 1853, have been alluded to elsewhere in this book.

Verdi was to see his *Traviata* taken completely into favour by the public, and it remains one of his greatest and most lasting successes.

In 1859 he married again, to Giuseppina Strepponi. They loved one another devotedly and their life together has been described as "perfect". Verdi was offered several honours—he was elected to Parliament, but resigned very soon, not wishing to take part in active politics. In 1875 Victor Emmanuel appointed him a Roman Senator, but it appears that he never attended the Chamber. In 1862 he first met the man who was to influence his work so strongly, and to whom Verdi gave his complete friendship. This was Arrigo Boito. Boito was an intellectual, and Verdi derived immense pleasure from his companionship and his lofty discussions.

Un Ballo in Maschera was produced in 1859 in Rome, and mention has also been made regarding the changing of the "setting" of this opera. I find the statement that "its success since [its production] and elsewhere has been moderate to say the least", but I see that this opera was given several presentations at La Scala in the 1925–1926 season; it was given at least four times at the Fenice in 1939 under the conductorship of Vittorio Gui, at Verona at the Arena in 1932 at least three times, and included in four separate seasons at Mantua from 1868 to 1889.

Again, I read that *La Forza del Destino* is "scarcely more than a name to be placed in the record"; this I find was given several times during two seasons at Mantua, at La Scala in 1929 and again in 1939. Of the San Carlo I have no records, but I believe that it was done there in 1938. This magnificent opera is dealt with by Jimmy Robertson. I have always regarded the overture as one of the most exciting pieces of music in opera, while that *finale* for the tenor, bass and soprano rises to magnificent heights.

Then came the request from Khedive Ismail Pasha that Verdi should write something "which should confer distinction upon the repertoire" of the Cairo Opera House. Early in 1870 the opera house was opened. *Aïda* was produced there on Christmas Eve, 1871. There is a belief that *Aïda* was written for the *opening* of the Cairo Opera House, but this is not correct, as I have shown.

Six weeks later it was given at Milan at La Scala under the direction of Verdi himself; he was recalled thirty-two times—*Aïda* was a triumph! You will hear the statement that *Aïda* is Wagnerian; this is sheer rubbish! It is a tremendous development when compared with Verdi's earlier operas, his mastery of orchestration is now complete, he "takes risks", as it were, because he is fully conscious of his own powers, but to stigmatize *Aïda* as Wagnerian on the score of a pageantry with music suitable for pageants is as unreasonable as the other statement that the trumpets in the opera play a melody which was an "adaptation" from Meyerbeer's *Prophète*.

After the great triumph of *Aïda*, Verdi appears to have passed through a "bleak" period. He felt that his genius had left him, and for hours, he tells us, he would wander about the streets of Venice sunk in the depths of depression. He even played with the idea of visiting Wagner, wondering if they might not exchange ideas. Verdi had never met the German, and they never did meet, although there must have been many opportunities for their doing so.

However, Verdi decided against attempting to use suggestions of others, or to superimpose ideas upon those which still flickered, although he felt that they died all too quickly, in his own mind. He returned to S. Agata; either his ideas would rise and live, either his ability to work would return, or he would write no more.

Thus twice the great musician came to somewhat similar decisions.

What influenced him? Was it his good friend Boito, or did he perhaps, idly turning over the pages of Shakespeare as he had once idly turned the pages of a libretto in Merelli's office, find phrases in the masterpiece of *Otello* which fired his imagination?

He began to write the score of *Otello* with Boito writing the words. The result was achieved sixteen years after the production of *Aïda*, when Verdi, at the age of seventy-four, gave the world one of the most noble

THE MEN WHO WROTE THE OPERAS

operas of all time. It was produced at La Scala, Milan, on February 5, 1887, and its success was immediate. Here was the Verdi of the "third period", and the work is described as being "far more careful in detail and more luxuriant than that of the earlier Italian school and his melody is more passionate and poignant in expression".

Otello has been called a "musicians" ' opera; it is said that there is possibly too much "technical perfection" for the "layman" while the trained musician is held entranced by the complete mastery and the "miraculous skill".

At the age of eighty Verdi produced *Falstaff*, again with Boito writing the "book"; it has been acclaimed as the greatest of all comic operas, and looking back we remember how the young Verdi, poor and almost unknown, had been given the libretto of a "comic opera" and how he had struggled over his task. One well-known writer on opera says, "Indeed it is clear that *Falstaff* can still teach something to composers who have definitely abandoned the school of Wagner."

Falstaff was produced at La Scala, Milan, in March 1893, amid much acclamation.

Verdi wrote little music that was not intended for operatic presentation, his chief work being his great *Requiem*, written in honour and memory of the Italian novelist and poet Alessandro Manzoni.

There, then, is the short history of Giuseppe Verdi, who died at the age of eighty-seven and three months. His wife, whom he had loved so tenderly, had died in 1897; his own death came on January 27, 1901.

He had travelled a long way since his parents contrived to pay 3*d.* a day for his lodging at Busseto; he had become identified with all the passionate ideals of freedom and national liberty, he had honours showered upon him: France gave him the Legion of Honour; his own King had made him a Roman Senator; his townsmen had elected him to Parliament; his house was full of presentation batons, with precious pieces of jewellery given to him as marks of admiration.

He remained, in spite of success and adulation, two things—great and simple.

It is only necessary to look at the splendid bust of him to be seen in Parma, to look long and intently at that fine head, noble brow and deeply-set eyes under their overhanging brows, to realize that this was a man of great mental and spiritual attainments.

He stated that he wished only for a simple funeral, and although over a hundred thousand people came from all over Europe to pay their last tributes to the great master, the funeral ceremonies were as simple as he had wished them to be.

He not only wrote music which was of the very first order, but he had a great and wonderful sense of character in his writing. Take, for example, the music written for Rigoletto, how it bears out and clarifies the character of the jester; how it swings and changes from murderous hate to the most exquisite tenderness. Compared with this development—musically—of the character, how frequently the music for the duke seems faintly vulgar. And how right it is that this should be so—for what is the duke but a sensualist and a professional amourist?

In the instance of Violetta in *La Traviata*, which is a very careful study indeed of a woman who is a complex character, she is passionate, often lightly foolish, weak and intensely pathetic. Compare the Violetta of Act I with the dying woman in that last tragic scene in Paris. This brings me again to one of my favourite contentions—that opera singers must be able to act.

Verdi, Heaven knows, does all he can with his music to denote these changes and developments, and, unless your *diva* is completely devoid of acting ability, surely she must realize what was in the master's mind and why he "developed" the character in his music.

Let me quote a very admirable comment upon this:

"The music in which the nature is portrayed is individual in a way that defies brief analysis. The famous solo scene at the end of Act I ('*Ah, Fors'e Lui*') might be taken as an example. Violetta's dawning realization of the meaning of real love is evoked in an *aria* which begins with slow-moving meditative phrases: the hectic frivolity of the life which she finds it so hard to abandon is reflected in the flashy waltz *allegro* which follows, and into which the strains of the tenor's declaration of love are suddenly projected; the sound of his voice echoing off-stage is a brilliant little operatic stroke of the kind in which Verdi excelled."

Here is another quotation from the same work which seems to me to be so admirable that I cannot resist using it. The reference is to Verdi's last opera, *Falstaff*.

"It needs close attention like a string quartet. The poetic atmosphere in which the comedy exists is lightened now by the pure lyric love music of Fenton and Ann Page, now clouded by Ford's jealous outbursts, now crackling with the mischief of the Wives, now heavy with the Fat Knight's mock heroic meditations. The sound of the laughter in *Falstaff* is an abiding joy."[1]

[1] *A Key to Opera*, by Frank Howes and Philip Hope-Wallace (Blackie).

ARRIGO BOITO (1842–1918)

Nerone

BOITO has his place here immediately after Verdi, who was not only his close friend, the composer for whom Boito wrote many "books" for operas, but in some ways the lives of the two men bear a resemblance. In other ways no two lives, no two men, could have been less alike.

Think of the rugged grandeur of Verdi's head, the massive effect of his features and something of the splendid lion which may be traced in his appearance. Boito, on the other hand, was very dark, with smooth hair, a well-trimmed moustache, and a general air of refinement. Their lives too, while holding similarities, began under very different circumstances. Verdi was the son of a peasant, Boito was the son of a highly successful painter, Cav. Silvestro Boito; his mother was a Polish countess, Josephine Radolinski.

Arrigo Boito was born in Padua on February 4, 1842. He was the younger of two brothers, and the elder Camillo was already past his school days when Arrigo began to show that intense interest in literature which was to bring forth such admirable achievements later. It appears that Camillo was delighted at the intelligence of his younger brother, and was happy to spend long hours giving him the benefit of his own brilliance, for he had been considered one of the most intellectual scholars in Padua for his age.

Not content with working hard under the tuition of Camillo, Arrigo, at the age of fourteen, declared that he wished to study music; he had already shown considerable aptitude for the art, and his parents willingly allowed him to leave Padua and enter the Conservatory of Milan.

It is easy to imagine how differently he lived in Milan from the manner in which Giuseppe Verdi spent his first months in that city. No doubt Boito went there well equipped with money, clothes, with suitable lodgings taken for him and having already a certain social standing as the son of a famous painter.

But, like Verdi, his early years at the Conservatory were not in any way successful. This boy who had studied so hard, and in whose high intelligence his family had such faith, was not hailed by the teachers at the Conservatory. His own teacher of musical composition, Mazzucato, reported to the Director, Lauro Rossi, that he showed so little promise that it might be well to consider his removal in order to make way for pupils of greater talent. Why this advice was not acted upon is not clear, but certainly Boito continued his studies, and at the same time wandered about the fine libraries of Milan amassing knowledge of the classics, and also studying languages which presented little or no difficulty to him.

He was a remarkable boy, Arrigo Boito—at this time he was barely fifteen years old, and yet already he was considering the possibilities in Goethe's *Faust* for a great opera. This resulted in the production, many years later, of his great masterpiece, *Mefistofele*.

He began to write essays, his style being particularly clear and pure. Being essentially modest, he was filled with surprise when a friend begged him to submit some of these to the Press—and they were immediately accepted, the editors clamouring for more work from this young student. Many of these essays were translated and Victor Hugo wrote complimenting the author.

It may have been that with this definite, if small, success came greater assurance, for certainly at this time his work at the Conservatory appears to have begun to make considerable headway. For his graduation work he produced in 1860 a cantata, *Il 4 Giugno*, which won a prize from the Government in the shape of an allowance which made it possible for him to travel and study music in other countries.

He was then eighteen years old, and two years later he produced in conjunction with a friend, Franco Faccio, a second cantata, *Le Sorelle d'Italia*. For this Boito wrote the whole of the libretto and half of the music.

Again Boito travelled, thanks to the Government allowance, and visited France, where he spent a considerable time in Paris, to Germany later, and finally to Poland, where he met for the first time his mother's family.

1866 finds him back in Milan, accepted as a "brilliant young intellectual", and given with his companions to long and erudite discussions on matters of philosophy and politics in the approved fashion of young intellectuals in all ages. Then occurred what is typical of the best type of those young men throughout the ages, who, while they were possibly at their happiest seated at the little tables of small cafés arguing and discussing, could yet forget that they were "thinkers" and become men of action when the call of their country reached them.

So in 1866 Boito and his immediate friends were among the youth of Italy who rushed to join Garibaldi in his fight for freedom and a united Italy. It is recorded that they behaved with great courage, and showed considerable heroism.

The war ended, and Boito appears to have found it impossible to settle down to work in Milan again; it may be that the longing to travel had again seized him, or that his experiences with the army of Garibaldi had unsettled him for his old life—however, he left for Paris, with a very warm letter of invitation from Victor Hugo.

He went to Paris in the early part of 1867, and for some reason which is not precisely known—for he was a sensitive and reserved fellow, not given to writing long and intimate letters concerning himself and his experiences—Paris did not hold its former appeal for him, and he went on to Poland to stay with one of his sisters who had married and settled there.

There he appears to have found peace and tranquillity, and his mind turned again to the idea of *Mefistofele*; he completed the great "Prologue in Heaven" and various other scenes. Then, satisfied that this opera was well on the way to completion, he returned to Milan. The directors of La Scala listened to as much of the work as was finished, they expressed their faith in it and promised to produce it during the following season, if Boito would finish it.

He worked feverishly, his heart very high, his determination stronger than ever—the opera was finished and delivered to the directors.

On March 5, 1868, when the composer had barely attained his twenty-sixth year, *Mefistofele* was produced at La Scala, and lasted for six hours. The reception was curious. There had been a great sense of excitement regarding this new opera, for Gounod's *Faust* had been produced in Paris in 1859, and had made a tremendous success, and had scored triumph after triumph all over Europe. Boito had been nervous concerning his own opera, his usual modesty made him uncertain of the success of his own work, so different in scope and treatment from that of Gounod.

Gounod had dealt only with the love adventures of Faust and their results, Boito had gone much deeper, and had dealt with much of the mysticism contained in Goethe's poem. The treatment of the opera was "un-Italian", and the audience were frankly puzzled though interested. Many of the critics declared that Boito's music was "Wagnerian", which criticism, let it be said, levelled against any musician in those days in Italy, was far from complimentary.

Milan was divided into two musical camps, the one acclaiming the opera as a masterpiece, the other decrying it and declaring that it was "merely exuberantly Germanic". So heated did the arguments grow that after the second performance the Milan authorities decided that it was not to be given again.

Boito, who, like many people with sensitive and thoughtful natures, possessed a strong strain of dogged pertinacity, set to work once more on his opera, and in 1875 it was again produced at Bologna in its present form to tremendous applause. The opera on which Boito had worked so long, the theme of which had never been long absent from his thoughts for nineteen years, was an unqualified success.

He had retained practically all of the "Prologue in Heaven"; there remained, too, the Grecian scene in Part 2, but he had changed the rôle for the baritone to one for the tenor voice.

The orchestration was then in a form which was considered "new"; the music was not merely used to supply beautiful melodies, but it became, as it were, a *commentary on the text*. Now, Boito had met Verdi in 1862, when began that friendship and intellectual companionship which was to last for the rest of their lives.

You may remember that in the life of Verdi I quoted from that excellent book *A Key to Opera*, and in the comments upon *Falstaff* there is a statement which refers to the various *types* of music used by Verdi to clarify the characters and the actual text—or "story". Now we find that Boito is virtually making his music in *Mefistofele* a *commentary* on the text.

At this time Verdi and Boito had been friends for thirteen years, and it is easy to imagine how the two men, whether in Venice, Genoa, or at S. Agata, had discussed and experimented with this idea which Verdi was to perfect in *Falstaff*.

Boito continued to work both at writing music and literature; he finished what was stated to be a very excellent book on Hero and Leander, and began to work on the music, but again and again he was dissatisfied, and finally became disheartened with the whole thing. He handed the "book" over to Bottesini, and later to Mancinelli, both of whom set it to music. Both settings failed to score a success when produced.

He then turned to occupy himself with the writing of an opera concerning which he was completely secretive, and after thirty years he was still at work, writing and rewriting, still refusing to talk about his work even to Verdi. Verdi, possibly amused, perhaps faintly irritated, at the silence and secrecy, referred to the work as "the opera I dare not name". The opera was *Nerone*, which, with one other—which has never been produced, *Orestiade*—were to give Boito work until his death.

He worked, he spent much time with Verdi and his wife, or living practically in retirement with his elder brother Camillo in Milan. He was given the title of Cavaliere, Ufficiale and Commendatore by the Government; he was a Chevalier of the Legion of Honour; he was appointed Inspector-General of Technical Education in the Conservatory of Milan, and he also became a senator.

Arrigo Boito died in Milan on June 10, 1918, at the age of seventy-six. His opera *Nerone* was produced in 1924 at La Scala. I have seen the statement that it was left unfinished and that Toscanini completed the score;

THE MEN WHO WROTE THE OPERAS

on the other hand I have read that Boito, when he finished the orchestration, wrote, "The End: Arrigo Boito."

The opera, which deals with the triumph of the spiritual over the material, and is concerned with the martyrdom of the Christian Fanuel, was admitted to be a greater musical work than *Mefistofele*, showing greater development and power. However, it did not make the same appeal and is very rarely offered to the opera-going public.

Mefistofele is still frequently given, and its popularity never seems to decrease. At the Metropolitan in New York it was one of the favourite and most successful rôles of Chaliapin; in Italy, Tancredi Pasero is the finest interpreter of the rôle of Mefistofele.

It may be noted that Boito, when he wrote his "books" or librettos—though the last word is scarcely applicable to the very fine and thoughtful work which he did, though technically it is no doubt correct—always signed these works with the name: Tobia Gorrio. This was an anagram of his own name.

199

GIACOMO PUCCINI (1858-1924)

Turandot

IT has been customary—outside Italy at least—to speak and write of
Puccini in a semi-patronizing tone, and again and again one hears the
words spoken tolerantly and with a slightly patronizing inflection: "Yes,
very tuneful, of course! But . . ."

Verdi, admittedly, takes pride of place, not because he is *better* than
Puccini, but because his work is cast in a grander mould. He is a kind of
Michael Angelo of music in opera, he gives us sheer beauty, masterly
compositions, and great dignity and knowledge; that Puccini did not, and
probably could not, produce work on these heroic lines is not to argue
that he could produce little that was not much below the standard
required to place him among the ranks of the great masters of opera.

Puccini, as Sardou declared, was "a man of the theatre", and for this
reason the stories on which he chose to base his operas are always—
with the exception of *Le Villi* ("The Wilis") and *Turandot*, where he
wandered into the world of imagination and tradition—credible. I
imagine that it was this complete "theatre sense" which sent him to
novelists or playwrights for his plots. But where the mastery of the man
is evinced is that he finds music for those plots which is "in the picture"
every time.

To turn to the man himself, for his life is interesting and in no way
the life of ease and continual success that many writers have tried to make
us believe. I have heard people state: "Ah, success came too easily to
Puccini! Had he faced more difficulties he might have written greater
music!"

With the production of *Le Villi* on June 8, 1884, at the Teatro dal
Verme, Milan, was the demonstration of a musical knowledge and ability
which had run through the family of Giacomo Puccini for a hundred and
seventy-two years. He was the last of a family of musicians, the first of
whom, also Giacomo, was born at Lucca, and studied in Bologna. In
1739 this first Giacomo was appointed "Musician to the Republic of
Lucca". He composed a certain amount of operatic music and several
pieces of church music. He died in 1781, and the second generation is
headed by his son, Antonio.

Antonio, who was born in 1747, studied in Lucca with his father

200

and Matteo Lucchesi; later he went to Bologna and studied with Parretti. He returned to Lucca, taking up the position which his father had held, and died in 1832 at the age of eighty-five, leaving behind him many compositions dealing with church music.

Now comes Dominico Puccini, born in 1771, who studied first at Lucca, then at Bologna and finally at Naples. This is the first time in the family history that the leaning towards operatic music begins to show more strongly than the ability to write ecclesiastical works. This Dominico left five operas which are reputed to have been produced with great success. Their names mean nothing to us, but they were *Quinto Fabio, Il Ciarlatano, L'Ortolanella, Le Freccie d' Amore*, and *La Capricciosa*. Their composer died at the early age of forty-four in 1815.

His son, Michaele, the father of Giacomo, was born in 1812, and was an orphan at the age of three years, he was brought up by his grandfather, Antonio. He, too, studied at Bologna, and then at Naples. He came back to Lucca as Professor and Director of the Musical Institute of the city. He was a composer of great ability, and has left two masses—one in G, the other in C, which are still regarded as being particularly beautiful. He also composed the music of an opera called *Antonio Foscarini*, which was left unfinished at his death, and a play named *Cattani*, which was produced and met with considerable success. He died at the age of fifty-two in 1864. The town settled an annual subsidy on his widow, Albina Magi, and deciding—such was their faith in the musical ability of this family of Puccini—that when he was old enough his father's position as choirmaster and organist should be given to the little Giacomo, who was then only five years old. The position was given for the time being to his uncle, Fortunato Magi.

The widow had very little money and a family of seven small children. The people of Lucca again recorded their belief in the hereditary musical ability of the family, and promised that Giacomo should also "inherit" his father's post as teacher at the Collegio Ponziano. Until he was sufficiently old the post was given to a very fine musician, the Abbot Nerici, who generously handed over part of his salary to Albina Puccini.

However, the small boy's talents were evident, and his mother, to whom he was devoted, contrived to keep house on the very small amount of money at her disposal. When the time came for the young Giacomo to enter the Milan Conservatory the necessary money presented a great difficulty. A great-uncle, Dr. Cerù, came forward to help, and a subsidy from Queen Margherita of Italy for 1200 lire for a year made it possible for Giacomo's studies to begin.

His progress was very rapid, his masters being Ponchielli (the composer of *La Gioconda*) and Bazzini. His composition for the final graduation at the Conservatory was *Capriccio Sinfonico*, and this was esteemed

201

so highly that Ponchielli advised Puccini to begin work on an opera immediately.

He chose an old Italian legend, and with Ferdinando Fontana as librettist, set to work on *Le Villi*. The work was finished in 1884, and was presented in Milan at the Teatro dal Verme. It had previously been submitted to the publishing house of Sonzogno, who were offering a considerable prize for an opera by an unknown and untried composer. *Le Villi* did not win the competition, in fact the score was sent in at the very last moment, Puccini not having time to make a fair copy. Arrigo Boito and Marco Sala, who had taken the trouble to read the opera, and knowing the financial difficulties which beset the young composer, in company with several other musicians, subscribed the necessary *lire* and had a fair copy made.

At the dal Verme the opera had a reasonable success, and was acquired by Ricordi, who commissioned Puccini to write another opera. Puccini embarked on *Edgar*. The libretto was again by Fontana, and was taken from a work by de Musset. The conception was daring, and the music contained all the youthful freshness and beauty which was to develop so strongly in the work of Puccini as years passed.

Edgar was produced at La Scala on April 21, 1889. There were many curtain calls, and Puccini appeared again and again—both with and without the cast; "the season closed with an impressive demonstration for Puccini . . . in answer to the shouting and cheers of the entire audience".

Thirty-five years later, on December 3, 1924, the funeral music from *Edgar* was heard in Milan Cathedral, when it was conducted by Toscanini on the occasion of Puccini's funeral.

But although he had won a measure of success, Puccini was still very badly off financially. Giulio Ricordi was making him an allowance for a year in order that he might live during the time he wrote *Edgar*, and again and again in Puccini's letters, both to Ricordi and to his family, we read of his money difficulties. Not that he allows himself to indulge in self-pity, but it is clear that the money problem worries him.

In the winter before the production of *Edgar*, *Le Villi* was given both at Brescia and Verona. Puccini had begun to work on *Manon*, and writes constantly to his brothers and sisters reporting his progress with the work, but says little as to his opinion of its quality.

In 1905 he writes to his sister Dide that he is going to Torre, which is the place where he loved to be, and where he found that he could work best. There in the quiet and tranquillity of the country he was free from the disturbances of a great city like Milan, and again and again in his letters occur references to the birds, trees and the beauty of the country.

Now, harking back to the year 1893, and the momentous night of

February 1, which set the seal on Puccini's success as a composer of music for the opera, *Manon* was produced at Turin. In the comments by the Press the following day on the work there is no indecision; one and all they acclaim the work as magnificent.

They "take pains" with their criticisms, the work is not dismissed as something trivial and not requiring proper analysis. The Turin musical critics were noted for their reserve and coldness, but they were unanimous in their praise.

The *Gazzetta Piemontese* said, at the end of a long account:

"Once more the four bars of the introduction, in the same key, return to recall the idea of the infinite [this is referring, of course, to the death of Manon] and the parenthesis is closed and the opera finished. But the clamorous demonstrations of the public are not ended so quickly. Their enthusiasm rises to a climax; they shout, they yell, they want Puccini."

Marco Parga was the first to attempt the libretto. He tells how Puccini met him in Savini's restaurant in the Galleria,[1] and asked him to undertake the work.

Everything appeared to be going smoothly. Praga worked in collaboration with Oliva, the poet, and in the summer they all went over to Cernobbio (on Lago di Como), where the Ricordi family were staying. Paolo Tosti was with them, the libretto was read, Tosti admired it. Everyone, including Puccini, appeared to be completely in accord.

Soon, however, Puccini began to ask for alterations, his keen theatrical sense was roused, and he kept seeing where improvements might be made; he once wrote that when he was composing he must be able to see his artists at work, meaning that unless a scene appeared so clearly to him that it became almost visual he could not write.

Praga became impatient and handed the whole libretto over to Oliva, who in his turn lost patience; finally Giacosa approached Luigi Illica, who took up the work.

This was the beginning of that collaboration which gave us the fine librettos of *La Bohème, Tosca* and *Butterfly*. Illica, writing years later to Riccordi, said, "*Manon* was the pleasant beginning of the later collaboration which certainly nothing but death could have ended."

On February 1, 1896, *La Bohème* was produced in Turin. The public were delighted with it, but the criticisms were little short of venomous. Gone were the praises which they had lavished on *Manon*. *La Stampa* accused Puccini of "composing his music hurriedly and with very little labour of selection or polishing"; it continued to state that the opera had

[1] In Milan.

left but little impression on the minds of the audience, and that it would leave no great trace upon "the history of our lyric theatre". The book was taken from the novel of Henri Mürger, and was prepared as a libretto by Illica and Giacosa.

Again the arguments began, again Puccini laid his demands before them, saying, "I do want to have my say, I will accept nobody's dictation." Ricordi kept writing and begging for haste, Giacosa replied that, as a poet, "I refuse to dash down anything that comes!" He offered to resign, and Puccini refused to allow this. Finally, after storms, arguments, suggestions, acceptances and many refusals, the opera was complete.

Here again we find Puccini's keen theatrical sense asserting itself. He writes to Ricordi, "I am annoyed by these trifling episodes which have nothing to do with the action of the drama." In writing of the scene of the Barrière d'Enfer he says: "This in my opinion is the weak act. Shall I be proved wrong? All the better! . . . The death of Mimi, with all that leads up to it, is very moving." It is interesting to read of Puccini quoting Verdi. He writes, "As for the *pp*'s and *ff*'s on the score, I have overdone them because, as Verdi says, when one wants *piano* one puts *ppp*."

Bohème was launched, and everywhere was greeted as a success. The melodies in this opera are many of them exquisite, and here Puccini demonstrates his ability to give what might be called a fair share to all his artists. Each part in *Bohème* has its moments which offer great opportunities, every character *has* character, and in almost every case each individual has a moment which will bring them attention and, if they are capable of demanding it, approbation.

He began, once *Bohème* was launched, to think about *Tosca*, which was to be taken from Sardou's great play in which Sarah Bernhardt made such a success. Puccini mentioned this idea to Illica, and later, when it appeared unlikely that he was still intent upon it, Illica mentioned it to Franchetti, and arranged to let him write the *libretto*. Then Puccini's interest awakened once more, and it needed all the skill and diplomacy of Illica and Ricordi to get the rights back again.

The first night of *Tosca* at the Costanzi in Rome has been mentioned elsewhere in this book; but throughout the composing of this work Puccini continues to make those small—or apparently small—suggestions which were of such immense value to the libretto.

He writes to Ricordi regarding the second act: "I have made some changes which I consider necessary, as for instance: *Come tu mi odii!*[1] is good, and *Tu mi odii?*[2] is impossible." He continues, "Why has the last line been cut out: *E avanti a lui tremava tutta Roma?*[3] I put it in, it serves my purpose. It is accordingly better to keep it."

[1] "How you hate me!" [2] "Do you hate me?"
[3] "And before him all Rome trembled."

Next came *Butterfly*, and here again there was the same difficulty over the libretto and Puccini producing new ideas at frequent intervals. The story was adapted by Belasco from a story by John Luther Long. Puccini saw the play, and was much impressed by it. Again he, Giacosa and Illica set to work. He worked very hard; he was not particularly well, but he never doubted that the work would be a tremendous success.

It seems impossible to doubt that the demonstration against it was not organized when it was given at La Scala on February 17, 1904. There was one performance only, and Ricordi, writing in one of the musical journals, comments upon the utterly unreasoning laughter of the audience, as, for example, when the maid of Butterfly "goes to pull up the blinds of the large window in the background".

Another journal reports: "Growls, shouts, groans, laughter, giggling, the usual single cries of *bis*, designed specially to excite the audience still more, these sum up the reception given by the public of the Scala to Giacomo Puccini's new work."

The opera was withdrawn by Puccini, Giacosa and Illica with the complete approval of Ricordi, and the performing fees were returned to the management despite their appeals to be allowed to give other performances. In spite of the fact that Puccini was only slowly recovering from a very serious injury, the result of a motor-car accident, he set to work at once on another arrangement of *Butterfly*. On May 28, 1904, it was given at the Teatro Grande at Brescia to a completely and utterly delighted audience.

It may be remarked that after the first disastrous performance at La Scala, on February 17, Rosina Storchio was leaving for America, where she was engaged to sing. Puccini, four days later, that is on February 22, was able to write to her a charming letter, in which there is no particular compassion for himself, but deep regret for the artists. He was critical of the American production, though the Press and the public were delighted with the opera; he also criticized the singing of the soprano. "She sings out of tune, and forces her voice, and it does not carry well in the large space of the theatre."

His next work was *La Fanciulla del West*, which was taken from David Belasco's play *The Girl of the Golden West*, which Puccini saw when he visited America. For this the librettists were Zangarini and Civinini. The work was promised its production at the Metropolitan, New York; this occurred on December 10, 1910, and the success was immediate. The first Italian performance was at the Costanzi in Rome on June 12, 1911. Here, too, the opera was declared to be brilliant. One paper said of Puccini, "He has never shown such a sure control of his genius and his skill as in this opera." Yet in spite of the praise given to it, this opera remains one of the least known of Puccini's operas; it may be that the setting is less attractive, and that the costumes lack the colour and splendour which have come to be associated with his work, for the music is of a very high order.

La Rondine was written when Puccini yielded to the persuasions of the directors of the Karltheater in Vienna to write an operetta. They arrived in Milan, these two directors, bringing with them Willner and Reichert to show him the libretto of La Rondine. Puccini did not dislike it, and began to work on it. He commissioned Adami to write the libretto in the traditional operetta manner and in Italian. The Vienese were to make the German translation. The work did not go well. Puccini wrote a piece here, a fragment there, but he was dissatisfied and finally wrote to Vienna that he could not compose an operetta. It must be opera or nothing!

Again he began to work, and into the writing of La Rondine he put much which was "limpid and scintillating" and the score was, we are told, "technically perfect". It was produced at Monte Carlo on March 17, 1917, and had a very real success. In the following May, it was given at Bologna and well received, but it never attained any great degree of popularity, and the production given in Vienna was not strikingly good.

In December 1918 Puccini's three one-act operas were produced in New York; they were successful and were given in Rome the following year. Their subjects vary greatly—Il Tabarro, which is a grim tragedy, Suor Angelica, which is mystical, and Gianni Schicchi, which is possibly the most amusing one-act opera ever written.

After attempting work on various stories, Puccini settled down to write his great opera Turandot. The opinions concerning the music of this work are still divided, the harmonies are broad and rich; true there are fewer of his usual lovely arias—it might be said that Turandot is on a larger and grander scale than his former works. It lacks perhaps the lovable qualities of Bohème, of Butterfly and of Tosca, but there are great masterful sweeps of melody which place this opera very high in the works of Puccini.

There is a wonderful atmosphere of horror and suspense created in the first act with the use of gongs and xylophones adding to the feeling of strain. Here, too, the music is a "commentary" on the text and action of the opera, as in the first act, when the guards attempt to drive the populace away from the palace with whips.

In the nostalgic musings of Ping, Pang and Pong there are some passages of tranquil beauty, and the tenor solo "Nessun Dorma" is a piece of sheer loveliness. Puccini longed to write the closing duet for Turandot and the Prince which should rank among the great love songs of the world. How much material he left in his notes we cannot tell; the work was finished by Alfano, who brought it to a successful conclusion after the

Master's death. Of the first performance at La Scala I have written in connection with the opera itself. He went to Brussels, as we know, taking with him thirty-six pages of composition and notes. He said that he could finish the work in three weeks.

Before he left for Brussels he wrote: "I am having a horrible time. This trouble in my throat is giving me no peace. I am going to Brussels to consult a well-known specialist. Will it be treatment? Or sentence of death? . . . The lines are good, exactly what were needed . . . so the duet is ready. As soon as I come back I shall get to work again."

The trouble in his throat had already been diagnosed as cancer, but this fact was concealed, mercifully, from Puccini.

In Brussels there were constant enquiries regarding his progress, but on November 26 Clausetti wrote, "The doctors are now saying that Puccini will certainly recover," and the doctor himself sent a message to the management of the Theatre de la Monnaie which said: "*Puccini en sortira*" ("Puccini will recover").

The end came three days later. The first presentation of Puccini's last opera was given at La Scala in April 1926.

Various opinions have been expressed concerning the character of Puccini. He has been stigmatized as "ordinary", "self-opinionated" and "boastful"; on the other hand he has been declared to have been essentially modest, rather shy, given to fits of melancholy, and loving simple things better than the noise, the luxury and the excitement of cities. One has only to read his letters, those letters which are so revealing, to realize the hours of toil he spent on his work, the way he altered and corrected because of his determination to give what he felt was not only his best but good theatre.

He said once, "There are certain fixed laws in the theatre: to interest, to surprise, to move"; and again, "I have the great weakness of being able to write only when my puppet executioners are moving on the scene"—and that is how it should be, surely.

He says in one of his letters: "If only I could be a purely symphonic writer! But that was not for me. I was born so many years ago . . . and Almighty God touched me with His little finger and said, 'Write for the theatre—mind, only for the theatre,' and I have obeyed the supreme command."

What was he like, this Puccini, this "man of the theatre"? I do not know if the statue of him still stands in La Scala, but here is a verbal picture of him by Renato Simoni: "Straight, tall, with shoulders squared and hat at a slight angle, his hands in his pockets, his step slightly swinging but strongly rhythmical, with his strong, sunburnt face, his suggestion of rough shyness and his good nature—sometimes boyish, and sometimes touched with compassion." Often when he was most depressed, when he gave way to melancholy, some apparently small thing would serve to suddenly illuminate his whole mental horizon, as for instance when Vittorio Gui wrote of him in a journal which had only a limited public, called *Pianoforte*. Puccini was delighted, and writes, "Gui has written a fine article on Puccini . . . it is the first voice that I have heard raised to vindicate me in the face of so many accusations and when . . . I have been forgotten or ignored."

He loved his home at Torre del Largo, near Lucca, and would willingly have spent every moment there, but late in the year 1921 he moved to Viareggio, because peat works had been opened at his former home and the noisy siren ruined the place for him.

There was a simplicity about him which is at times almost touchingly childlike, as when he writes to one of the Ricordi staff in Milan, to announce that he has bought a bicycle.

He adds: "Payable, however, by monthly instalments. You will have a visit from the manager of the firm of A. Schlegel, 36 Foro Bonaparte, whom will you please pay on my behalf seventy lire as the first instalment, and fifty lire every month afterwards. I shall pay it up completely at my return to Milan in October."

From Paris he writes: "I am sick of Paris! I am panting for the fragrant woods; I pant for the wind that blows free from the sea; I savour with wide nostrils its iodic salty breath and stretch my lungs to breathe it!

"I hate pavements!

"I hate palaces!

"I hate capitals!

"I hate columns!

"I love the beautiful column of the poplar and the fir. I love the vault of shady glades; and I love like a modern druid to make my temple, my house, my studio therein!"

One last quotation from a letter written to Ricordi. He writes again from Paris:

"I am not very happy here. I should like to be away now for the sake of my work. I cannot work here. I am suffering too much from nervous excitement. . . . An invitation to dinner makes me ill for a week. I am made like that, it is useless to insist. I wasn't born for a life of drawing-rooms and parties. What good does it do to expose myself to the risk of behaving like a cretin and an imbecile? I am made so—and you know me, but Tito does not, and he constantly insists that I must make an effort to smarten up. I don't want to make comparisons, because it would be ridiculous, but Verdi has always pleased himself in these matters, and—had not such a bad little career!"

So it would appear that Giacomo Puccini was at heart a simple man in his real taste, in the life which he preferred, and that he was not the swaggering creature some people have believed, intent only on achieving popular and easy success.

If Verdi were a giant in his genius and outlook, we must at least admit—in the words of Renato Simoni—that Puccini was "straight and tall".

GIOACHINO ROSSINI (1792-1868)

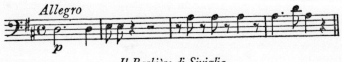

Il Barbière di Siviglia

TURNING to that valuable work *A Key to Opera*, which I have mentioned before, I find this comment on Rossini. Writing of contemporary Italian opera at the time of this composer, the comment is: "With Rossini it put forth new and gorgeous flowers, with Bellini and Donizetti it gained new elegiac and slightly effeminate pathos. . . . With Verdi, passion, masculine vigour and a new depth of expressive power."

Rossini was born at Pesaro, and is sometimes referred to as the "Swan of Pesaro". His family were poor people, his father being the town trumpeter of Lugo, and also the Inspector of Abbatoirs for the district. The elder Rossini had a great inclination to mix himself up with matters political, and in the disturbances of 1790, "backed the wrong horse" in his choice of parties. He found himself thrown into gaol when the faction which he had opposed attained power.

His wife took the small Gioachino with her to Bologna where, having some musical ability, she obtained an engagement in a travelling opera company in which she was to sing the *buffa* rôles. When her husband was released from prison, he joined her—with his trumpet— and played in the orchestra.

Young Rossini was left behind in Bologna where he was lodging with one of the local pork butchers. It may have been while here that Rossini developed his taste for good food, for of all towns in Italy Bologna was reputed to specialize most notably in food, the nickname of the town being "La Grassa".

He was already longing to study music, and became a pupil of one Prinetti, who earned his living teaching the harpsichord. As a teacher he could scarcely have been a great success, for it is recorded that he could only play with one finger!

The pork butcher about this time apprenticed Rossini to a black-smith, a trade which was unlikely to make much appeal to the boy, who, except for music, was not strikingly addicted to hard work, then or at any time.

He found a new teacher, Tesei, who recognized that the boy had promise and gave him excellent instruction. His progress was astonishingly rapid, and when only ten years old was able to earn a little money by singing in the church where his master was choirmaster and organist. At thirteen Rossini sang in Paer's opera, *Camilla*, and when not actually on the stage went into the orchestra and assisted there in company with his father, who had returned from tour complete with the rest of the family, and the—once official—trumpet. The boy was intent on his singing and managed to get lessons from the old tenor, Babbini. However, soon after his voice broke and he had to abandon his singing lessons.

About this time, because he was always an amusing and gay little fellow, he gained the valuable friendship of Chevalier Giusti, who had both wealth and education. Through his influence the boy was able to enter the Bologna Conservatory, where he studied under Padre Mattei who had been one of the teachers of Donizetti. He not only became absorbed in the study of counterpoint, but began to learn the cello, and was able before long to take part in chamber music concerts.

He had written a cantata and an overture which had actually been performed when he met another influential friend, the Marquis Cavalli. He was given a commission to write an opera for the Teatro San Mose at Venice. He also conducted an orchestra, gave lessons, acted as accompanist, in fact was ready to do anything which might earn him a little money.

His first opera was *La Cambiale di Matrimonio* and was produced when Rossini was eighteen. It was sufficiently well received to get him further commissions, meanwhile he wrote a cantata, *Didone Abbandonata*. In 1811 his second opera *L'Equivoco Stravagante* was produced in Bologna, and soon afterwards another called *Demetrio e Polibio* was given at the Teatro Valle. Almost immediately followed *L' Inganno Felice* and *L'Occasione Fa Il Ladro*, both of which were produced in Venice.

The first opera by Rossini to be given at La Scala was *La Pietra del Paragone* in 1812; this was very successful, and wonderfully given by a brilliant company of artists.

On February 6, 1813, we read in the chronicles of the Fenice "*Trionfali accoglienze al 'Tancredi' del ventunenne Gioachino Rossini*" ("The triumphal acknowledgment of the opera *Tancredi* by the twenty-one year old Gioachino Rossini"); in the same opera house the first performance of his *Sigismondo* was given on December 26, 1813, and on February 2, 1823, Rossini is again represented at La Fenice with his opera *Semiramide*. The comment here is, "*Tepide accoglienze alla 'Semiramide' di Rossini; dopo alcune modifiche introdotte dall'autore l'opera trionfa*".

Rossini was much liked in Venice where he had numbers of friends who all delighted to entertain him and give banquets in his honour. In 1815, through the influence of his friend Barbaja, Rossini was appointed as Musical Director of the San Carlo at Naples. He found that this city did not receive him with open arms as Venice had done, there were *cabals* and jealousies mostly emanating from the musicians of the town; but Rossini was easy-going, shrugged his shoulders and dismissed the whole matter.

While in Naples he wrote *Elizabeth, Queen of England* (*Elizabetta, Regina d' Inghilterra*), and soon after its production Rossini was called to Rome and ordered to fulfil the contract which he had made with the directorate there for two operas. The first one, as I have recorded in the history of the Rome theatre, was not an outstanding success, but the second was the famous, ever popular *Il Barbière di Siviglia*. Of the arguments and discussions which waged round this opera, of its first performance, and of the contentions of Paisiello I have also written. Sufficient to say that this remains the most popular of Rossini's works, and that after its initial performance he made certain alterations.

It would appear that Rossini was one of those furious workers who, once work is finished, has no more wish to make changes and alterations. He was asked to write a new overture to *Il Barbière*, he merely used the overture of *Elizabetta, Regina d' Inghilterra*, and after the fiasco of the song by Almaviva, which I have also mentioned, he used the tenor *aria "Ecco Ridente in Cielo"*, which was originally written for *Aureliano*, which was one of Rossini's operas produced at La Scala with no success whatever.

The San Carlo was burnt in 1816, but when it was rebuilt—which it was very quickly—Barbaja—that extraordinary man who should, by rights, have a book devoted to his life and his strange character—gave Rossini an even better position than that which he had previously held.

While in Naples Rossini composed his *Otello*, which was produced at the Teatro del Fondo in 1816. This was his first attempt at writing tragedy, and was well received although it was far surpassed by the great work of Verdi which was produced in 1887. In this production at Naples appeared the singer Isabella Colbran, to whom Rossini was married in 1822.

In the five years which followed *Otello*, Rossini wrote *Cenerentola, La Gazza Ladra*, and his oratorio-opera *Moses in Egypt* was given at the San Carlo, and was successful, though the "scenic effects" were too much for the technical appliances and machinery when it came to the passage of the Red Sea!

Later, after his marriage, possibly for his honeymoon, Rossini went to Vienna, where *Cenerentola* was given to a delighted audience; he remained there for some time, and repeated the social success which he had previously enjoyed in Venice.

212

In 1823 *Semiramide* was given at the Fenice, with the comment that I have already quoted. However, in this case it would appear that Rossini made the necessary alterations, and failure was changed to success. This opera, which seems to have vanished from the repertoire of opera companies, was produced in New York in 1826, 1855 and again in 1890, when the soprano and contralto rôles were sung by Patti and Scalchi with marked success.

We next find Rossini in Paris, where he was appointed Director of the Théatre des Italiens; he held this position for eighteen months, but any work which needed regular and careful attention was apt to bore him, he grew to hate his appointment, and there was general dissatisfaction not only on his side but on the side of the other controlling members of the theatre management. Rossini resigned, and was made "Inspector-General of Song"—with a salary as handsome as the title!

In 1829 he wrote *Guillaume Tell*, which was originally in five acts and which he reduced to three by taking out the third act and running the fourth and fifth acts into one. As it was originally written this opera would have run well over five hours. It was written in the French style, and possibly Rossini as an Italian did not find this easy to him. It lacks spontaneity, and although the music is heroic and often rises to great heights, and—to quote from Gustav Kobbé's excellent work on opera, there is always a feeling that "the sudden cuckoo is with difficulty restrained in its box and may at any time pop out and join in the proceedings". As with *Tancredi*, so in *Guillaume Tell*, the overture is still played very frequently, and equally frequently with disastrous results to poor Rossini's music.

This was Rossini's last opera, and he retired doing nothing more except to write his beautiful *"Stabat Mater"*.

He retired to Bologna, where he and his wife lived in happy contentment; they were both well provided with this world's goods and Rossini was able to indulge his tastes as a *gourmet* and a *bon vivant*.

He disliked the bustle and excitement of the theatre, and much preferred a leisurely and tranquil existence. It is said that during this period of retirement he went back to one of the pleasures of his youth— cooking special dishes of which he was abnormally fond. His wife died in 1845, and in 1847, when he was fifty-five, he married for the second time. His wife was Olympe Pelissier, who he had met first when he was in Paris.

He moved to Florence, where he mixed with the many musicians in that city, but still made no attempt to write. He was not particularly well, already he had been forced to go to Paris for a serious operation. He disliked the climate of Florence though he loved the town. In 1855

213

he returned to Paris, where again he was popular with everyone for his amusing conversation, his general good humour, and his geniality.

His portraits show him as a very stout man, with a kindly, humorous expression; he worked hard only when there was definite work to be done, and once he had succeeded in saving sufficient money to keep him in the comfort which he loved, he retired—at the age of thirty-seven.

GAETANO DONIZETTI (1797-1848)

Allegretto moderato

Bra-vo, bra-vo — Don Pa-squa-le! —
Don Pasquaie

GAETANO DONIZETTI was born in Burgamo, that lovely and fascinating city which overlooks so much of the beautiful country where Colleone is buried, and where the new opera house is named for the composer of *Don Pasquale*. There is also an older theatre, which when I last tried to enter had been turned into a Fascist Headquarters or something equally unromantic and dreary. This stands in the old town, Burgamo Alta, which is by far the most interesting part of the place. The modern town, which lies far below—for old Burgamo is built on a hill—is clean, busy and rather painfully modern.

It seems uncertain as to what trade or profession Donizetti's father belonged, either he was a small tradesman, or an equally small government official.

Gaetano studied music while very young in his native city, and later went to Bologna where he studied with Mattei; leaving there he was a pupil at the Naples Conservatory. His studies ended, Donizetti's father wished his son to take up teaching—a common happening with young men who had studied music and also wished to compose, when their families were not too well endowed with this world's goods. This was, at that time, a recognized thing—study music, and then return home to teach. This alternative to actual composition was the one which was offered to Puccini when he left the Conservatory at Milan. Young Donizetti refused, his father continued to urge him, and finally the relations between the son and his father grew so strained that Gaetano left home and joined the army.

I find a record that it was in the army he wrote his first opera, *Enrico di Borgogna*, while he was stationed with his regiment in Venice. Also that the opera was produced in that city and had considerable success. In the chronicles of the Fenice, however, the first mention I can find of Donizetti is that of February 4, 1836, when his opera *Belisario* was produced with success. The first opera, *Enrico di Borgogna*, was first presented, according to one authority, in 1818.

Donizetti was a most rapid worker, and within a year had finished his second opera, *Il Falegname di Livonia* (The Carpenter of Livonia).

OPERA IN ITALY

This was produced at Mantua in 1818, and must have been at one or other of the old theatres of Mantua, as the Teatro Sociale was not opened in that city until 1822.

His third opera—produced the next year, 1820—was not a success, but *Zoraide di Granata*, which was produced in Rome in 1822, set the seal of public approval on the work of the young composer. He was carried in triumph to the Capitol, where he was presented with a laurel wreath and granted exemption from future military service.

For the following six years Donizetti worked as hard as ever, he wrote with almost incredible rapidity, and was inclined to be slightly intolerant of composers who worked slowly and with difficulty. When he was told that Rossini had written the *Barber of Seville* in thirteen days, Donizetti shrugged his shoulders and said, "No wonder—he is so lazy."

In 1830 he completed *Anna Bolena*, which was well received not only in Italy but in many other European countries. In the London production the great Lablache, one of the greatest bassos in history, played the part of Henry VIII. Two years later Donizetti wrote one of his best-known works, *L'Elisir d'Amore*, which was produced in Milan.

I find records of two other operas, *L'Ajo nell' Imbarazzo*, which was offered at the Mantua Teatro Sociale in 1828, and *Olivo e Pasquale*, given there in 1829. *L'Elisir d'Amore* was written when Donizetti was strongly influenced by Rossini—"that lazy fellow"—and the quack doctor, Dulcamara, is one of the most amusing *buffo* figures in Italian opera. The plot is slight, but the music has great charm. In this opera Donizetti begins to show more markedly his *pénchant* for using certain instruments to obtain special effects; in *L'Elisir d'Amore* this is shown in the bassoons which introduce the flowing beauty of *"Una furtiva lagrima"*. Later he was to use the same device in *Lucia*, this time the harps and the flute obbligato in the introduction of the Mad Scene are noticeable. *Lucia di Lammermoor* was produced in Naples at the San Carlo, on September 26, 1835, later in England—in English—and also in New York. The rôle is a favourite among sopranos and among the most successful in this rôle have been Patti, Melba, Tetrazzini and Galli-Curci.

Lucia scored a great success in Naples and its composer was offered a professorship in the Royal College of Music in that city. He remained in Naples for four years, only leaving for the production of his opera, *Marino Faliero*, at the Théatre des Italiens in Paris in 1835. Later he returned to Paris and stayed there for a considerable time, but on his first visit he found the Parisiens talking of nothing but Bellini and his work, *I Puritani*.

Returning to Naples he was made Director of the college, and at this time he produced a small but charming work, *Il Campanello di Notte*. This was said to have been written for a small and impecunious

216

opera company, the director of which came to Donizetti to beg him to write something for his company in order to "set them on their feet once more". This the composer good-naturedly did, even writing the libretto himself. *Il Campanello di Notte* was written in just over a week!

In 1839 Donizetti found himself at loggerheads with the authorities in Naples, who refused to allow his opera *Poliuto* to be produced. The composer gave up his post at the College and went back to Paris, taking his opera with him. It was successfully produced there, and Donizetti took over the management of the Salle Ventadour where a number of his operas were produced.

While he was in Paris, we find that his work was not neglected in Italy, *Anna Bolena, Torquato Tasso, Il Furioso, Belisario, Gemma di Vergy, Lucia di Lammermoor* and *Parisina* all being given at Mantua between 1834 and 1838.

At the Fenice on February 18, 1837, *Pia de' Tolomei* was given for the first time, followed on January 30, 1839, by what is noted in the chronicles of the Fenice as *"Insuccesso di Maria de Rudenʒ di Donizetti"*. Not a *fiasco*, you notice, but certainly not a popular reception.

Lucreʒia Borgia was written and produced in Italy in 1833, but its Paris production was not until 1840, when Victor Hugo visited the opera some weeks after the opening, when it was running most success-fully, and obtained an injunction on the grounds that without his per-mission the libretto had been made from his tragedy of the same name. Donizetti immediately changed the name to *La Rinegata*, and the opera was redressed—in Turkish costume! The run continued.

In 1840 both *La Favorita* and *La Fille du Régiment* were produced in Paris. *The Daughter of the Regiment* was produced in Italy at La Scala in October 1840, and in England—with Jenny Lind—in 1847. Among other operas which he composed about this time were *Marino Faliero, Roberto Devereaux, La Regina di Golconda* and *Il Furioso all' Isola di S. Domingo.*

He left Paris in 1841 and returned to Italy, later visiting Vienna, where his *Linda di Chamounix* was produced at the Kärutherthor on May 19, 1842. This opera contains what is regarded as one of the com-posers best *arias*: in the first act Linda sings *"O Luce di Quest' Anima"*, which is written in a beautifully light and attractive manner. The story itself is simple and unpretentious and this has perhaps led to its "old-fashioned" air; it is not that the music is not admirable, but the story has grown out of date to modern audiences. It is one of those conventional plots where after trials and tribulations everyone "lives happy ever after".

Donizetti returned to Paris in 1843 when he wrote *Don Pasquale*, one of his greatest successes and a first-rate piece of comedy. This was

produced in Paris on January 4, 1843: its first Italian performance I have
failed to find, but it was certainly presented in Mantua in the Spring of
1844.

I quote from the admirable book entitled *Opera Nights* of Ernest
Newman, in which he says of this opera:

> "The wit and humour of this music, the composition of which is
> said to have occupied Donizetti no more than eleven days, ensured
> popularity for the work from the beginning. It was first performed
> in Paris on January 4, 1843, with a cast that sends our thoughts back
> wistfully to the great days when singing *was* singing: Lablache was
> the Pasquale, Tamburini the Malatesta, Mario the Ernesto and Grisi
> the Norina."

He continues, after a eulogy on the work of the other artists:

> "As for Lablache opera has perhaps never seen or heard his like
> before or since. He was equally great in serious or comic rôles.
> Henry Chorley . . . described him as 'taking him all for all the most
> remarkable man whom I have ever seen in opera'. He was of gigantic
> stature, 'yet one never felt on the stage how huge he was'."

Mr. Newman continues by insisting that the part of Don Pasquale
should never be "clowned", and how right he is. He adds:

> "Pasquale, for all his amorous foolishness, was a gentleman in an
> epoch when good breeding still counted for something."

Donizetti followed *Don Pasquale* with a rather gloomy and dull
opera, *Don Sebastian*, which when produced was a failure, and which
disappeared into the limbo of forgotten operas.

The composer himself was beginning to suffer from those terrible
signs of exhaustion and melancholy. He had for many years been "burning the candle at both ends", he had loved pleasure and excitement,
and his work had been tremendous. At fifty-two he was a very sick
man, suffering from cerebro-spinal trouble. He had probably suffered
from the existence of this disease for many years, and he had done
nothing to delay its progress.

This brilliant creature, who had written sixty-four operas—of which
at least three are still great favourites with the opera-going public in
many countries, of which several are still able to make their appearance
in the repertoire of the great opera companies from time to time and be
assured of a warm welcome—who could when necessary write his own

libretti as he did for *Don Pasquale* and that charming *Il Campanello di Notte*, became paralysed in 1845, at the age of fifty-two. For nearly eighteen months the unfortunate man was in a lunatic asylum, and in October 1847 he was taken to Burgamo, where he died on April 8, 1848.

His portraits show him as good-looking in a rather ineffective way; he certainly does not appear to be the man of almost boundless energy which he certainly was.

His early work shows the influence of Rossini—or it might be more just to say that it proved his admiration for Rossini—his later work matures and in it can be found many of the idioms in music which Verdi was to use with such effect and to give to the world in their most perfect form. In making these comparisons it must be clearly understood that while none of these composers "copied" or based their work upon that of composers who had preceded them, the *influence* of the earlier composers is traceable. These great musicians had their finger on the "public pulse"; they sensed, more generally than not, what the public liked and in which direction the taste of their audiences would lie. They, as good servants of the public, and in the service of the evolution and development of opera, took advantage of their knowledge.

I find in my notes the recording that Donizetti was given in La Scala, when *Lucia di Lammermoor* was presented in 1922. *La Favorita* was given at the Arena Verona in 1938, with Stignani, Malipiero, Maria Basiola and Tancredi Pasero. The conductor was Capuana. *L'Elisir d'Amore* was given in 1936 at the Arena with Schipa and Carosio. The conductor being Serafin.

In 1934 there was a memorable performance in the Arena with Toti dal Monte and Borgioli, when Marinuzzi was the conductor.

VINCENZO BELLINI (1801-1835)

Allegro marziale

Norma

IT has become customary to adopt a slightly patronizing tone when speaking or writing of Vincenzo Bellini, to state that he had not the humour of a Rossini, nor the grandeur of a Verdi—both of which facts, if facts they are, do not of necessity damn him as a composer. Remember that, as this young man was only thirty-four when he died, his gifts could scarcely have come to fruition. Admittedly he was limited in his instrumentation, but that was surely a fault of his immaturity, and owing to the fact that he had not yet complete mastery of the opportunities which with greater experience he might have taken full advantage. His harmonies have been described as "somewhat static" and this again may have been a fault of his youth. On the other hand there is a gracious warmth in his music, occasionally it rises to heights of real grandeur, and several times his dramatic instinct is unerring and effective.

It has been said that his music was like a "large guitar"; on the other hand, certain authorities hold that Chopin "owed much to Bellini". If he had not genius, or even remarkable talent, there were moments when he flung all that he had—and it represented a great deal—into his music, and the result is the lasting beauty of such *arias* as *"Casta Diva"* and *"Non Giunge Uman Pensiero"*. *"Ah! Non Giunge"* remains one of the favourite *arias* for sopranos, its brilliance is unmistakable, and it is not merely the bright, scintillating, hard brilliance of a mere "show piece": there is tenderness and a kind of "shining" tranquillity.

As for *"Casta Diva"*—where Bellini used one of his favourite devices in allowing the chorus to hold the essential melody, while the soprano enlarges and elaborates it—the sheer beauty of this work cannot be questioned, much less denied.

I find in one comment upon this opera the following, *"Norma* has dignity and beauty when it is sung with conviction as well as with adequate skill, but a mediocre performance makes it painfully ridiculous." That of course is a plea for "Divas who can act", but the fact that *Norma* in the hands of a poor singer is painfully ridiculous is no fault of Bellini's, surely!

Neither can Bellini be dismissed as merely having written "charming music of no great depth". There are passages of great dignity and even severity in both *Norma* and *La Sonnambula*—and although neither of these operas are given very frequently, they are never completely omitted from the repertoire of the great opera houses.

Vincenzo Bellini was born in Catania, in Sicily, where his name is still held in the highest affection and admiration. His father was an organist, and, I have read, also a fine performer on the cembalo.[1] With the assistance of some of the local nobility, it was possible for Bellini to obtain the best possible musical education. The expenses of a period of study being guaranteed, he entered the Naples Conservatory in 1819.

Bellini's first opera, *Adelson è Salvina*, was produced in Naples; among the audience was Barbaja, that energetic and alert man of business, who was always on the look out for new talent in his capacity of manager of La Scala in Milan and also of the San Carlo. Barbaja immediately commissioned the young composer to write an opera for the San Carlo; this was completed and produced in a few months, and *Bianca e Fernando* was a success with Naples audiences.

Barbaja gave a second commission, this time for a work to be given at La Scala, and he promised that the great tenor Rubini should be engaged for it. *Il Pirata* was duly produced at the Milan House and attracted considerable attention. The rather over-decorated music which audiences had come to expect from Rossini was replaced with those simple melodies for which Bellini came to be so well known. The contemporary criticisms of *Il Pirata* say that Rubini sang these melodies so beautifully and with such distinction that Bellini's opera could not have been better received.

The opera was later produced in London, as was *La Straniera*, which had its first Italian presentation at La Scala in 1829. This opera was not a great success, and even in other cities in Italy it failed to make a favourable impression. On March 11, 1830, *I Capuletti ed i Montecchi* (a version, of course, of *Romeo and Juliet*) was given for the first time at the Fenice in Venice, Grisi was in the cast, and the opera is reported to have been "*Esito magnifico*". Bellini's work does not appear in Venice again until 1833, when *Beatrice di Tenda* was given in March of that year. This is described with terse brevity as "*Scarso successo di Beatrice di Tendra*".

After this failure Bellini found as a librettist the famous Romani, who was the most distinguished writer of libretto of the day and who was willing to work in conjunction with the young composer. The result of their joint labours was *La Sonnambula*, which was produced at La Scala and acclaimed as an immediate success.

The story is simple, not to say ingenuous, but the music—though

[1] A small piano or harpsichord.

Bellini still continued to use a limited instrumentation—is charming and held a great warmth and sentiment. The *aria "Ah, Non Giunge"* has been referred to already, and the rôle of Armina became very popular with sopranos, both Patti and Albani sang it with great success, as did Jenny Lind and Grisi.

After this production the friendship between Bellini and the genial Rossini developed, and the elder man took an interest in Bellini which never weakened for the rest of the young man's tragically short life.

On December 26, 1831, Bellini's greatest triumph—*Norma*—was produced at La Scala. The story is of ancient Britain, and the music rises to great heights of dignified and severe beauty, while retaining the simplicity to which Bellini adhered. The opera was a great success, and is still given—when sopranos can be found who are capable of singing the rôle of Norma. The last time I heard this work was at the Arena at Verona, with Cigna and Pasero singing. The production was admirable, the orchestra was in charge of Marinuzzi, and the cast also included Ebe Stignani and Parmeggiani. The presentation took place in July 1935, and under a deep blue, starlit sky in that vast Arena, and with the magnificent stage setting, the melodies seemed to gain in beauty and intensity. Never have I heard *"Casta Diva"* sung so wonderfully, and even now I have only to put on the recording of this opera to be transported mentally to the Arena of Verona, and I see again the beautifully staged opera, hear the fine orchestra, and hear Cigna's voice to the "accompaniment" of the chorus.

It may be recorded here that for the centenary of Bellini's birth, as a *"solenne commemorazione per l' autore della Norma"*, this opera was given at the Costanzi (now the Teatro dell' Opera) in Rome, and Gabriele d'Annunzio recited an Ode which he had written in praise of Bellini and his music.

Norma was a success everywhere, and when it was given in Mantua, where his *Straniera* had been coldly received, it is recorded as a veritable triumph, and "marking a historic page in the opera of Italy".

Bellini went to England and from there to Paris, to visit his friend Rossini, and here he was commissioned to write an opera for the Théatre des Italiens. He worked hard, they say even "feverishly", and *I Puritani* was produced on January 25, 1835, with Grisi as Elvira, and Rubini as Arturo. While this opera does not attain the heights reached in *Norma*, it gives magnificent opportunities for the tenor—Arturo—and the soprano.

Gustav Kobbé records that it was while singing the duet in the second act of *I Puritani*, that Antonio Galassi, the great Italian baritone, lost his voice. He says, "I heard break and go to pieces the voice of Antonio Galassi, the great baritone of the heyday of Italian opera at the

THE MEN WHO WROTE THE OPERAS

Academy of Music.[1] '*Suoni la tromba!*' He could sound it no more. The career of a great artist was at an end."

I Puritani was given in London on May 21, 1835, when it was called *I Puritani ed i Cavalieri;* in the September of that year Bellini broke down through over-work. He had never been a robust man, and his delicate constitution gave way under the demands which he had made upon it. He was on a visit to Puteaux near Paris, when he contracted some kind of internal infection, and died on September 23, 1835.

He was only thirty-four.

In his native town of Catania, the piano on which he worked out his early compositions is still preserved, and when I was there last, almost immediately after the liberation of Sicily by the Allies, the custodian of the little Bellini museum talked to me at great length about Bellini and his music. He spoke with that affection which exists for such people as Bellini in the minds of men who, while they could never have known him, have come to have a feeling of genuine sentiment for him through their knowledge of his work.

We gather that Bellini was a lovable person, delicate and given to fits of melancholy, but possessing a kindliness and modesty which endeared him to everyone.

There is a monument to him in Naples, and also in Catania, where the opera house is called after him, as is one of the smaller theatres in Naples.

NOTE.—I find that in the spring of 1868 *Giulietta e Romeo* by Bellini, with the last act written by Vaci (also spelt Vacci), was given at the Sociale at Mantua. It is recorded as being a complete failure at its first presentation. (*Cadde disastrosamente alla prima rappresentazione.*) Was this an attempt to rewrite *I Capuletti ed i Montecchi*, which was produced as an *Esito magnifico* in Venice on March 11, 1830, or was it another opera altogether? I have been unable to find further trace of it, or to obtain any information regarding it.

New York.

AMILCARE PONCHIELLI (1834-1886)

La Gioconda

PONCHIELLI might be classed among the "one opera composers"; he will be, and is known to posterity and present opera lovers almost solely through his magnificent work *La Gioconda*. This work is not only remarkably popular, but it richly deserves to be so, and it seems strange that the man who could write such harmonies, who could devise such fine dramatic moments, in whom the characterization of his characters is so fully developed, should not have succeeded more widely.

He was born in the province of Cremona, and as a child his musical talent was so unmistakable that he was admitted to the Conservatory of Milan at the age of nine years. He remained there until he was over twenty, when his first opera—*O Promessi Sposi*, which was, of course, based upon the novel of that name—was produced at Cremona. The opera appears to have been successful, and for the next fifteen years Ponchielli produced a number of operas and at least two ballets. The names of the operas are unfamiliar to us, two were produced at Cremona and one at Piacenza.

His first ballet, *Le Due Gemelle* (The Two Twins), which had a considerable success, was given at La Scala in 1873. Another ballet, *Clarina*, from his pen was given at La Scala the same year. Ponchielli was retained by the Scala management for three years, during which time he wrote a cantata in honour of the reinterment of Donizetti's body at Burgamo in 1875.

In April 1876 *La Gioconda* was produced at La Scala, and was an immediate success. The writer of the book was the famous—probably the most famous of all writers for opera—Arrigo Boito.

The popularity of *La Gioconda* has never waned, and it is given frequently. The music is masterly, descriptive and highly dramatic. In Ponchielli's work there were many pieces of instrumentation which obviously influenced both Mascagni and Leoncavallo. It may be that it lays claim to be "penny plain and tuppence coloured", but it remains a fine and virile piece of work, and an opera which provides magnificent opportunities for those artists who are capable of taking them.

Ponchielli did little more of any significance after *La Gioconda*;

in 1881 he became maestro di Cappella in Burgamo, where it is said that he carried out his duties with "dignity and fidelity". He died in Milan in 1886, his last work being a hymn to Garibaldi. During the time that Ponchielli was teaching in Milan some years before the production of *La Gioconda*—probably while he was actually employed at La Scala writing ballets—two of his pupils were the young Puccini and Mascagni.

RUGGIERO LEONCAVALLO (1858-1919)
PIETRO MASCAGNI (1863-1945)
UMBERTO GIORDANO (1867-——)

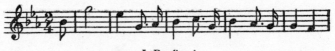

I Pagliacci

THESE first two composers may well be dealt with together, for there is a certain similarity between them. Here are two more of the "one opera" composers, though neither of them produced anything which even remotely approached the dignity and artistry of Ponchielli's *La Gioconda*.

Their claim to fame rests on the two short operas which are now almost invariably given in the same "bill" and which are referred to by a certain type of opera-goers as *Cav.* and *Pag.*

Leoncavallo was born in Naples, and studied at the Conservatory there; he also showed considerable talent for the pianoforte, studied with a teacher named Siri, and later studied literature at the University of Bologna.

His first opera was based on the life of the unfortunate young English poet, Chatterton. The opera progressed and one impresario was so impressed by it that he said that he would produce it as soon as Leoncavallo had finished it. The work done, the composer went in search of the impresario—who had disappeared leaving the poor young man in very straitened circumstances.

It was then that Leoncavallo began his wanderings which led him as far afield as Egypt. He gave music lessons, he accompanied, and gave concerts on the piano.

He returned to Italy and began to compose what was to have been his masterpiece, a trilogy called *Crepusculum*. He submitted the first part in a still unfinished state to Ricordi, who promised to publish it. As time passed and this first part, *I Medici*, still remained unpublished, Leoncavallo began to work on *I Pagliacci*, writing the libretto as well as the music. He worked desperately hard, finished the work, and offered it to the publisher Sonzogno, who had published *Cavalleria Rusticana* by Mascagni two years previously. *I Pagliacci* was produced at the Teatro dal Verma in 1892, its success was instantaneous, and it was soon established as a popular favourite.

226

On the strength of this success, Leoncavallo's earlier work was brought out; *I Medici* was produced in 1893, but failed to please the audience, and the other two parts of the trilogy were never finished. *Chatterton* was produced in Rome in 1896, but also failed. Leoncavallo's next opera was *La Bohème*, but it failed possibly because it was produced two months after the first performance of Puccini's opera on the same theme and taken from the same novel by Henri Mürger.

In 1900 Leoncavallo completed his opera *Zaza*, which was produced at the Teatro Lirico in Milan, but its reception was cold. Here and there throughout the opera there are fragments of music which are full of melody, though nothing ever rises to great heights.

The German Emperor, who was greatly taken by Leoncavallo's work, commissioned him to write an opera which should laud and exalt the Hohenzollern family. The story is that of Frederick II, and when it was produced at the Berlin Royal Opera House, under "the gracious and immediate patronage of the Emperor and the Court", not even this somewhat questionable advantage could atone for the fact that the music was dull and uninspired, while being at the same time pompous and lacking in real melodies.

In 1906 Leoncavallo toured with *I Pagliacci* which he conducted himself, and visited all the important cities of Europe. The opera was produced at Covent Garden on May 19, 1893, and again given at Leicester —in English—on June 15, 1893.

He also toured Canada and the United States, where he completed *La Jeunesse de Figaro*, which was produced and failed.

In 1913 his opera *Zingari* was produced at San Francisco, where it failed, as it had done when produced in London a year previously. Leoncavallo died at Montecatini, the celebrated Italian *"bagni"*, on August 9, 1919.

The music of *I Pagliacci*, which bears some resemblance to the *Cavalleria* of Mascagni, is not of a particularly high order. The story of the opera is sordid and even brutal. When one remembers how Puccini was accused of writing a "decadent opera" when he produced *Tosca*, it is a source of astonishment that Leoncavallo did not suffer from the same denunciation. Poor Puccini! Only the other day I read, to me, the astonishing statement that *The Geisha* had a certain historic importance, owing to its obvious influence on Puccini's *Madame Butterfly*! The one—*Butterfly*—taken from a short story by Luther Long and the drama by Belasco; the other with the book by Owen Hall and the music by Sidney Jones. One produced at Daly's in London and an immediate success, the other produced eight years later at La Scala where it was a failure, and only succeeded after Puccini made drastic alterations. I have searched Puccini's letters for any reference to either hearing or referring to the music of Sidney Jones—I can find none.

Cavalleria Rusticana

Pietro Mascagni, who preceded Leoncavallo, must rank as the better composer because with all his faults there is in *Cavalleria* a kind of rough, if crude, sincerity and one or two passages of real, if not particularly exalted, beauty.

He was the son of a baker living in Livorno (Leghorn) and his father had not the slightest wish that his son should follow music as a career. He opposed the idea with great firmness, and when Pietro contrived to enter the Instituto Luigi Cherubini in his native town, he did so without telling his father what he had done. When his father discovered that the boy was actually studying music, he was furiously angry, and Mascagni's hopes might have been dashed to the ground had not his uncle come forward with an offer to adopt the youth and also pay for his future musical education.

Mascagni was held in esteem by his teachers, and composed a Symphony in C Minor and a Kyrie in honour of Cherubini. Later his cantata *Filanda* was given an "honourable mention" at a competition held at the International Exhibition in Milan. (It may be noted that *Filanda* was revived in Florence at the Teatro Comunale for a very brief run.)

Baron de Lardarel, a nobleman of Livorno, offered to send Mascagni to the Conservatory of Milan, but for reasons which are not clear Mascagni did not settle down to the life and left, joining a travelling orchestra, making a poor living and going from one small and unimportant company to another.

He married and went to live at Cerignola, where he earned some kind of a living by teaching the piano and also being director of the local school of music. At this time the publishers Sonzogno—to whom it will be remembered Leoncavallo submitted his *I Pagliacci*, though at a later date—were offering a prize for the best one act opera. Mascagni submitted his *Cavalleria Rusticana*, a work on which he had worked while touring round Italy. He was awarded the prize and the opera was produced in Rome on May 17, 1890.

The first performance must have been extraordinary, for soon after the early part of this short opera the whole house was in a state of wild excitement and enthusiasm; the critics were full of nothing but praise for the work, and in a night Mascagni had become one of Italy's most celebrated people. He wrote to his father at Livorno, "*La mia posizione è assoluta mente cambiata.*"[1] "But it seems fantastic!" he adds.

His next work was *L'Amico Fritz*, which was given in Rome the following year and was received without much enthusiasm, though it has still occasional presentations given, and is heard fairly frequently on the Italian Radio. The work is pleasant, tuneful but not outstanding.

However, this failure did not affect in any way the world-wide success of *Cavalleria*, and it is recorded that "it was impossible to visit any café in Europe without hearing the music of this opera; it was played in all restaurants, by all orchestras, not only in Italy but in Austria, Germany and England".

Guglielmo Ratcliff was produced in 1895, but it was so gloomy and heavy that the Italians disliked it; in 1896 Mascagni completed *Zanetto* but this—although the critics admitted that he had taken more care in the writing—did not prove acceptable.

Two years later, in 1898, Mascagni completed *Iris* which was something of a rather mild success, but one critic wrote, "Mascagni must have written this opera for his own pleasure, for it most certainly gave none to the audience." The scenes were set in Japan, and the story was filled with intense gloom. This was given in the Metropolitan in New York in 1906 and 1928.

Mascagni's next work was *Le Maschere*, produced in 1901, and he had the idea of arranging for the production of this opera to take place on the same night in no less than seven Italian opera houses. The opera was produced at the Costanzi at Rome on January 17, 1901. The reception was cool, while at Genoa the audience would not allow the opera to be finished so great was their dislike for it. The chronicles of the Fenice at Venice—which, incidentally, state that *Le Maschere* was only given in five opera houses not seven as is sometimes stated. The production was a failure in Venice, and is described as "*Si fischiano Le Maschere di Mascagni*".

In 1903 Mascagni toured America, but the tour was a failure, for several reasons including what appears to have been bad management and an indifferent company.

He returned to Italy to find that his position as director at Pesaro had been filled in his absence, and his financial state was far from good. He was, however, given the appointment of Director to the National School of Music in Rome.

He wrote *L'Amica*, which was produced with moderate success in

[1] "My position is absolutely changed."

Monte Carlo in 1905; this was followed by *Isabeau*, produced in Buenos Aires in 1911, and also in January 1912. This opera had its first presentation at the Fenice, Venice, and on the same night at La Scala. It has been given more frequently of late years, and some of the presentations have been memorable (*see* Jimmy Robertson's notes). In 1921 *Il Piccolo Marat* was produced in Rome with considerable—if not very lasting—success. It was given with a new *décor* at La Scala in 1938, though not one of the "star" operas of the season which contained *Macbeth, Maruf, Nerone, Fidelio* and *Turandot*.

Mascagni died in Rome on August 2, 1945.

His music probably attained its highest peak in *Isabeau*, which is referred to during its production in Mantua in 1912, when it was given several times during the season, as always having a "happy reception" with this very critical audience.

Fedora

Umberto Giordano was born at Foggia in 1867. He was the son of an artizan, who wished him—these parents of Italian composers seem to have always "run true to type" with very few exceptions—to follow his father's trade. However, the providential neighbour arrived and offered to send the boy to Naples when he had finished the musical education which he could obtain in Foggia.

He worked hard, and left home for the Naples Conservatory, where he studied for nine years, it is recorded, "with great diligence". His first effort at opera was a rather "youthful" production called *Marina*, but it was considered sufficiently good for it to interest that very "go-ahead" publisher, Sonzogno, whose name occurs so often in connection with the works of the more youthful of Italian composers. He was commissioned to write another opera, and chose for its theme *Mala Vita*, a play which was popular at the time but of which the plot was not particularly pleasing. The work attracted considerable attention when it was produced in Rome in 1892, although much of the attention given was due to the plot and not to the music. If it was produced at the Costanzi it was not considered worthy of record in the chronicles of that opera house for I find no mention of it.

Giordano followed this with *Regina Diaz*, produced at Naples in

1894 with no success whatever. Two years later he completed his opera *Andrea Chénier*, which was produced at La Scala, Milan, and was an immediate success. The work was acclaimed everywhere for its beauty and excellence; it not only played to crowded houses in Italy but also all over Europe. In this work Giordano achieved his greatest success; musically the opera is filled with lovely melodies and the whole work shows not only a masterly knowledge of the orchestration and instrumentation, but an ability to write melodiously and with great "smoothness".

This opera was given at the New York Academy of Music in 1898, and later at the Manhattan Opera House and in Boston.

Giordano continued to work without ceasing: like so many of these composers the urge to write music was insistent. He embarked on a musical version of Sardou's great drama, *Fedora*. This was produced at the Lirico, Milan, in 1898, and apart from the music, great excitement and even amusement was caused by the fact that "bicycles are introduced, a truly modern note". Not that the bicycles were ridden, but the mere fact that they were wheeled on to the stage caused as much interest as did the hansom cab and horse introduced into the dramatic play, *Zaza*.

The success of *Fedora* was considerable, and at that very critical opera house, Mantua, where it was given in January 1899, it is recorded that the success was extraordinary, and that the audience consisted not only of the people of Mantua but from Verona, Brescia and Cremona. The opera had been produced at the Teatro Lirico in Milan previously. The performance is stated to have been *"Esito felicissimo"*.

I heard this opera three times at Bologna in 1946, and I must admit that it impressed me greatly. It may not have the limpid beauty of many of the passages in *Andrea Chénier*, but for its fine story, the dignified scenery taken in conjunction with the music which is often very melodious, and has fine passages of musically dramatic work, it remains memorable. I also had the privilege of watching the soprano at work on the part, and as these "rehearsals" took place under the direction of an Italian opera star who has long since retired and now gives instruction in production, it was both interesting to watch, and, I might add, instructive. To see the character of Feodora emerge, to notice small touches which were introduced from time to time until the complete character—with the voice not detracting from the characterization but enriching it—emerged, was an experience which any actress might value highly.

In 1915 Giordano composed *Madame Sans Gene*, the story of the celebrated laundress of Napoleon. This was produced in Italy and later at the Metropolitan, New York, but in both countries its success was not outstanding, and it has been dropped from the repertoires. Since then, except for an opera which was given in New York, and which achieved only a *succès d'estime*, Giordano has not produced anything for the operatic stage.

It may be said that while Giordano's work is uneven, while his work is not consistently brilliant, he has a style which is undoubtedly higher in quality than the majority of Italian composers of the last fifty years. To dismiss him as comparatively insignificant is unfair; he never rose to the great heights of Verdi or Puccini, but at least two of his operas still find a place in the repertoires, and rightly so.

FINAL NOTE

La Traviata (Verdi)

I HAVE derived great pleasure from the writing and arranging of this book, fulfilling an ambition of my own and Jimmy Robertson's to "one day write a book about opera". I have already stated that this is not a book for the specialists, neither is it written by a specialist, except the parts which are from Jimmy's pen—and not mine.

There must be hundreds, thousands of men and women who served in Italy during the war, who made their first excursions into opera in this country. I remember when the talk of giving opera to the troops was first mooted, I heard many statements that "you'll never get English and Americans to go to listen to opera". There were many "head-shakings" and gloomy prophecies! Opera was offered, not as something of "educational value" but as entertainment, and everywhere the opera houses were packed. Houses were "sold out" long before the performance, audiences listened with attention and appreciation, they came not once but many times. Catania, Naples, Bari, Rome, Florence, Padua, Venice, Trieste and Udine all remember the Allied troops as being most admirable and attentive audiences.

The old belief that opera was a "high-brow" and essentially difficult form of entertainment has been killed—let us hope for ever. True, there are operas where the music is difficult to comprehend completely at the first or even second hearing; there are plots which are involved and improbable but these are in the minority. In the main the stories of the operas may be slightly melodramatic and highly coloured—as in *La Gioconda* or *Un Ballo in Maschera*—but nothing could be more simple and straightforward than both the plot and the music of *La Bohème* or *Rigoletto*. Personally, I have always to wrinkle my brows a little to remember exactly what is happening in *Il Trovatore*, but the beauty more than compensates for any mental exercises in recollection.

Opera must be studied if one is to understand its "soul". By that word I do not mean that students of opera must delve into heavy and often highly technical books, the soul of opera never lives in those pages. Study by listening, listen not only once to a great opera but as often as your time and purse will allow. For these great works are like some fine tapestry or splendid painting. With each visit new beauties are apparent,

233

new details appear, and take their proper place in the scheme, and slowly the listener comes to comprehend what was in the mind of the composer as he wrote. Opera ceases to be a series of "tunes I remember", a number of *arias* strung together with a thread of incidental orchestral music. We no longer wait impatiently for the *arias* which are familiar to us: "*O Patria! Quanto Mi Costi!*", "*Vissi d'Arte*", "*Questo e Quello Per Me Pari Sono*", or even the great "*Casta Diva*" as isolated "numbers"; we know that they are part of the plan, the scheme of the work to which we listen to—with our greater knowledge—as a whole, complete and satisfying.

In England at the moment there is a great *risorgimento* of opera, in no less than three theatres in London may it be heard, and although to my mind opera should always be sung in the language in which it was originally written and not in a translation, yet there is always the loveliness of the music and the wonder of the orchestration.

Although it is not absolutely "safe" to judge voices which are heard only on the radio, yet the ability to listen to opera given in great foreign opera houses is a great boon, and an immense aid to complete understanding.

Then too, there are the magnificent gramophone records which, if you will treat them with due care and respect, can give you tremendous help in your study of opera.

And this study is not a dull, painstaking business, it is both thrilling and satisfying; when you begin to realize that you are "piecing" the music together in proper proportion, when you can both hear and understand why this phrase or that is played and then replayed possibly several times in other acts, you will experience a sense of excitement and pleasure. No longer are Verdi, Puccini, Rossini and Bellini mere names to you, they emerge as people you know and understand, whose art you begin to comprehend.

So listen to that "linked sweetness long drawn out" for your joy and pleasure, hear too:

> "The melting voices through mazes running,
>   Untwisting all the chains that tie
>   The hidden soul of harmony."

N. J.

CURTAIN

Fasano,
Lago di Garda,
Italy.